First Workshop on Natural Language Processing for Turkic Languages (SIGTURK 2024)

Bangkok, Thailand
15 August 2024

ISBN: 979-8-3313-0176-7

Printed from e-media with permission by:

Curran Associates, Inc.
57 Morehouse Lane
Red Hook, NY 12571

Some format issues inherent in the e-media version may also appear in this print version.

Association for Computational Linguistics
209 N. Eighth Street
Stroudsburg, Pennsylvania 18360

Phone: 1-570-476-8006
Fax: 1-570-476-0860

acl@aclweb.org

Additional copies of this publication are available from:

Curran Associates, Inc.
57 Morehouse Lane
Red Hook, NY 12571 USA
Phone: 845-758-0400
Fax: 845-758-2633
Email: curran@proceedings.com
Web: www.proceedings.com

SIGTURK 2024

The First Workshop on Natural Language Processing for Turkic Languages (SIGTURK 2024)

Proceedings of the Workshop

August 15, 2024

Association for Computational Linguistics (ACL)
317 Sidney Baker St. S
Suite 400 - 134
Kerrville, TX 78028
USA
Tel: +1-855-225-1962
acl@aclweb.org

Preface

Welcome to the First Workshop on Natural Language Processing for Turkic Languages (SIGTURK 2024), held on August 15, 2024, in Bangkok, Thailand, and online.

This inaugural workshop received 25 submissions, out of which 9 papers were accepted as archival publications and 7 as non-archival. All 16 accepted papers will be presented as posters in addition to oral presentations.

We are excited to bring together researchers working on NLP for Turkic languages and hope this workshop will foster collaboration and advance the field. The program includes invited talks, oral presentations, and a poster session showcasing the latest work in this area.

We thank all authors for their submissions, the program committee for their thorough reviews, and our invited speakers for sharing their expertise. We look forward to engaging discussions and new connections made at SIGTURK 2024.

SIGTURK 2024 Organizers

Organizing Committee

Organizers

Duygu Ataman, New York University
Mehmet Oguz Derin
Sardana Ivanova, University of Helsinki
Abdullatif Köksal, Ludwig-Maximilians-Universität München
Jonne Sälevä, Brandeis University
Deniz Zeyrek, Middle East Technical University

Program Committee

Organizers

Duygu Ataman, New York University
Mehmet Oguz Derin
Sardana Ivanova, University of Helsinki
Abdullatif Köksal, Ludwig-Maximilians-Universität München
Deniz Zeyrek, Middle East Technical University
Jonne Sälevä, Brandeis University

Reviewers

Duygu Ataman, New York University
Necva Bölücü, CSIRO
Cagri Coltekin, University of Tuebingen
Mehmet Oguz Derin, Mehmet Oguz Derin
Orhan Firat, Google
Omer Goldman, Bar Ilan University
Mammad Hajili, Microsoft
Sardana Ivanova, University of Helsinki
Murathan Kurfali
Abdullatif Köksal, Ludwig-Maximilians-Universität München
Constantine Lignos, Brandeis University
Aziza Mirsaidova
Saliha Muradoglu
Jonne Sälevä, Brandeis University
Francis M. Tyers, Indiana University, Bloomington
Jonathan Washington, Swarthmore College
Deniz Zeyrek, Middle East Technical University
Arzucan Özgür, Boğaziçi University
Adnan Öztürel, Google
Gözde Gül Şahin, Koç University

Table of Contents

Program

Thursday, August 15, 2024

09:00 - 09:10	*Opening remarks*
09:10 - 10:30	*Morning session 1: Invited speech*
10:30 - 11:00	*Coffee break*
11:00 - 12:30	*Morning session 2: Oral presentations*
12:30 - 13:30	*Lunch*
13:30 - 14:50	*Afternoon session 1: Oral presentations*
14:50 - 15:30	*Afternoon session 2: Invited speech*
15:30 - 16:00	*Coffee break*
16:00 - 17:00	*Poster session*
17:00 - 17:40	*Afternoon session 3: Invited speech*
17:40 - 18:00	*Closing remarks*

Unsupervised Learning of Turkish Morphology with Multiple Codebook VQ-VAE

Müge Kural
KUIS AI, Koc University
mugekural@ku.edu.tr

Deniz Yuret
KUIS AI, Koc University
dyuret@ku.edu.tr

Abstract

This paper presents an interpretable unsupervised morphological learning model, showing comparable performance to supervised models in learning complex morphological rules of Turkish as evidenced by its application to the problem of morphological inflection within the SIGMORPHON Shared Tasks. The significance of our unsupervised approach lies in its alignment with how humans naturally acquire rules from raw data without supervision. To achieve this, we construct a model with multiple codebooks of VQ-VAE employing continuous and discrete latent variables during word generation. We evaluate the model's performance under high and low-resource scenarios, and use probing techniques to examine encoded information in latent representations. We also evaluate its generalization capabilities by testing unseen suffixation scenarios within the SIGMORPHON-UniMorph 2022 Shared Task 0. Our results demonstrate our model's ability to distinguish word structures into lemmas and suffixes, with each codebook specialized for different morphological features, contributing to the interpretability of our model and effectively performing morphological inflection on both seen and unseen morphological features [1].

1 Introduction

In this paper, we introduce an interpretable unsupervised morphological learning model that achieves performances comparable to supervised models in the acquisition of complex morphological rules of Turkish. We demonstrate its abilities in addressing one of the most studied problems in the literature, morphological inflection in the SIGMORPHON Shared Tasks (Cotterell et al., 2016, 2017, 2018; Vylomova et al., 2020; Pimentel et al., 2021; Kodner et al., 2022; Goldman et al., 2023).

The unsupervised acquisition of morphological rules in humans is a natural process during language learning. This involves the analysis of word structures, recognition of stems and affixes, association of consistent meanings, and the integration of these elements into novel combinations, as explained by Clark (2017). These rules govern the appropriate structure of words to convey their intended meanings. For instance, when forming the present participle of the verb *"to bike"* it becomes *"biking,"* not *"bikeing"* necessitating the exclusion of the last vowel. Similarly, when evaluating the feasibility of a goal, we consider its *"attainability" (attain+able+ity)*, not *"attainityable" (attain+ity+able)*; maintaining the correct sequence of suffixes is crucial in this context. Given the inherent ability of humans to learn morphology unsupervisedly, it is essential to develop unsupervised neural models that can replicate this process. This analogy suggests that it should be feasible for a model to acquire morphological rules without explicit supervision.

In the intersection of computation and morphology, researchers have developed computational approaches to explore human morphology learning theories and address practical applications like spell checking, correction, automatic speech recognition, and statistical machine translation. The two-level morphology model (Koskenniemi, 1983), prevalent in the early stages, highlights the complexity of morphology, incorporating phonological alterations beyond a simple arrangement of morphemes. For example, in Turkish words like *bahçemden* and *garajımdan*, both indicating movement from a possessed place, the morpheme sequences differ (*+m+den* vs. *+ım+dan*) based on Turkish phonological rules. Two-level morphology dissects this into lexical and phonological levels, resulting in the correct surface forms. Finite-state transducers, exemplified by a Turkish morphological analyzer (Oflazer, 1993), have been utilized

[1] Our code, data and experimental results are available at https://github.com/mugekural9/unsup-morph-vqvae.

Proceedings of the First Workshop on Natural Language Processing for Turkic Languages (SIGTURK 2024), pages 1–17
August 15, 2024 ©2024 Association for Computational Linguistics

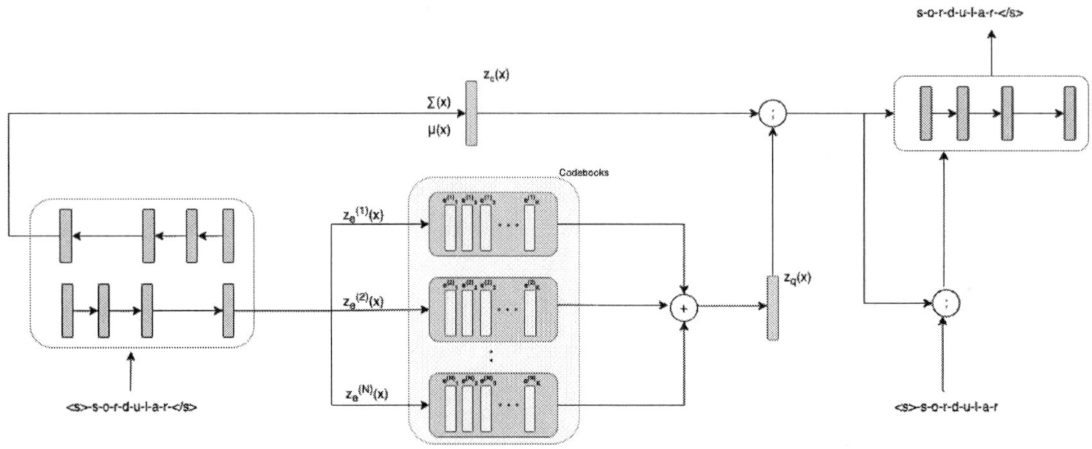

Figure 1: Our model: Multiple Codebook VQ-VAE

to study morphological processes across languages within the two-level formalism.

To evaluate unsupervised models from a morphological standpoint, it is essential to establish expectations for a model proficient in "learning" morphology. As outlined in (Goldsmith et al., 2017), the questions an unsupervised morphology learner should address include identifying component morphemes in words, recognizing alternative forms (allomorphs) like *-ler* and *-lar* in Turkish, understanding conditions for their usage, explaining alternative forms through phonological generalizations, determining permissible combinations of feature specifications, and unraveling morphological realization of each combination.

In this work, we propose the Multiple Codebook Vector Quantized Variational Autoencoder (VQ-VAE) (Van Den Oord et al., 2017) as an unsupervised morphology learner for text. Our approach entails establishing a continuous space and utilizing multiple codebooks. The model integrates codebook entries with the continuous space to generate words. We expect the model to discretize various morphological features in codebooks, thereby representing a word's lemma in continuous space. For example, one codebook may encode person features (e.g., 1st person singular, 3rd person plural), another may represent the tense of the word (e.g., present, future, past), and a separate codebook may handle the polarity of the word (positive or negative).

We evaluate our model's performance in morphological inflection, addressing the challenges it faces in learning crucial abilities such as allomorph recognition, phonological generalizations, and the realization of diverse morphological feature combinations. Additionally, we examine its generalization capabilities under both high and low resource data scenarios by testing it on unseen suffixation scenarios within the SIGMORPHON-UniMorph 2022 Shared Task 0 (Kodner et al., 2022). To gain insights into the model's learning, we further employ probing techniques for interpreting encoded information within latent representations.

Our primary contributions are:

- We introduce a novel and interpretable unsupervised model that achieves comparable performance to supervised models in learning the morphological rules of Turkish.
- The model exhibits robust performance in both high and low-resource scenarios for morphological inflection tasks.
- The model segregates word lemmas into continuous variables and their suffixes into discrete variables within codebooks. Additionally, across random runs, the model specializes each codebook with a unique morphological feature, thereby enhancing its interpretability.

2 Model

We extend the idea of Vector Quantised-Variational Autoencoders (VQ-VAE) (Van Den Oord et al., 2017) for text. The original VQ-VAE is an encoder-decoder model that aims to model image and speech data using discrete latent variables picked from a codebook having embeddings. The encoder outputs are replaced with the nearest vectors in l_2 distance from the codebook. Then, the codebook embeddings are fed to the decoder, and the data reconstruction is aimed. In our model, we employ multiple codebooks, in contrast to the original VQ-VAE that uses only one. Additionally, we incorporate continuous variables, following the approach of the original VAE. Our expectation is that the model will specialize each codebook to capture distinct morphological features of a word, and as a result, the continuous space will be utilized to encode the lemma of a word. Specifically, we construct a VQ-VAE model with continuous and discrete variables with the following blocks: bidirectional GRU encoder, low-dimensional continuous space, varying number of codebooks for discrete space, and a unidirectional GRU decoder, as seen in Fig. 1. While the continuous part is regulated by KL divergence to standard Gaussian prior as in regular VAE, the discrete latent variables are obtained with quantization through multiple codebooks. The encoder q with parameters ϕ has the last forward hidden state $\overrightarrow{h_t}$, and the last backward hidden state $\overleftarrow{h_t}$ with d dimensional vectors. The mean μ and variance σ are learned by applying a linear transformation to the last backward hidden state $\overleftarrow{h_t}$. Then, using μ and σ, we estimate the continuous latent variable z_c. To make the learning step differentiable, we use the reparameterization trick (Kingma and Welling, 2013) and calculate $z_c = \mu_\phi(x) + \sigma_\phi(x) * \epsilon$ where $\epsilon \sim N(0,1)$.

For quantization, we define the latent embedding space of codebooks as $e \in R^{N \times K \times D}$ where N is the number of codebooks, K is the number of entries in each codebook, D is the dimension of each embedding vector $e^{(n)}$ in the codebook. The $\overrightarrow{h_t}$ vector from the encoder is then linearly transformed into N vectors with dimension D. For each linearly transformed vector from encoder $z_e^{(n)}(x)$, the nearest embedding from $codebook^{(n)}$ is calculated:

$$\mathrm{q}(\mathrm{z}_q^{(n)} = k|x) = \begin{cases} 1 & \text{for k} = \text{argmin}_j ||z_e^{(n)}(x) - e_j^{(n)}||_2 \\ 0 & \text{otherwise} \end{cases} \tag{1}$$

Then we sum the quantized vectors $z_q^{(1)}, z_q^{(2)}, ...z_q^{(N)}$ and obtain $z_q(x)$ vector. We finally concatenate the quantized vector with the continous vector and feed it to the decoder as an initial hidden state. At each time step of decoding, we concatenate the continous vector z_c, quantized vector z_q, and the target token embedding.

The total objective for our model becomes:

$$\begin{aligned} L = \; & E_{z_c \sim q_\phi(z|x)}[\log p(x|z_c, z_q)] \\ & + \sum_{n=1}^{N} ||sg[z_e^{(n)}(x)] - e^{(n)}||_2^2 \\ & + \sum_{n=1}^{N} \beta ||z_e^{(n)}(x) - sg[e^{(n)}]||_2^2 \\ & - KL(q(z_c|x)||p(z_c))\} \end{aligned} \tag{2}$$

The initial component of the loss involves the reconstruction loss, where the model conditions on the continuous latent variable z_c and discrete latent variable z_q to reconstruct the observed data x. The subsequent element pertains to the overall vector quantization loss for each vector $z_e^{(n)}(x)$. Similar to the original VQ-VAE, the stop gradient operation (denoted as sg) is employed to facilitate the learning of codebook embeddings $e^{(n)}$. This operation ensures that the gradient of the applied term becomes zero during forward computation, converting it into a non-updated constant. In the second term, to minimize the l_2 distance between encoder outputs and codebook embeddings, only the codebook embeddings are updated. The third term involves updating only the encoder outputs, weighted by the parameter β to prevent the encoder outputs from growing faster than the codebook embeddings. Lastly, in the fourth term, we regulate the continuous vector using a standard Gaussian distribution.

3 Evaluation

In this section, we evaluate the performance of our unsupervised model in morphological inflection (see Section 3.1) and probe the latent variables of the model for morphological features (see Section 3.2). We conduct further evaluation of our model in the context of Sigmorphon-UniMorph 2022 Shared Task 0 (Kodner et al., 2022) in Section 3.3.

3.1 Morphological Inflection

At morphological inflection problem, a model takes a word's lemma and a morphological feature set as input, and generates the inflected target form of the word.

```
e.g.:
vermek + V;DECL;OBLIG;PL;2;NEG;PST
-> vermemeliydiniz
```

Morphological inflection, highlighted in (Cotterell et al., 2016), is crucial for generating and analyzing words in a language based on inflected forms. This task aids in understanding word shapes and suffixation patterns, allowing models to generalize to unseen words by learning inflection rules. Particularly challenging in languages like Turkish with rich inflectional morphology, the task involves learning various morphological processes.

3.1.1 Experiments

For this problem, we conduct experiments using 4, 6, 8, and 12 codebooks, each containing 6, 8, and 12 entries. To determine the convergence of the model, we evaluate model's copying exact match accuracy and model's sampling quality: This involves sampling vectors from the continuous space and using a fixed entry combination from codebooks. We expect to observe inflections of different lemmas sharing the same suffix. This approach ensures that the model leverages the codebooks to generate a word. We provide results for the best model with 4 codebooks and 8 entries per codebook. Full results of models with different codebook-entry configurations can be found in the Appendix C.

	train	test
# total words	404896	1446
# unique lemma	588	536
# unique feature sets	703	616

Table 1: Dataset statistics

We filter the Turkish Unimorph dataset (McCarthy et al., 2020) for verbs. The dataset includes triples in the format (lemma, inflected form, feature set), such as (çıkarmak, çıkaracağım, V;DECL;IND;SG;1;POS;FUT). We augment the dataset with verbs from the large training set of Turkish in Sigmorphon 2022 Shared Task-0 (Kodner et al., 2022). In this way we have a dataset with 404,896 words, featuring 588 unique lemmas and 703 unique morphological feature sets. For evaluation, we also use the shared task test set which contains 1,446 verbs. It's important to note that all lemmas and feature sets are encountered during training, although not together in the same triple. Further details can be found in Appendix B.

During training, our unsupervised model relies solely on observing the raw surface forms of words without explicit morphological feature sets. To address the inflection task using our unsupervised model, we initially associate codebook entries with the corresponding feature sets. This process involves the following steps: At test time, we present all target words in the test set to the model and observe its selection of codebook entries for each word while copying them. For example, to map the relevant codebook entries for a feature set like V;DECL;IND;SG;1;POS;FUT, we identify the most frequently selected codebook entries when copying words with this specific feature set. We then use these mapped entries in conjunction with a word's lemma to inflect it into the target form with that particular feature set. This inflection, using the mapped entries, is referred to as a top-1 match. Moreover, we track the second most frequently chosen codebook entries, labeling it as a top-2 match.

3.1.2 Baselines

We use the baseline models provided by the recent SIGMORPHON Shared Tasks, which have been consistently employed in previous iterations of the shared task.

Unsupervised We use the non-neural baseline model provided by the shared task as an unsupervised baseline model. The model initially aligns input/output training examples using the Levenshtein distance. The system presupposes that each input-output pair can be segmented into a prefixation part (`Pr`), a stem part (`St`), and a suffixation part (`Su`), based on the presence of initial or trailing zeroes in the inputs or outputs. Subsequently, the system extracts a set of prefix-changing rules based on the `Pr` pairings and a set of suffix-changing rules based on `St+Su` pairings. During generation, the longest suffix rule that is applicable to a lemma form to be inflected is employed.

We also perform unsupervised training on the closely related work by Zhou and Neubig (2017), initially trained using a mix of supervised and semi-supervised approaches. Their semi-supervised method involves reconstructing target and source words using inferred labels and training MLP classifiers for each morphological feature label. They employ a continuous vector for encoding word lemmas, regularized by KL divergence towards a standard Gaussian prior. Morphological feature encoding utilizes MLPs as discriminative classifiers, incorporating the Gumbel-Max trick for differentiating discrete latent variables. An attention mechanism facilitates feature label inference, and

Lemma	Feature set	Codebook entries	Inflected word
dondurmak	V;OBLIG;SG;2;POS;PST;INTR	7;5;6;3	dondurmalı mıydın
ekşimek	V;OBLIG;SG;2;POS;PST;INTR	7;5;6;3	ekşimeli miydin
sanmak	V;DECL;PL;1;POS;PST;INFR	1;1;0;0	sanmışız
ölçmek	V;DECL;PL;1;POS;PST;INFR	1;1;0;0	ölçmüşüz
götürmek	V;DECL;PL;1;NEG;FUT;INFR	1;7;5;6	götürmeyecekmişiz
taşmak	V;DECL;PL;1;NEG;FUT;INFR	1;7;5;6	taşmayacakmışız

Table 2: Inflection results. The model employs the same codebook combinations for identical feature sets and can apply different harmony rules, such as *-meli miydin* / *-malı mıydın* and *-mışız* /*-müşüz* and *-meyecekmişiz* /*-mayacakmışız*.

the lemma vector, attention vector, and target token are concatenated to the decoder at each time step. KL annealing scheduling and input operation dropout are employed to prevent posterior collapse during generation. However, in our unsupervised setups, the model struggles to distinguish lemmas and suffixes as effectively as in supervised cases. We are unable to identify any specifications for classifiers related to morphological features, preventing us from mapping the morphological features to classes. Consequently, the model's capability to perform morphological inflection is hindered. Additional details can be found in the Appendix E.

Supervised We employ a baseline from the recent years of the shared tasks (Pimentel et al., 2021; Kodner et al., 2022; Goldman et al., 2023), which inspired many other works on the inflection problem such as Yang et al. (2022); Merzhevich et al. (2022); Forster and Meister (2020); Canby et al. (2020), specifically a character-level transducer proposed by Wu et al. (2021). This transducer is based on transformers, utilizing special position and type embeddings for morphological features and word characters. In their approach, positional encodings for features are set to 0, as the order of features is not considered important, and only word characters are counted. Additionally, a special type token is introduced to indicate whether a token represents a feature or a word character.

3.1.3 Results & Analysis

The model achieves a 94% accuracy in top-1 matches and a 98% accuracy in top-2 matches for inflection, as shown in Table 3. While the unsupervised baseline exhibits poor performance on the task, the supervised baseline demonstrates nearly perfect performance, and our results indicate comparable performance to that model. We also investigate the model's codebook selection for given words. Our findings reveal that **the model selects the same codebook-entry combinations for words that share the same suffix**, as shown in Table 4. Moreover, by employing these identical entries, **the model learns to apply morphosyntactic rules, preserving vowel harmony** as illustrated in Table 2. By employing the top-2 match selection instead of the top-1, 56 errors were resolved, with 2 errors pertaining to lemma corrections and the remaining errors involving suffix adjustments. Therefore, the results indicate that **the model performs strongly in inflection by effectively mapping the appropriate suffix to the codebook entries.**

Model	E.M. Acc.
Ours (top-1 match)	0.94
Ours (top-2 match)	**0.98**
Baseline (Unsupervised)	0.38
Baseline (Supervised)	0.99

Table 3: Performance of models on verbs in morphological inflection: Our model demonstrates comparable performance to the supervised baseline, achieving nearly 100% accuracy. E.M. Acc.: Exact match accuracy.

3.2 Probing

Probing is a technique used to interpret neural models by identifying encoded information in their representations. The use of classifiers enables us to evaluate if these representations correspond to human classification patterns. For morphological evaluation, a probing procedure can be employed to analyze the morphological features of words. In this section, we evaluate our model's ability to capture the tense, person, and polarity features of verbs (e.g., *okuyacaklar* -> 3rd person plural, future tense, positive).

Codebook entries	Words
7;5;3;7	fotoğraf çekiyor olmalıydın süründürüyor olmalıydın yontuluyor olmalıydın eğleniyor olmalıydın
2;7;5;6	programlattırmayacakmışım süründürtmeyecekmişim kırdırtmayacakmışım göndermeyecekmişim
4;5;5;6	kanıtlamadıydınız birleşmediydiniz eğilmediydiniz dolmadıydınız

Table 4: Model's codebook entry selections. It employs the same entry combinations for words that have the same suffix. Combination 1: (past perfect cont. tense) Combination 2: (negative inferential future tense). Combination 3: (negative past tense)

	Person	Tense	Polarity
z_c	0.25	0.48	0.63
z_q	0.99	0.98	0.86
cbook-0	**0.98**	0.50	0.52
cbook-1	0.20	**0.88**	0.54
cbook-2	0.20	0.54	**0.75**
cbook-3	0.18	0.49	0.73
baseline	0.18	0.48	0.52

Table 5: Model's probing results. Codebooks are specialized for different morphological features, while continuous part exhibits significantly lower performance. cbook: codebook.

3.2.1 Experiments

We analyze the representation of morphological features in both continuous vector and discrete codebook vectors. To achieve this, we maintain fixed model parameters and introduce a linear layer on the model's continuous latent variables z_c, quantized variables which are separate codebook embeddings, and their sum z_q. This linear layer is trained to predict the morphological feature. The 'person' feature encompasses 6 classes: singular and plural for 1st, 2nd, and 3rd persons. The 'tense' feature consists of 3 classes: present, past, and future. Finally, the 'polarity' feature comprises 2 classes: positive and negative. We use the majority of classes in the test set as our baseline.

3.2.2 Results & Analysis

As indicated in Table 5, the continuous vector z_c, intended to encode the lemma, exhibits performance close to the baseline score for each morphological tag classification. This was anticipated since it is not supposed to contain information related to the suffix. Conversely, the quantized vector z_q encodes a significant portion of suffix-related information and effectively clusters the words in its space (refer to Fig. 2). Notably, there is a clear distinction in the person tag for words within codebook-0, whereas the other codebooks exhibit performances comparable to the baseline. Regarding the tense feature, codebook-1 seems to encode that information. However, for polarity, there isn't a significant discrimination, as codebook-2 and codebook-3 display similar performances. The results suggest that **across random runs, the model specializes distinct codebooks for different morphological features.** Full results can be found in Appendix D.

In summary of Sec. 3.1 and Sec. 3.2, we present a model that encodes lemmas into continuous vectors, translating morphological features in the suffix into codebook entries. We also show that these codebooks specialize in various morphological features, such as Person, Tense, and Polarity. Furthermore, we demonstrate the model's capability to inflect a lemma with a suffix mapped in codebook entries, generating a newly inflected word not encountered during training.

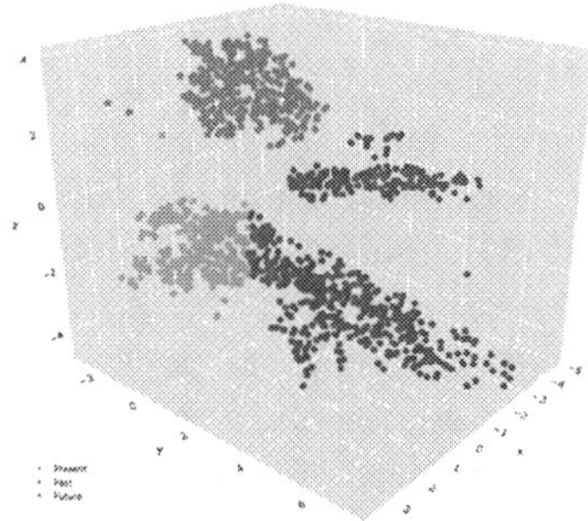

Figure 2: Visualization of tense probe logits in quantized vector z_q. The model clusters words based on tense suffixation.

3.3 Evaluation on SIGMORPHON-UniMorph 2022 Shared Task 0

In this section, we show that our **model exhibits comparable performance even in low-resource scenarios when compared to supervised models.** In the SIGMORPHON 22 Shared Task 0 (Kodner

Gold target	Ours
büyüyor olacaklar	büyümüş olacaklar
kullanıyor olmamalısınız	kullanıyor olmamalıyız
delecek olmayacakmışız	deler olacakmışız
dedikodu yaparlardı	dedikodu yapacaklardı
hareket ediyorsun	hareket ediyor olmalısın

Table 6: Model's errors with unseen feature sets. Although it correctly identifies lemmas, it struggles to inflect them into the accurate target forms.

et al., 2022), the primary focus is to evaluate the capacity of models in generalizing to unseen lemmas and features. The task includes conditions of both large and small datasets, organized based on overlaps in lemmas and features. We focus on scenarios with lemma overlap in the task, where test pair lemmas are included in the training data, but their feature sets are novel.

3.4 Experiments

We filter the original large dataset of Turkish, reducing it from 7,000 to 5,273 instances by selecting only verbs. In the test set, we have 1,446 instances with 731 featuring both overlap and 715 showing lemma overlap, implying the presence of words with novel feature sets. Our model is trained using 6 codebooks, each containing 8 entries.

3.5 Models

All models, except Flexica (Sherbakov and Vylomova, 2022), use transformers in a supervised fashion. CLUZH (Wehrli et al., 2022) is a character-level neural transducer handling edit actions like insertion, deletion, substitution, and copy. UBC (Yang et al., 2022) improves Wu et al. (2021) with reverse positional embeddings for better suffix handling. TüM-M (Merzhevich et al., 2022) also adapts Wu et al. (2021) for predicting a distribution over states of FST. OSU (Elsner and Court, 2022) uses a transformer with an analogical exemplar model for inflection, effective when target cell examples are available. Flexica employs refined alignment patterns, learning transformation patterns through maximal continuous matches between lemmas and inflected forms. Extraction involves finding the longest common substring, recursively extending until no more common characters are found, and then enriching patterns with concrete characters from training samples.

System	E.M. Acc.
UBC	0.98
CLUZH	0.92
OSU	0.48
Flexica	0.38
TüM-M	0.22
Ours (top1-match)	0.81
Ours (top2-match)	0.88

Table 7: Performance of submitted systems for verbs in the large training condition in the SIGMORPHON-UniMorph 2022 Shared Task-0. E.M. Acc.: Exact match accuracy.

3.6 Results & Analysis

As indicated in Table 7, our model surpasses three systems in both top-1 and top-2 matches. In top-2 matches, our model achieves a 88% accuracy with 171 mistakes out of 1,446 test instances. Despite having no unseen lemma between our training and test set, almost half of the test set comprises words with novel feature sets. We observe that our model accurately captures 91% of cases for seen feature sets, while for unseen feature sets, the model correctly generates 85% of the words.

Error analysis We analyze our model's errors in top-2 matches for seen and unseen features. We observe that 63% of ours models errors cause because of the unseen feature sets. Out of errors, the models generated novel words that were not encountered during training. As seen in Table 6, in most of the cases, our model fails to form the correct inflected target word due to incorrect suffixation. However, we observe that the model still preserves harmony rules, such as the -meli/-malı obligation suffix, where models CLUZH and OSU struggle. For instance, with the lemma ending with the vowel *a*, such as açılmak, it should be *açılmalıyım*, not *açılmeliyim*. Similarly, with the lemma *asmak* and the related 3rd person plural, it should be *asmalısınız*, not *asmamelisiniz*. In these examples, our model is able to preserve vowel harmony where CLUZH and OSU fail.

4 Importance of Directionality

In this section, we investigate the impact of our directional choice, where we assign the last backward hidden state $\overleftarrow{h_t}$ to the continuous vector, aimed at encoding the lemma, and the last forward hidden state $\overrightarrow{h_t}$ to the codebooks, intended to encode morphological features in the suffix. Given the structure of Turkish, where the lemma typically starts on the left and suffixation occurs on the right, we anticipate this approach to be effective, introducing a form of inductive bias. To understand its effect, we concatenate the last forward and backward hidden states $[\overrightarrow{h_t}; \overleftarrow{h_t}]$, and input the resulting vector into both the continuous vector and the codebooks. We conduct experiments with 4, 6, and 8 codebooks, each having 6, 8, and 12 entries, while maintaining other model dimensions. The experiments with three different random initializations reveal three types of observed problems: (1) Suffix information is not entirely encoded in the discrete part, but partially encoded in the continuous part with lemma. (2) Lemma information is not entirely encoded in the continuous part but is partially embedded in the discrete part with suffixes, leading to a significant increase in codebook entry usage. This suggests that the model does not effectively cluster words based on suffixation, instead encoding most of the word information into the codebooks. (3) Lemma information is entirely encoded in the discrete part, while suffix information is entirely encoded in the continuous part. We give futher evidences for these problems in Appendix F).

In every setup, the lack of separation between lemma and suffix into continuous and discrete parts interferes with mapping morphological tags to codebook entries. Thus, morphological inflection cannot be performed well. While the problems are partially observed in several runs of the model with an inductive bias, we could still achieve good convergence in most setups, which is a challenge to replicate without incorporating directionality. Consequently, we argue that **the directionality helps the model in distinguishing between lemma in the continuous and suffix in the discrete parts.** Nevertheless, further experiments without directionality may provide better insights.

5 Related Work

The unsupervised study of morpheme boundaries dates back years. Harris (1955)'s pioneering work introduces a heuristic based on letter successor/predecessor tokens, counting the different letters after a morpheme candidate x. Subsequent works enhance this approach by analyzing the frequency distribution of successor tokens and calculating entropy to measure predictability.The Morfessor family, including Morfessor Baseline (Creutz and Lagus, 2002), Morfessor FlatCat (Grönroos et al., 2014), and Morfessor EM+Prune (Grönroos et al., 2020), utilizes generative models for language morpheme learning. Morfessor Baseline optimizes parameters through MAP estimation, adhering to the Minimum Description Length principle. Morfessor EM+Prune starts with a seed lexicon of the most frequent subwords and prunes during training. Additionally, Adaptor Grammar (Johnson et al., 2006) and MorphAGram (Eskander et al., 2020) contribute to unsupervised morphological segmentation, incorporating adaptors like the Pitman-Yor Process (Pitman and Yor, 1997). Further work involves leveraging semantic features of words through neural networks for unsupervised morphological segmentation (Üstün and Can, 2021; Üstün et al., 2018). Previous work in morphological inflection includes supervised learning techniques. Durrett and DeNero (2013) employs alignment and learns edit operations, while Kann and Schütze (2016) proposes a neural approach using an encoder-decoder architecture with soft attention (Bahdanau et al., 2015) and stacked GRUs (Cho et al., 2014). Anastasopoulos and Neubig (2019) proposes data augmentation by generating hallucinated data in lemma-feature tag-target pairs. They replace shared substrings longer than three characters with random characters, resulting in hallucinated lemma-tag triples. Some probing studies on RNNs include Shi et al. (2016); Conneau et al. (2018). Criticisms regarding probe reliability and classification limitations have prompted the consideration of simpler probes, emphasizing information-theoretic measures over accuracy (Hewitt and Liang, 2019; Voita and Titov, 2020; Pimentel et al., 2020). The studies also explore causal relations and latent ontologies, providing insights into feature usage and representations (Vanmassenhove et al., 2017; Elazar et al., 2021; Giulianelli et al., 2018; Lasri et al., 2022).

6 Conclusion & Future Work

This work presents a novel and interpretable unsupervised model for learning Turkish morphological rules, performing comparably to supervised models, particularly in low-resource settings. The model separates the lemma of words into continuous variables and their suffix into discrete variables within codebooks. Across multiple runs, it customizes each codebook with distinct morphological features, contributing to enhanced interpretability.

Future work may involve exploring different morphological tasks, such as unsupervised paradigm completion and unsupervised paradigm clustering.

Limitations

Our proposed model incorporates the bidirectionality of the encoder as a bias in its architecture, leveraging it to capture the structure of Turkish, with word lemmas on the left and suffixation on the right. Therefore, while it is expected to perform well with similar agglutinative languages, further experimentation is necessary to adjust the directionality for languages with varying morphological typologies.

Our other limitation relates to the part of speech in our dataset. Focusing on a word-level dataset without contextualization, we exclusively include verbs to minimize ambiguity, significantly when context alters word structure. For instance, the Turkish word "*çizmem*" can mean both "I do not draw" (*çiz+me+m*, verb) and "my boot" (*çizme+m*, noun) depending on the context. The model may struggle to identify the lemma and select the correct codebooks in such cases. Additionally, we cannot constrain the model to generate a lemma exclusively for a verb or noun, leading to inconsistencies between the lemma and the codebooks during word generation. Therefore, it is also essential to incorporate word contextualization to improve this work further.

Ethics Statement

We foresee no ethical concerns related to the methods outlined in this paper.

Acknowledgements

We gratefully acknowledge the support of the KUIS AI Center at Koç University, Istanbul, for this work.

References

Antonios Anastasopoulos and Graham Neubig. 2019. Pushing the limits of low-resource morphological inflection. In *Proceedings of the 2019 Conference on Empirical Methods in Natural Language Processing and the 9th International Joint Conference on Natural Language Processing (EMNLP-IJCNLP)*, pages 984–996, Hong Kong, China. Association for Computational Linguistics.

Dzmitry Bahdanau, Kyunghyun Cho, and Yoshua Bengio. 2015. Neural machine translation by jointly learning to align and translate. *CoRR*, abs/1409.0473.

Marc Canby, Aidana Karipbayeva, Bryan Lunt, Sahand Mozaffari, Charlotte Yoder, and Julia Hockenmaier. 2020. University of Illinois submission to the SIGMORPHON 2020 shared task 0: Typologically diverse morphological inflection. In *Proceedings of the 17th SIGMORPHON Workshop on Computational Research in Phonetics, Phonology, and Morphology*, pages 137–145, Online. Association for Computational Linguistics.

Kyunghyun Cho, Bart van Merrienboer, Dzmitry Bahdanau, and Yoshua Bengio. 2014. On the properties of neural machine translation: Encoder–decoder approaches. In *SSST@EMNLP*.

Eve V Clark. 2017. Morphology in language acquisition. *The handbook of morphology*, pages 374–389.

Alexis Conneau, Germán Kruszewski, Guillaume Lample, Loïc Barrault, and Marco Baroni. 2018. What you can cram into a single $&!#* vector: Probing sentence embeddings for linguistic properties. *ArXiv*, abs/1805.01070.

Ryan Cotterell, Christo Kirov, John Sylak-Glassman, Géraldine Walther, Ekaterina Vylomova, Arya D. McCarthy, Katharina Kann, Sabrina J. Mielke, Garrett Nicolai, Miikka Silfverberg, David Yarowsky, Jason Eisner, and Mans Hulden. 2018. The CoNLL–SIGMORPHON 2018 shared task: Universal morphological reinflection. In *Proceedings of the CoNLL–SIGMORPHON 2018 Shared Task: Universal Morphological Reinflection*, pages 1–27, Brussels. Association for Computational Linguistics.

Ryan Cotterell, Christo Kirov, John Sylak-Glassman, Géraldine Walther, Ekaterina Vylomova, Patrick Xia, Manaal Faruqui, Sandra Kübler, David Yarowsky, Jason Eisner, and Mans Hulden. 2017. Conll-sigmorphon 2017 shared task: Universal morphological reinflection in 52 languages. In *CoNLL Shared Task*.

Ryan Cotterell, Christo Kirov, John Sylak-Glassman, David Yarowsky, Jason Eisner, and Mans Hulden. 2016. The SIGMORPHON 2016 shared task—morphological reinflection. In *Proceedings of the 2016 Meeting of SIGMORPHON*, Berlin, Germany. Association for Computational Linguistics.

Mathias Creutz and Krista Lagus. 2002. Unsupervised discovery of morphemes. In *Proceedings of the ACL-02 Workshop on Morphological and Phonological Learning*, pages 21–30. Association for Computational Linguistics.

Greg Durrett and John DeNero. 2013. Supervised learning of complete morphological paradigms. In *NAACL*.

Yanai Elazar, Shauli Ravfogel, Alon Jacovi, and Yoav Goldberg. 2021. Amnesic probing: Behavioral explanation with amnesic counterfactuals. *Transactions of the Association for Computational Linguistics*, 9:160–175.

Micha Elsner and Sara Court. 2022. OSU at SigMorphon 2022: Analogical inflection with rule features. In *Proceedings of the 19th SIGMORPHON Workshop on Computational Research in Phonetics, Phonology, and Morphology*, pages 220–225, Seattle, Washington. Association for Computational Linguistics.

Ramy Eskander, Francesca Callejas, Elizabeth Nichols, Judith L. Klavans, and Smaranda Muresan. 2020. Morphagram, evaluation and framework for unsupervised morphological segmentation. In *LREC*.

Martina Forster and Clara Meister. 2020. SIGMORPHON 2020 task 0 system description: ETH Zürich team. In *Proceedings of the 17th SIGMORPHON Workshop on Computational Research in Phonetics, Phonology, and Morphology*, pages 106–110, Online. Association for Computational Linguistics.

Mario Giulianelli, John Harding, Florian Mohnert, Dieuwke Hupkes, and Willem H. Zuidema. 2018. Under the hood: Using diagnostic classifiers to investigate and improve how language models track agreement information. In *BlackboxNLP@EMNLP*.

Omer Goldman, Khuyagbaatar Batsuren, Salam Khalifa, Aryaman Arora, Garrett Nicolai, Reut Tsarfaty, and Ekaterina Vylomova. 2023. SIGMORPHON–UniMorph 2023 shared task 0: Typologically diverse morphological inflection. In *Proceedings of the 20th SIGMORPHON workshop on Computational Research in Phonetics, Phonology, and Morphology*, pages 117–125, Toronto, Canada. Association for Computational Linguistics.

John A. Goldsmith, Jackson L. Lee, and Aris Xanthos. 2017. Computational learning of morphology.

Stig-Arne Grönroos, Sami Virpioja, and Mikko Kurimo. 2020. Morfessor EM+Prune: Improved subword segmentation with expectation maximization and pruning. In *Proceedings of the Twelfth Language Resources and Evaluation Conference*, pages 3944–3953, Marseille, France. European Language Resources Association.

Stig-Arne Grönroos, Sami Virpioja, Peter Smit, and Mikko Kurimo. 2014. Morfessor FlatCat: An HMM-based method for unsupervised and semi-supervised learning of morphology. In *Proceedings of COLING 2014, the 25th International Conference on Computational Linguistics: Technical Papers*, pages 1177–1185, Dublin, Ireland. Dublin City University and Association for Computational Linguistics.

Zellig S. Harris. 1955. From phoneme to morpheme. *Language*, 31(2):190–222.

John Hewitt and Percy Liang. 2019. Designing and interpreting probes with control tasks. *ArXiv*, abs/1909.03368.

Mark Johnson, Thomas Griffiths, and Sharon Goldwater. 2006. Adaptor grammars: A framework for specifying compositional nonparametric bayesian models. *Advances in neural information processing systems*, 19.

Katharina Kann and Hinrich Schütze. 2016. Med: The lmu system for the sigmorphon 2016 shared task on morphological reinflection. In *SIGMORPHON*.

Diederik P Kingma and Max Welling. 2013. Auto-encoding variational bayes. *arXiv preprint arXiv:1312.6114*.

Jordan Kodner, Salam Khalifa, Khuyagbaatar Batsuren, Hossep Dolatian, Ryan Cotterell, Faruk Akkus, Antonios Anastasopoulos, Taras Andrushko, Aryaman Arora, Nona Atanalov, Gábor Bella, Elena Budianskaya, Yustinus Ghanggo Ate, Omer Goldman, David Guriel, Simon Guriel, Silvia Guriel-Agiashvili, Witold Kieraś, Andrew Krizhanovsky, Natalia Krizhanovsky, Igor Marchenko, Magdalena Markowska, Polina Mashkovtseva, Maria Nepomniashchaya, Daria Rodionova, Karina Scheifer, Alexandra Sorova, Anastasia Yemelina, Jeremiah Young, and Ekaterina Vylomova. 2022. SIGMORPHON–UniMorph 2022 shared task 0: Generalization and typologically diverse morphological inflection. In *Proceedings of the 19th SIGMORPHON Workshop on Computational Research in Phonetics, Phonology, and Morphology*, pages 176–203, Seattle, Washington. Association for Computational Linguistics.

Kimmo Koskenniemi. 1983. Two-level model for morphological analysis. In *IJCAI*.

Karim Lasri, Tiago Pimentel, Alessandro Lenci, T. Poibeau, and Ryan Cotterell. 2022. Probing for the usage of grammatical number. In *ACL*.

Arya D. McCarthy, Christo Kirov, Matteo Grella, Amrit Nidhi, Patrick Xia, Kyle Gorman, Ekaterina Vylomova, Sabrina J. Mielke, Garrett Nicolai, Miikka Silfverberg, Timofey Arkhangelskiy, Nataly Krizhanovsky, Andrew Krizhanovsky, Elena Klyachko, Alexey Sorokin, John Mansfield, Valts Ernštreits, Yuval Pinter, Cassandra L. Jacobs, Ryan Cotterell, Mans Hulden, and David Yarowsky. 2020. UniMorph 3.0: Universal Morphology. In *Proceedings of the Twelfth Language Resources and Evaluation Conference*, pages 3922–3931, Marseille, France. European Language Resources Association.

Tatiana Merzhevich, Nkonye Gbadegoye, Leander Girrbach, Jingwen Li, and Ryan Soh-Eun Shim. 2022. SIGMORPHON 2022 task 0 submission description: Modelling morphological inflection with data-driven and rule-based approaches. In *Proceedings of the 19th SIGMORPHON Workshop on Computational Research in Phonetics, Phonology, and Morphology*, pages 204–211, Seattle, Washington. Association for Computational Linguistics.

Kemal Oflazer. 1993. Two-level description of turkish morphology. *Literary and Linguistic Computing*, 9:137–148.

Tiago Pimentel, Maria Ryskina, Sabrina J. Mielke, Shijie Wu, Eleanor Chodroff, Brian Leonard, Garrett Nicolai, Yustinus Ghanggo Ate, Salam Khalifa, Nizar Habash, Charbel El-Khaissi, Omer Goldman,

Michael Gasser, William Lane, Matt Coler, Arturo Oncevay, Jaime Rafael Montoya Samame, Gema Celeste Silva Villegas, Adam Ek, Jean-Philippe Bernardy, Andrey Shcherbakov, Aziyana Bayyr-ool, Karina Sheifer, Sofya Ganieva, Matvey Plugaryov, Elena Klyachko, Ali Salehi, Andrew Krizhanovsky, Natalia Krizhanovsky, Clara Vania, Sardana Ivanova, Aelita Salchak, Christopher Straughn, Zoey Liu, Jonathan North Washington, Duygu Ataman, Witold Kieraś, Marcin Woliński, Totok Suhardijanto, Niklas Stoehr, Zahroh Nuriah, Shyam Ratan, Francis M. Tyers, Edoardo M. Ponti, Grant Aiton, Richard J. Hatcher, Emily Prud'hommeaux, Ritesh Kumar, Mans Hulden, Botond Barta, Dorina Lakatos, Gábor Szolnok, Judit Ács, Mohit Raj, David Yarowsky, Ryan Cotterell, Ben Ambridge, and Ekaterina Vylomova. 2021. SIGMORPHON 2021 shared task on morphological reinflection: Generalization across languages. In *Proceedings of the 18th SIGMORPHON Workshop on Computational Research in Phonetics, Phonology, and Morphology*, pages 229–259, Online. Association for Computational Linguistics.

Tiago Pimentel, Josef Valvoda, Rowan Hall Maudslay, Ran Zmigrod, Adina Williams, and Ryan Cotterell. 2020. Information-theoretic probing for linguistic structure. *ArXiv*, abs/2004.03061.

Jim Pitman and Marc Yor. 1997. The two-parameter poisson-dirichlet distribution derived from a stable subordinator. *The Annals of Probability*, pages 855–900.

Andreas Sherbakov and Ekaterina Vylomova. 2022. Morphology is not just a naive Bayes – UniMelb submission to SIGMORPHON 2022 ST on morphological inflection. In *Proceedings of the 19th SIGMORPHON Workshop on Computational Research in Phonetics, Phonology, and Morphology*, pages 240–246, Seattle, Washington. Association for Computational Linguistics.

Xing Shi, Inkit Padhi, and Kevin Knight. 2016. Does string-based neural mt learn source syntax? In *EMNLP*.

Ahmet Üstün and Burcu Can. 2021. Incorporating word embeddings in unsupervised morphological segmentation. *Natural Language Engineering*, 27(5):609–629.

Ahmet Üstün, Murathan Kurfalı, and Burcu Can. 2018. Characters or morphemes: How to represent words? Association for Computational Linguistics.

Aaron Van Den Oord, Oriol Vinyals, et al. 2017. Neural discrete representation learning. *Advances in neural information processing systems*, 30.

Eva Vanmassenhove, Jinhua Du, and Andy Way. 2017. Investigating 'aspect' in nmt and smt: Translating the english simple past and present perfect.

Elena Voita and Ivan Titov. 2020. Information-theoretic probing with minimum description length. *ArXiv*, abs/2003.12298.

Ekaterina Vylomova, Jennifer White, Elizabeth Salesky, Sabrina J. Mielke, Shijie Wu, Edoardo Maria Ponti, Rowan Hall Maudslay, Ran Zmigrod, Josef Valvoda, Svetlana Toldova, Francis Tyers, Elena Klyachko, Ilya Yegorov, Natalia Krizhanovsky, Paula Czarnowska, Irene Nikkarinen, Andrew Krizhanovsky, Tiago Pimentel, Lucas Torroba Hennigen, Christo Kirov, Garrett Nicolai, Adina Williams, Antonios Anastasopoulos, Hilaria Cruz, Eleanor Chodroff, Ryan Cotterell, Miikka Silfverberg, and Mans Hulden. 2020. SIGMORPHON 2020 shared task 0: Typologically diverse morphological inflection. In *Proceedings of the 17th SIGMORPHON Workshop on Computational Research in Phonetics, Phonology, and Morphology*, pages 1–39, Online. Association for Computational Linguistics.

Silvan Wehrli, Simon Clematide, and Peter Makarov. 2022. CLUZH at SIGMORPHON 2022 shared tasks on morpheme segmentation and inflection generation. In *Proceedings of the 19th SIGMORPHON Workshop on Computational Research in Phonetics, Phonology, and Morphology*, pages 212–219, Seattle, Washington. Association for Computational Linguistics.

Shijie Wu, Ryan Cotterell, and Mans Hulden. 2021. Applying the transformer to character-level transduction. In *EACL*.

Changbing Yang, Ruixin (Ray) Yang, Garrett Nicolai, and Miikka Silfverberg. 2022. Generalizing morphological inflection systems to unseen lemmas. In *Proceedings of the 19th SIGMORPHON Workshop on Computational Research in Phonetics, Phonology, and Morphology*, pages 226–235, Seattle, Washington. Association for Computational Linguistics.

Chunting Zhou and Graham Neubig. 2017. Multi-space variational encoder-decoders for semi-supervised labeled sequence transduction. *arXiv preprint arXiv:1704.01691*.

A Hyperparameter details

For our main model used in Section 3.1 and Section 3.2, the configuration includes a bidirectional GRU encoder with a hidden size of 256, an unidirectional GRU decoder with a hidden size of 1024, a continuous vector of 100 dimensions, 4 codebooks with 8 entries per each codebook, 128 dimensions in each codebook entry, 128 dimensions in encoder-decoder input token embeddings, decoder input dropout set to 0.2, a batch size of 64, Adam optimizer with β values of (0.5, 0.99), a learning rate of 0.0005, KL weight of 1.0 with an annealing strategy starting from epoch 5, and a total of 50 epochs.

For our main model used in Section 3.3, the configuration comprises a bidirectional GRU encoder with a hidden size of 256, an unidirectional GRU decoder with a hidden size of 256, a continuous vector of 100 dimensions, 6 codebooks with 8 entries per each codebook, 128 dimensions in each codebook entry, 128 dimensions in encoder-decoder input token embeddings, decoder input dropout set to 0.1, a batch size of 16, Adam optimizer with β values of (0.5, 0.99), a learning rate of 0.0005, KL weight of 0.05 with an annealing strategy starting from epoch 10, and a total of 500 epochs.

B Dataset Preprocessing in Section 3.1

We firstly acquired the Unimorph dataset [2], which initially contained 570,420 examples in the format of (lemma, target, tags). We eliminated duplicate examples with identical targets, reducing the count to 536,701. Subsequently, we filtered out target words from the SIGMORPHON-UniMorph 2022 Shared Task 0 development and test data unless they were also present in the shared task's large training set of Turkish, resulting in 533,708 instances. Further refinement involved selecting only words with "V" tags in their feature list, yielding 404,896 instances. For the test set, we also filtered out shared task test data words with "V" tags, leaving us with 1,446 instances. This procedure led to one instance of a triple overlap between the training and test sets (out of all 1,446 instances).

[2]https://github.com/unimorph/tur/blob/master/tur

C Different codebook-entry configurations

Test acc.	0.93
Inflection acc. (Top-1)	0.30
Inflection acc. (Top-2)	0.40
Train # used entries	1122
Test # used entries	577

Table 8: 4x6 Training results. KL=1.0.

	Person	Tense	Polarity
z_c	0.27	0.54	0.95
z_q	0.96	0.86	0.59
cbook-0	0.31	**0.72**	0.54
cbook-1	0.18	0.48	**0.56**
cbook-2	**0.72**	0.52	0.53
cbook-3	0.26	0.53	**0.56**
baseline	0.18	0.48	0.52

Table 9: 4x6 Probing accuracy results.

Test acc.	0.87
Inflection acc. (Top-1)	0.48
Inflection acc. (Top-2)	0.74
Train # used entries	11891
Test # used entries	1259

Table 10: 4x12 Training results. KL=1.0.

	Person	Tense	Polarity
z_c	0.28	0.48	0.71
z_q	0.96	0.96	0.98
cbook-0	**0.75**	0.49	0.53
cbook-1	0.30	0.62	**0.86**
cbook-2	0.20	0.59	0.53
cbook-3	0.19	**0.67**	0.69
baseline	0.18	0.48	0.52

Table 11: 4x12 Probing accuracy results.

Test acc.	0.94
Inflection acc. (Top-1)	0.54
Inflection acc. (Top-2)	0.83
Train # used entries	12089
Test # used entries	1270

Table 12: 6x6 Training results. KL=1.0.

	Person	Tense	Polarity
z_c	0.26	0.51	0.64
z_q	0.98	0.95	0.83
cbook-0	0.50	0.50	0.55
cbook-1	0.20	0.61	0.54
cbook-2	0.20	**0.69**	**0.78**
cbook-3	0.19	0.57	0.57
cbook-4	**0.65**	0.57	0.55
cbook-5	0.19	0.57	0.53
baseline	0.18	0.48	0.52

Table 13: 6x6 Probing accuracy results.

Test acc.	0.99
Inflection acc. (Top-1)	0.72
Inflection acc. (Top-2)	0.92
Train # used entries	23104
Test # used entries	1291

Table 14: 6x8 Training results. KL=0.5.

	Person	Tense	Polarity
z_c	0.25	0.51	0.64
z_q	0.99	0.95	0.87
cbook-0	**0.85**	0.51	0.52
cbook-1	0.18	0.48	0.56
cbook-2	0.20	**0.90**	0.53
cbook-3	0.33	0.54	0.63
cbook-4	0.18	0.50	0.65
cbook-5	0.19	0.50	**0.85**
baseline	0.18	0.48	0.52

Table 15: 6x8 Probing accuracy results.

Table 16: Summary of training and probing results. We present the best performances of various configurations with KL values of 0.2, 0.5, and 1.0. Since models employing 12-codebooks exhibit poor performance in both inflection and probing tasks; we exclude them from our analysis.

Test acc.	0.99
Inflection acc. (Top-1)	0.82
Inflection acc. (Top-2)	0.95
Train # used entries	31197
Test # used entries	1327

Table 17: 6x12 Training results. KL=0.5.

	Person	**Tense**	**Polarity**
z_c	0.30	0.51	0.74
z_q	0.99	0.95	0.91
cbook-0	0.20	**0.78**	0.68
cbook-1	0.20	0.55	0.67
cbook-2	0.19	0.68	**0.74**
cbook-3	0.18	0.49	0.59
cbook-4	0.67	0.62	0.54
cbook-5	**0.68**	0.52	0.66
baseline	0.18	0.48	0.52

Table 18: 6x12 Probing accuracy results.

Test acc.	0.99
Inflection acc. (Top-1)	0.87
Inflection acc. (Top-2)	0.96
Train # used entries	27073
Test # used entries	1312

Table 19: 8x6 Training results. KL=0.5.

	Person	**Tense**	**Polarity**
z_c	0.26	0.49	0.65
z_q	0.98	0.86	0.95
cbook-0	0.19	0.48	0.53
cbook-1	**0.84**	0.49	0.54
cbook-2	0.68	0.49	0.53
cbook-3	0.18	0.49	0.57
cbook-4	0.20	0.60	0.59
cbook-5	0.18	0.50	0.71
cbook-6	0.19	**0.65**	**0.89**
cbook-7	0.27	0.62	0.54
baseline	0.18	0.48	0.52

Table 20: 8x6 Probing accuracy results.

Test acc.	0.99
Inflection acc. (Top-1)	0.84
Inflection acc. (Top-2)	0.95
Train # used entries	29251
Test # used entries	1277

Table 21: 8x8 Training results. KL=0.5.

	Person	**Tense**	**Polarity**
z_c	0.28	0.53	0.71
z_q	0.99	0.99	0.99
cbook-0	0.20	0.66	0.54
cbook-1	0.36	0.50	0.60
cbook-2	0.19	0.58	0.67
cbook-3	0.19	**0.68**	0.82
cbook-4	0.19	0.49	0.57
cbook-5	0.64	0.49	0.53
cbook-6	**0.90**	0.66	0.53
cbook-7	0.20	0.58	**0.96**
baseline	0.18	0.48	0.52

Table 22: 8x8 Probing accuracy results.

Table 23: Summary of training and probing results. We present the best performances of various configurations with KL values of 0.2, 0.5, and 1.0. Since models employing 12-codebooks exhibit poor performance in both inflection and probing tasks; we exclude them from our analysis.

D 5 Different random runs with 4x8 codebooks

Test acc.	0.98
Inflection acc. (Top-1)	0.73
Inflection acc. (Top-2)	0.82
Train # used entries	2656
Test # used entries	811

Table 24: RUN 1: Training results.

	Person	**Tense**	**Polarity**
z_c	0.25	0.50	0.75
z_q	0.99	0.90	0.65
cbook-0	0.20	0.53	0.55
cbook-1	0.49	0.50	0.54
cbook-2	0.21	**0.81**	**0.63**
cbook-3	**0.58**	0.49	0.56
baseline	0.18	0.48	0.52

Table 25: RUN 1 Probing accuracy results.

Test acc.	0.95
Inflection acc. (Top-1)	0.39
Inflection acc. (Top-2)	0.59
Train # used entries	3085
Test # used entries	933

Table 26: RUN 2: Training results.

	Person	**Tense**	**Polarity**
z_c	0.29	0.50	0.69
z_q	0.98	0.88	0.81
cbook-0	0.19	**0.64**	0.51
cbook-1	**0.90**	0.55	0.52
cbook-2	0.18	0.49	0.54
cbook-3	0.20	0.62	**0.74**
baseline	0.18	0.48	0.52

Table 27: RUN 2 Probing accuracy results.

Test acc.	0.98
Inflection acc. (Top-1)	0.94
Inflection acc. (Top-2)	0.98
Train # used entries	2621
Test # used entries	779

Table 28: RUN3: Training results.

	Person	**Tense**	**Polarity**
z_c	0.25	0.48	0.63
z_q	0.99	0.98	0.86
cbook-0	**0.98**	0.51	0.52
cbook-1	0.20	**0.88**	0.53
cbook-2	0.20	0.55	**0.74**
cbook-3	0.18	0.50	0.72
baseline	0.18	0.48	0.52

Table 29: RUN 3 Probing accuracy results.

Test acc.	0.95
Inflection acc. (Top-1)	0.74
Inflection acc. (Top-2)	0.93
Train # used entries	2624
Test # used entries	921

Table 30: RUN 4: Training results.

	Person	**Tense**	**Polarity**
z_c	0.27	0.54	0.68
z_q	0.92	0.88	0.83
cbook-0	0.21	**0.72**	**0.79**
cbook-1	0.30	0.50	0.50
cbook-2	0.45	0.54	0.56
cbook-3	**0.50**	0.48	0.62
baseline	0.18	0.48	0.52

Table 31: RUN 4 Probing accuracy results.

Test acc.	0.98
Inflection acc. (Top-1)	0.96
Inflection acc. (Top-2)	0.97
Train # used entries	2478
Test # used entries	736

Table 32: RUN 5: Training results.

	Person	**Tense**	**Polarity**
z_c	0.25	0.49	0.67
z_q	0.95	0.96	0.90
cbook-0	**0.59**	0.49	0.54
cbook-1	0.33	0.52	**0.78**
cbook-2	0.35	**0.64**	0.56
cbook-3	0.18	0.58	0.70
baseline	0.18	0.48	0.52

Table 33: RUN 5 Probing accuracy results.

E Related Model: MSVAE

We experiment with 4,6 and 8 MLP classifiers, each designed with 8 classes for every morphological feature. Additionally, we adjust the KL ratio to 1.0 to encourage the model to use discrete vectors from the classifiers. We observe that the model uses a small subset of classes for the test set, (which originally had 616 unique feature sets) suggesting that it exclusively relies on the continuous vector and does not make use of the discrete vectors from the classifiers. Consequently, the model fails to differentiate the lemma via the continuous part and the suffix-related morphological features via the classifiers. This results in inconsistencies in sampling as seen in Table 36, generating different suffixations even when the same morphological classes are given as input for the word.

Setting	Copy acc.	# Used Classes
4x8	0.94	53
6x8	0.96	54
8x8	0.96	60

Table 34: Training results of MSVAE with various number of classifiers.

Predicted classes	Words
2;6;6;6	bıkıyor olacaktım iyileşiyor olmayacaklar mıymış gizlenmez misiniz açılmalı mıydınız
5;4;1;1	kaynaştırılıyor olmalı mıyım hava atacak olacak mıymışsın güzelleştiriyor olacakmışsınız öğretiyor olmayacaklar mıydı
7;6;1;1	gülünçleşir olmayacakmışsın buharlaşıyor olacak mısınız fındık kıracak olacaklarmış ilerletiyor olmayacaklar mı

Table 35: Model's classifications with 4x8 MLPs. The model fails to use combinations specific to the same suffix.

sample 1	otostop çekermişsin
sample 2	darılmalı mıydık
sample 3	üzmemişlermiş
sample 4	sünüyor olmaz mıydı
sample 5	havlu atıyor muydunuz

Table 36: Sampled words with 4x8 MLPs. Continous vectors are sampled from a Gaussian distribution, and a specific class combination is selected from the classifiers. We do not observe consistent patterns in suffix usage.

F Importance of Direction

Problem (1): Suffix information is not entirely encoded in the discrete part, but partially encoded in the continuous part with lemma. An example of this case occurs with a model with 4 codebooks and 8 entries. The model only achieves a 12% accuracy in top-1 match and 18% accuracy in top-2 match for inflection. This is confirmed by sampled words as in Table 37 and probing experiments as seen in Table 38.

sample 1	bulamadı mı
sample 2	dalamadı mı
sample 3	coşmadım mı
sample 4	kopmadım
sample 5	boyamadım

Table 37: Sampled words with 4x8 codebooks. Continuous vectors are sampled from a Gaussian distribution, and a specific entry combination is selected from the codebooks. The model exhibits a slight inconsistency with respect to suffix.

	Person	**Tense**	**Polarity**
z_c	0.67	**0.70**	**0.88**
z_q	**0.97**	0.63	0.72
cbook-0	0.55	0.64	0.53
cbook-1	0.20	0.50	0.70
cbook-2	0.19	0.59	0.67
cbook-3	0.36	0.49	0.54
baseline	0.18	0.48	0.52

Table 38: Probing results for the model with 4-codebooks x 8-entries with no inductive bias. Suffix-related information is encoded into a continuous vector, which is expected to solely represent the lemma.

Problem (3): Lemma information is entirely encoded in the discrete part, while suffix information is entirely encoded in the continuous part. An example of this case occurs with a model with 6 codebooks and 6 entries. The model achieves a 3% accuracy in top-1 match and 9% accuracy in top-2 match for inflection. This is confirmed by sampled words as in Table 39 and probing experiments as seen in Table 40.

sample 1	canlandırılmış mıymış
sample 2	canlandırtılmış mıydık
sample 3	canlandırtılmışız
sample 4	canlandırılmıştım
sample 5	canlandırılmış olmamalıyız

Table 39: Sampled words with 6x6 codebooks. Continuous vectors are sampled from a Gaussian distribution, and a specific entry combination is selected from the codebooks. The model uses the same lemma but alters the suffixation, which is expected to be the opposite.

	Person	**Tense**	**Polarity**
z_c	**0.99**	**0.83**	**0.97**
z_q	0.30	0.63	0.50
cbook-0	0.30	0.49	0.54
cbook-1	0.20	0.48	0.56
cbook-2	0.20	0.48	0.65
cbook-3	0.20	0.49	0.53
cbook-4	0.19	0.61	0.60
cbook-5	0.20	0.48	0.54
baseline	0.18	0.48	0.52

Table 40: Probing results for the model with 6-codebooks x 6-entries with no inductive bias. Suffix-related information is encoded into a continuous vector, which is expected to solely represent the lemma.

Open foundation models for Azerbaijani language

Jafar Isbarov*
The George Washington University
Department of Computer Science
0000-0001-8404-2192
jafar.isbarov@gwmail.gwu.edu

Kavsar Huseynova*
Baku Higher Oil School
Information Technology Department
0009-0007-0362-9591
kavsar.huseynova.std@bhos.edu.az

Elvin Mammadov
Baku Higher Oil School
Information Technology Department
0009-0005-9237-9736
elvin.mammadov.std@bhos.edu.az

Mammad Hajili
Microsoft
0000-0002-9522-2137
mammadhajili@microsoft.com

Abstract

The emergence of multilingual large language models has enabled the development of language understanding and generation systems in Azerbaijani. However, most of the production-grade systems rely on cloud solutions, such as GPT-4. While there have been several attempts to develop open foundation models for Azerbaijani, these works have not found their way into common use due to a lack of systemic benchmarking. This paper encompasses several lines of work that promote open-source foundation models for Azerbaijani. We introduce (1) a large text corpus for Azerbaijani, (2) a family of encoder-only language models trained on this dataset, (3) labeled datasets for evaluating these models, and (4) extensive evaluation that covers all major open-source models with Azerbaijani support.

1 Introduction

Large language models (LLMs) have seen a sudden rise in popularity in recent years. Both open-source and proprietary models have seen wide adoption across various industries. This boost has not been shared equally across different regions, however, mostly due to the slow osmosis of these technologies into low-resource languages. Azerbaijani language falls on the "other" side of this barrier, with its 24 million speakers worldwide.

While some models have a limited understanding of the Azerbaijani language, only paid models offered by OpenAI have seen some level of adoption in the industry. Open-source models are being created with multilingual or Azerbaijani-only capabilities, but the community is not as keen to adopt them. This is possibly due to the limited exploration of these models' potential. This paper encompassed several lines of work that share a common goal - promoting open-source foundational models for Azerbaijani. Our contributions are as follows:

1. DOLLMA: A new text corpus of 651.1 million words in Azerbaijani that can be used for pre-training LLMs.
2. aLLMA: A new family of BERT-class models trained on this dataset from scratch.
3. Three labeled datasets that can be used for benchmarking foundation models in Azerbaijani:
   - 3.1. AZE-SCI: A text classification dataset.
   - 3.2. AZE-NSP: A next-sentence prediction dataset.
   - 3.3. CB-MCQ: A closed-book question-answering dataset.
4. A benchmark for several natural language understanding (NLU) tasks in Azerbaijani. It contains our newly introduced models and other existing open-source alternatives.

*Equal contribution

Proceedings of the First Workshop on Natural Language Processing for Turkic Languages (SIGTURK 2024), pages 18–28
August 15, 2024 ©2024 Association for Computational Linguistics

1.1 Foundation Models

While language modeling has a long history, transformer-based large foundation models can be considered a recent phenomenon. These models have a disproportionately high number of trainable parameters, made possible due to the highly parallelizable nature of the transformer architecture. Their development takes place in two stages: Pre-training and fine-tuning. Pre-training is performed on Web-scale text corpora, while fine-tuning is performed on smaller and higher-quality data to adapt the model to a specific task. (Minaee et al., 2024)

Foundation models exist for various modalities, including language, vision, and speech. Language foundation models are usually classified as encoder, decoder, or encoder-decoder models. Encoder models are used for tasks that require language understanding, such as sentiment analysis and extractive question-answering. Encoder-decoder and decoder-only models are better suited for generative tasks, such as machine translation and text summarisation. *Our work concentrates on encoder-only models.* Our main inspiration is the BERT model family by (Devlin et al., 2019) and its derivatives.

In the rest of the paper, a foundation model refers to a language model trained on a vast amount of unlabeled text data that can be fine-tuned for various downstream tasks. A large language model refers to a foundation language model with at least tens of millions of parameters.

1.2 Modeling Azerbaijani

The majority of LLMs are either monolingual English models or multilingual models that do not support Azerbaijani. Very few multilingual models support Azerbaijani, and only recently monolingual Azerbaijani models are beginning to emerge.

This slow progress can be explained by several factors. A smaller market and less investment is an obvious explanation, but the field faces more fundamental challenges that would not be immediately solved by more funding. One of these is the state of digitalization of the language. Most of the electronic books in Azerbaijani are scanned books. Only books published since the 1990s are written in the last version of the Azerbaijani Latin alphabet [1], which creates another barrier. Yet another challenge is the small size of the community that's devoted to the development of open-source language models for Azerbaijani. The challenges regarding digitalization and script differences are further discussed in the third section.

An idea that is often heard regarding Azerbaijani LLMs is that we can simply go for the models developed for Turkish since languages are so similar. Azerbaijani and Turkish languages are not as similar as it is publicly perceived. According to (Salehi and Neysani, 2017), Azerbaijanis scored 56% of receptive intelligibility in spoken Turkish. Differences in written language are not any smaller. Based on the methodology offered by (Gupta et al., 2019), a 44% similarity score has been calculated between the vocabularies of the two languages [2]. Due to these significant differences, Turkish LLMs are not useful in machine learning tasks for Azerbaijani.

The paper is structured as follows. The next section gives a brief overview of previous works on foundational language models, and language modeling on Azerbaijani. The third section introduces DOLLMA, a new text corpus, and outlines the methodology, challenges we faced, and future works. The fourth section introduces aLLMA, a new family of monolingual encoder-only language models. The fifth section introduces several benchmarks for evaluating encoder-only Azerbaijani language models. These benchmarks are used to evaluate newly introduced models, as well as existing alternatives. The sixth section presents these benchmarks' results.

2 Previous works

The use of neural networks for language modeling can be traced back to the early 2000s. (Bengio et al., 2000) and (Mikolov et al., 2010) had created neural networks that outperformed traditional state-of-the-art model. (Schwenk et al., 2006) uses neural networks for machine translation.

These models and their derivatives were task-specific. The idea of creating a foundational language model that could later be adapted (i.e., fine-tuned) to specific tasks was popularized only after the introduction of the transformer architecture by

[1]There was an older version of the Azerbaijani Latin alphabet introduced by the Soviets in 1922. This followed several variations until 1939 when the alphabet was replaced with a Cyrillic alternative. Azerbaijan started the transition to an updated Latin alphabet in 1991, which was completed in 2001.

[2]`https://www.ezglot.com/most-similar-languages?l=aze`

(Vaswani et al., 2017). The earliest foundational language model that gained wide adoption was BERT by (Devlin et al., 2019) and later variations like RoBERTa (Liu et al., 2019).

BERT was an encoder-only model, therefore more suitable for problems that could be formulated as a subset of the classification problem. Generative foundation models came out around the same time, in the example of GPT-1 (Radford and Narasimhan, 2018), GPT-2 (Radford et al., 2019), and T5 (Raffel et al., 2019). While the GPT series continued with closed-source, enterprise models, other alternatives quickly emerged with superior performance. The most famous of these was the LLaMA series, which directly or indirectly resulted in the development of hundreds of open-source language models. (Touvron et al., 2023).

Early foundation models were trained on English text, but multilingual models quickly emerged. Google had released multilingual BERT alternatives, and mGPT by (Shliazhko et al., 2023) was an early variation of the GPT architecture for multiple languages. XLM-RoBERTa by (Conneau et al., 2020) was a larger and more successful alternative to mGPT and was quickly adopted worldwide.

XLM-RoBERTa was also one of the first (if not the first) foundation models that supported Azerbaijani. We are aware of only one academic work that has concentrated on the development of foundational language models for Azerbaijani. (Ziyaden et al., 2024) have trained a RoBERTa model on the Azerbaijani split of the OSCAR dataset (Ortiz Suárez et al., 2020). This work is a first of its kind for Azerbaijani and a very valuable starting point. However, it does not concentrate on the development of a foundation model. Its main focus is improving model performance by text augmentation. Therefore, they do not perform a systematic evaluation of the model. They have released one RoBERTa model, without different sizes, which is yet another limiting factor in the adoption of the work. Unfortunately, this model has not been included in our evaluation benchmarks because they have not released a tokenizer that is compatible with their model.

There have also been some community attempts to create such open-source models. A series of RoBERTa models were developed by continuing the pre-training phase on a small Azerbaijani dataset (Hajili, 2024c). Alas Development Center has developed a series of decoder-only LLMs for Azerbaijani [3], but they offer no explanation regarding their approach, and the models failed to pass initial sanity checks.

3 Text corpus

A large text corpus is a prerequisite for training a large language model. For reference, GPT-2 and RoBERTa both were trained on OpenWebText (Liu et al., 2019), consisting of 13.5 billion tokens, which is roughly equivalent to 10 billion words. Original BERT models were trained on 3.3. billion words. While these numbers have exploded in recent years, the success of these models suggests that similarly effective models can be trained on similarly sized datasets.

The largest corpora that existed at the beginning of our work were OSCAR, which contained 316 million words in Azerbaijani, and Colossal Clean Crawled Corpus (C4) with 1.7 billion words. Introduced by (Raffel et al., 2020), C4 is one of the most widely used datasets in the pretraining stage of LLMs. C4 is labeled by language and contains 1.83 million documents tagged as Azerbaijani. Upon further inspection, however, we discovered a significant portion of this text is not only in different languages, but also in different alphabets (Armenian, Georgian, and Cyrillic). In addition, the C4 dataset contains a significant amount of informal text. This can be a valuable resource, but it is outside the scope of our work. Considering all of these points, we decided against using it. OSCAR (Ortiz Suárez et al., 2020) dataset is also derived from CommonCrawl. It suffers from the same problems, so it was not included in our corpus either.

Due to these limitations, we decided to curate a new dataset specifically for pre-training LLMs that understand Azerbaijani. This new corpus is called DOLLMA (**D**ataset for **O**pen **L**arge **L**anguage **M**odels in **A**zerbaijani).[4] The first and current version of this dataset contains Azerbaijani Wikipedia, Translated English Wikipedia (incomplete), news, blogs, books, and Azerbaijani laws. This dataset contains about 651.1 million words.[5] New versions

[3]`https://github.com/interneuron-ai/project-barbarossa`

[4]`https://huggingface.co/datasets/allmalab/DOLLMA`

[5]Words were counted with a simple whitespace tokenizer.

Data source	Word count	Upscale	Final count	Source
English Wikipedia	194.0M	4	776.0M	(BHOS AI R&D Center, 2024)
Azerbaijani Wikipedia	40.0M	6	245.0M	(aLLMA Lab, 2024c)
News	238.9M	1	238.9M	BHOS AI R&D Center
Books I	2.5M	20	50.0M	aLLMA Lab
Books II	131.7M	4	526.8M	LocalDoc
Blogs	0.9M	20	17.5M	aLLMA Lab
Azerbaijani laws	44M	6	264M	(aLLMA Lab, 2024e)
Total	651.1M	-	2118.2M	-

Table 1: Data sources used to generate the DOLLMA corpus. English Wikipedia has been translated with open-source models by the BHOS AI team.

of DOLLMA will incorporate the Common Crawl data.

Books. We attempted to create a large book corpus but faced several challenges. Most of the available electronic books in Azerbaijani are scanned copies. Publishers rarely offer electronic books that are suitable for text extraction. As of 9 May 2024, Qanun Publishing, the largest publishing house in Azerbaijan, offers 52 PDFs or EPUBs on its website. The remaining books, which were sampled from the Azerbaijan National Library [6], Children's Library [7], and other sources, are all scanned copies that have occasionally passed through an OCR model. For OCR, Tesseract (Smith, 2007) was chosen due to its multilingual support and open-source availability. We scanned thousands of books and manually sampled and analyzed them. Tesseract failed to capture guillemets, which is widespread in older Azerbaijani books. It also mixed up "m" with "rn" in scanned books. This happened often enough to decrease the quality of the text substantially. Due to these limitations, we decided against using OCR output altogether as training data. Instead, we opted for two datasets:

1. Books I contains a small number of hand-picked books.

2. Books II contains a higher number of books with less detailed processing.

Wikipedia. We used dumps provided by the Wikimedia Foundation to create a new version of Azerbaijani Wikipedia. Both the data (aLLMA Lab, 2024d) and cleaning scripts [8] are publicly available. BHOS AI team leads another initiative where they are using open-source translation models to translate English Wikipedia into Azerbaijani (BHOS AI R&D Center, 2024). While this dataset offers little in terms of linguistic variety, it provides an invaluable knowledge base to train the models. Therefore, it was included in the final corpus.

News. There is an abundance of news datasets for Azerbaijani. However, we decided against using a very large news corpus, since it offers little variety in terms of language. In our experience, models trained on news datasets do not learn the language comprehensively, possibly because the news contains little to no creative writing, first- and second-person narration, and dialogue. Due to these limitations, only two news datasets were included. One contains text scraped from several news platforms, and the other contains news and updates from Azerbaijan National Library. The BHOS AI team provided both datasets.

Blogs. Another data source was blog posts collected from various websites. Instead of scraping a large number of websites for their blogs, several blogs were manually picked due to their high-quality text and informative content.

Laws. The last part consisted of Azerbaijani laws, all of which are publicly available. We have also released this as an independent text corpus (aLLMA Lab, 2024e).

You can see a summary of these sources and their accompanying upscaling ratios in Table 1. Upscaling ratios were decided rather arbitrarily. We decided against upscaling the news since they of-

[6]`https://www.millikitabxana.az/`

[7]`https://www.clb.az/`

[8]`https://github.com/ceferisbarov/azwiki`

fer little linguistic variety. Azerbaijani Wikipedia was upscaled higher than the translated English Wikipedia to account for the lossy translation process. Azerbaijani laws offer higher-quality text than Azerbaijani Wikipedia but offer less variety both in terms of content and form. Considering this, we upscaled them at the same level. Blogs and Books II datasets were hand-picked and constituted the highest-quality text in our corpus. Therefore, their upscaling ratio was the highest. Books II had mediocre quality, mostly due to the challenges of extracting text from PDF files. We upscaled it at the same level as the English Wikipedia.

A major shortcoming of DOLLMA is imbalanced domain distribution. While the dataset contains a substantial amount of text on Azerbaijani laws, it is lacking in terms of first-person narrative, and STEM fields. It is also heavily Azerbaijan-centric, which may or may not be an issue depending on the final goal.

Deduplication has not been performed since none of the sources has the potential of overlapping with another (i.e., Wikipedia and News, or Books and Laws). However, the addition of a deduplication stage is important if this corpus is to be expanded further.

Later versions of DOLLMA will include several major changes:

1. Add deduplication to the pipeline. This will allow us to incorporate potentially overlapping text sources.

2. Create a large-scale book corpus.

3. Improve domain distribution.

4. Incorporate web-scraping datasets such as OSCAR and C4.

We believe that these changes will open up new possibilities for modeling the Azerbaijani language. At the current state, however, taking into account time and hardware limitations, our dataset was sufficient to continue to the modeling stage.

4 Pre-training

Using DOLLMA, we have developed a series of foundational language models called aLLMA (**a** **L**arge **L**anguage **M**odel for **A**zerbaijani). aLLMA has been trained in three sizes: small, base, and large. Base and large correspond to the original BERT models $\text{BERT}_{\text{BASE}}$ and $\text{BERT}_{\text{LARGE}}$ (Devlin et al., 2019). Small architecture was borrowed from (Bhargava et al., 2021). Architectural details of these models can be found in Table 2. aLLMA-SMALL[9] and aLLMA-BASE[10] have been trained and are included in our benchmarks. aLLMA-LARGE will be released before September, 2024 and the benchmarks will be updated accordingly.

We recognize two alternative approaches to the problem of modeling a low-resource language:

- Continue the pertaining step of an existing multilingual foundation model.

- Pre-train a foundation model from scratch.

aLLMA models were developed with the latter approach. While the benchmarks contain several models that have been trained with the former method, no detailed analysis of the performance difference is provided. This is left as a future research area.

The pre-training task was only masked language modeling. The next sentence prediction task constitutes one of our benchmarks but is not included in the pre-training stage. Training loss of aLLMA-SMALL and aLLMA-BASE models can be found in Figure 1.

One major limitation of the original BERT paper was static masking. If tokens are masked before the training process, then even with multiple epochs, the model will always have to predict the same token. We borrow the idea of dynamic masking from (Liu et al., 2019). Instead of masking tokens before the training, tokens are masked on demand. This results in various masking patterns on the same text samples. Since our model is trained from scratch on an Azerbaijani-only dataset, using existing multilingual tokenizers offered no advantages. A WordPiece tokenizer[11] was trained on a weighted version of DOLLMA, with a vocabulary size of 64k. We have not performed a systematic evaluation to find the optimal vocabulary size. (Kaya and Tantuğ, 2024) have researched the impact of vocabulary size on the performance of Turkish language models. Since both Azerbaijani and Turkish are

[9] `https://huggingface.co/allmalab/bert-small-aze`

[10] `https://huggingface.co/allmalab/bert-base-aze`

[11] `https://huggingface.co/allmalab/bert-tokenizer-aze`

Model	Hidden Size	Num. Attention Heads	Num. Hidden Layers	Num. Parameters
aLLMA-SMALL	512	8	4	45.9M
aLLMA-BASE	768	12	12	135.2M
aLLMA-LARGE	1024	16	24	369.5M

Table 2: Architectural differences among the aLLMA models.

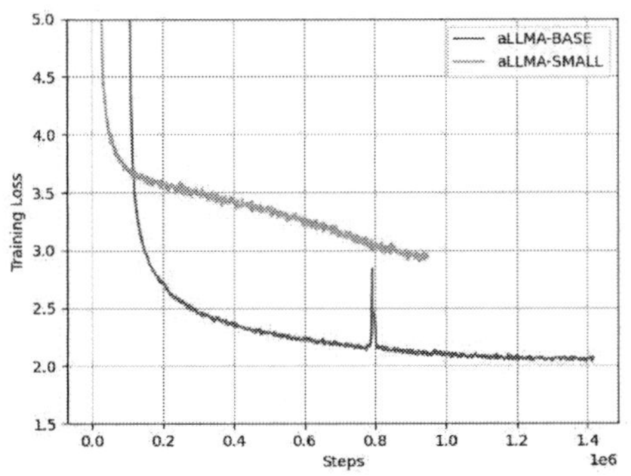

Figure 1: Training loss for aLLMA-SMALL aLLMA-BASE and aLLMA-LARGE models.

agglutinative languages and share similar morphological features, we used the results of this research as a guide. While (Kaya and Tantuğ, 2024) recommends increasing this number further, anything above that would be too computationally expensive for us.

5 Benchmarks

This section presents the tasks that were used to evaluate the natural language understanding capabilities of foundation models in Azerbaijani. All of these tasks are a form of classification since the models are encoder-only. We created three new datasets - text classification (AZE-SCI), closed-book multiple-choice questions (CB-MCQ), and next-sentence prediction (AZE-NSP) as a part of this project. Four more datasets (WikiANN, translated MRPC, translated SQuAD, and LDQuAd) were borrowed from the open-source community.

For each task, all models were trained with the same hyperparameters (learning rate, number of epochs, etc.). In almost all cases, models were undertrained - the project had hardware and time constraints and we were trying to get comparative results rather than functioning models. The source code for all experiments is being released, and the reader can generate better-performing models by simply training longer. Benchmarks have been summarized in Table 3.

5.1 AZE-SCI

AZE-SCI dataset contains titles, topics, and subtopics of dissertations written at Azerbaijani universities and institutes. Subtopics were ignored and only topic labels were used for classification. Being the simplest out of all, this dataset offers a traditional text classification challenge. (Hajili, 2024a)

5.2 AZE-NSP

The next-sentence prediction task allows us to assess the higher-level understanding capabilities of the models. We were unable to find such a dataset in Azerbaijani and decided to build one ourselves. Several books were compiled and split into paragraphs. A sentence pair was extracted from each paragraph and divided into two parts. The second sentence served as the true label, while randomly sampled sentences from other parts of the same book functioned as distractors. Special care was taken to ensure that there was no overlap between this dataset's source text and the pre-training data. (aLLMA Lab, 2024b)

5.3 CB-MCQ

The most challenging task given to the models was a closed-book multiple-choice question-answering dataset, collected from various websites. Its content is mostly middle- and high-school topics, but also contains topics like a driver's exam and state service examination. (aLLMA Lab, 2024a)

All of the tested models failed to learn this model even at a basic level. Due to this, we have decided against testing all models and including them in the leaderboards. This benchmark remains an open challenge for Azerbaijani language modeling. It has been released publicly on the Hugging Face platform to promote further research.

Dataset	Num. of samples	Task	Source
AZE-SCI	5.76k	Text classification	(Hajili, 2024a)
MRPC (translated)	3.67k	Paraphrase identification	(Eljan Mahammadli, 2024)
WikiANN	12k	Named entity recognition	(Pan et al., 2017)
SQuAD (Translated)	54.1k	Extractive QA	(Hajili, 2024d)
LDQuAd	154k	Extractive QA	(LocalDoc, 2024)
AZE-NSP	9.15k	Next sentence prediction	(aLLMA Lab, 2024b)

Table 3: Benchmarks.

5.4 Existing datasets

Several open-source datasets were sampled as an evaluation criterion. Some of these datasets were discarded due to low quality or small size. In the end, we decided on WikiANN, translated SQuAD, LDQuAd, and translated MRPC.

5.4.1 WikiANN

WikiANN is a multilingual named entity recognition dataset sampled from Wikipedia articles (Pan et al., 2017). The dataset contains 12 thousand samples in Azerbaijani. The text is tokenized and location, person, and organization entities are labeled. Since the tokenized version of the dataset does not match our tokenizer, each token was re-tokenized separately and a tag was assigned to each new token.

5.4.2 SQuAD

Question-answering problems usually demand more robust language understanding and therefore serve as a better criterion than simpler classification tasks. There is no original open-book question-answering dataset in Azerbaijani. The Stanford Question Answering Dataset (SQuAD) is one such dataset in English. We used a translated and reindexed version of the original (Hajili, 2024d).

5.4.3 LDQuAd

LDQuAd is a native Azerbaijani alternative to the SQuAD dataset. It contains 154,000 thousand samples, about 30% of which have no answer. Upon further inspection, we realized that most samples with a "no answer" label actually had a correct answer. It is possible that indices were generated automatically with a string search, and some answers were not found, resulting in mislabeled samples. Due to this, we discarded all samples with no answer. (LocalDoc, 2024)

5.4.4 MRPC

Microsoft Research Paraphrase Corpus (MRPC) (Dolan and Brockett, 2005) is an English dataset that is used in NLU benchmarks like GLUE. Each sample contains two sentences and a label of whether or not two sentences are paraphrased versions of each other. We used a translated version of the corpus (Eljan Mahammadli, 2024).

6 Results

Initial tests were performed on dozens of foundation models and some were deliberately left out of the final analysis due to their inferior performance. The final benchmark includes four model categories:

Multilingual foundation models. BERT-BASE-MULTI is a multilingual version of the original BERT model. XLM-RoBERTa-BASE and XLM-RoBERTa-LARGE are some of the best-performing multilingual models (Conneau et al., 2020). mDeBERTa-v3-BASE is a multilingual version of DeBERTa v3 model (He et al., 2023)).

Multilingual models further pre-trained for Azerbaijani. BERT-BASE-AZE (Hajili, 2024b) and RoBERTa-BASE-AZE (Hajili, 2024c) have been further pre-trained on a small and high-quality Azerbaijani dataset. Their base models are RoBERTA-BASE, BERT-BASE-MULTI, and DeBERTa-BASE, respectively.

Models pre-trained from scratch. aLLMA-SMALL and aLLMA-BASE are the only monolingual Azerbaijani models. aLLMA-LARGE is still being trained.

Baseline models. The original English-only BERT-BASE was added as a baseline for the multilingual models. BERT-SCRATCH refers to the models trained on a specific task without pre-training weights. It functions as a baseline for all models in the benchmark.

Model name	Size	AZE-SCI	MRPC	WikiANN	SQuAD	AZE-NSP	LDQuAd
XLM-RoBERTa-LARGE	560M	89.76	82.41	92.35	**75.70**	33.46	83.48
mDeBERTa-v3-BASE	279M	87.13	**83.71**	91.87	72.27	**78.84**	85.29
XLM-RoBERTa-BASE	278M	86.99	70.90	90.29	70.97	74.96	85.17
RoBERTa-BASE-AZE	278M	89.17	81.25	91.62	70.36	76.98	85.44
BERT-BASE-AZE	178M	88.80	80.12	**92.35**	69.42	74.12	64.41
BERT-BASE-MULTI	178M	86.88	79.92	91.67	68.92	72.46	83.48
BERT-SCRATCH	135M	73.31	65.36	72.95	16.11	50.73	26.60
BERT-BASE	108M	76.73	75.00	90.94	55.51	62.12	74,88
ALLMA-BASE	135M	**90.84**	79.74	91.26	71.30	75.95	**86.26**
ALLMA-SMALL	46M	88.06	71.77	90.07	59.89	70.23	80.80

Table 4: Azerbaijani NLU benchmark. All metrics are F1 score. Blue models are multilingual. Orange models are multilingual models that have been further pre-trained for Azerbaijani. Green models were trained from scratch only for Azerbaijani. Black models serve as baseline.

You can find the results in Table 4. mDeBERTa-v3-BASE and aLLMA-BASE have the best overall performance. Figure 2 compares the performance of BASE models.[12] aLLMA-BASE outperforms all other models of similar size in 4 out of 6 benchmarks. Comparing BERT-BASE-AZE with BERT-BASE-MULTI shows that further pre-training of multilingual models can result in some performance improvement, but also model collapse (compare their performance in LDQuAd benchmark). However, a more comprehensive analysis is required before we can make generalizations about the effects of continued monolingual pre-training on multilingual models.

BERT-SCRATCH performs particularly well on AZE-SCI, MRPC, and WikiANN tasks. We believe this has two explanations. The first is that these tasks can be solved partially with statistical information from the input text, while this is not possible with the other tasks. The second is that the random baseline in these tasks is relatively high, while SQuAD and LDQuAd have very low random baselines.

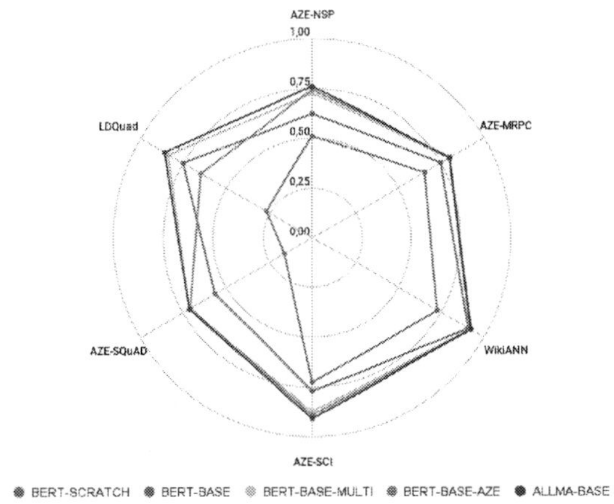

Figure 2: Performance comparison among BERT models of the same configuration. aLLMA-BASE outperforms the other models in 4 out of 6 benchmarks.

These results demonstrate several points regarding foundation models for low-resource languages:

1. *Pre-training from scratch on a monolingual dataset is a viable strategy for building a low-resource LLM.* aLLMA-BASE has competitive performance against larger models de-

[12]The difference in number of parameters between these models is due to varying vocabulary sizes. Otherwise, their architectures are identical.

spite being trained only on the DOLLMA corpus.

2. *Multilingual models offer competitive performance even in languages that they were undertrained for.* Azerbaijani has not been the focus in any of these multilingual models (XLM-RoBERTa, mDeBERTa-v3-BASE, or BERT-BASE-MULTI). Despite this, they outperform most models in some tasks.

3. *Even monolingual English foundation models can be useful for fine-tuning on a downstream task and perform better than training a model from scratch.* BERT-BASE was included in our research as a baseline but exceeded our expectations. This suggests that the state-of-the-art English models can be utilized for certain NLU tasks in Azerbaijani. This remains a potential research area.

It is still possible that we have missed some high-quality models and we are open to feedback regarding this. Our work can be strengthened by finding or creating new benchmarks. We hope that this work will lay the foundations for such developments.

7 Conclusion

Despite some academic and community attempts to create a foundation model for Azerbaijani, this problem has not received systemic treatment. We tackle this issue by introducing a new family of foundation models for the language and benchmarking these models and other existing alternatives. To compensate for the lack of datasets suitable for benchmarking LLMs in Azerbaijani, we introduce text classification, closed-book question-answering, and next-sentence prediction datasets.

This work can be extended in several ways. The simplest improvement would be **training larger models on larger corpora**. Our project does not achieve this due to time and hardware limitations. aLLMA models are not a final product, but an early prototype. A larger training corpus, more advanced hardware, and a better-optimized training process will certainly result in more robust foundation models for Azerbaijani.

A more urgent work, however, is **extending the benchmarks** by creating more labeled task-specific datasets and adding other existing models to the leaderboards.

Including the next-sentence prediction task in the pre-training phase can increase the performance of aLLMA models further.

Another ambitious direction would be using our corpus to **develop a generative foundation model.** This paper concentrated on encoder-only models because it is a simpler problem to solve and it has more immediate applications. Nevertheless, generative language models have wide-ranging industrial applications and demand a systemic treatment.

Acknowledgements

This work has been funded by PRODATA LLC and performed at aLLMA Lab 11 . We would like to thank Haim Dror and Mirakram Aghalarov for the invaluable discussions that led to this project. We would also like to thank the BHOS AI team for their close collaboration throughout the project. All of the data and code that has been created as part of this project is going to be publicly available under permissive licenses.

References

aLLMA Lab. 2024a. az-multiple-choice-questions (revision eb9cd4f).

aLLMA Lab. 2024b. Aze-nsp (revision c59f4f8).

aLLMA Lab. 2024c. azwiki (revision 65d6610).

aLLMA Lab. 2024d. azwiki (revision 65d6610).

aLLMA Lab. 2024e. eqanun (revision 8f99a3a).

Yoshua Bengio, Réjean Ducharme, and Pascal Vincent. 2000. A neural probabilistic language model. In *Advances in Neural Information Processing Systems*, volume 13. MIT Press.

Prajjwal Bhargava, Aleksandr Drozd, and Anna Rogers. 2021. Generalization in NLI: Ways (not) to go beyond simple heuristics. In *Proceedings of the Second Workshop on Insights from Negative Results in NLP*, pages 125–135, Online and Punta Cana, Dominican Republic. Association for Computational Linguistics.

BHOS AI R&D Center. 2024. Translated_english_wikipedia_on_azerbaijani (revision 077a718).

Alexis Conneau, Kartikay Khandelwal, Naman Goyal, Vishrav Chaudhary, Guillaume Wenzek, Francisco Guzmán, Edouard Grave, Myle Ott, Luke Zettlemoyer, and Veselin Stoyanov. 2020. Unsupervised cross-lingual representation learning at scale. In *Proceedings of the 58th Annual Meeting of the Association for Computational Linguistics*, pages 8440–8451, Online. Association for Computational Linguistics.

Jacob Devlin, Ming-Wei Chang, Kenton Lee, and Kristina Toutanova. 2019. BERT: Pre-training of deep bidirectional transformers for language understanding. In *Proceedings of the 2019 Conference of the North American Chapter of the Association for Computational Linguistics: Human Language Technologies, Volume 1 (Long and Short Papers)*, pages 4171–4186, Minneapolis, Minnesota. Association for Computational Linguistics.

William B. Dolan and Chris Brockett. 2005. Automatically constructing a corpus of sentential paraphrases. In *Proceedings of the Third International Workshop on Paraphrasing (IWP2005)*.

Eljan Mahammadli. 2024. glue-mrpc-azerbaijani (revision b60caf0).

Prabhakar Gupta, Shaktisingh Shekhawat, and Keshav Kumar. 2019. Unsupervised quality estimation without reference corpus for subtitle machine translation using word embeddings. In *2019 IEEE 13th International Conference on Semantic Computing (ICSC)*, pages 32–38.

Mammad Hajili. 2024a. azsci_topics (revision 26b9a83).

Mammad Hajili. 2024b. bert-base-cased-azerbaijani (revision 0cad0fa).

Mammad Hajili. 2024c. roberta-base-azerbaijani (revision 40f7699).

Mammad Hajili. 2024d. squad-azerbaijani-reindex-translation (revision f48f8fe).

Pengcheng He, Jianfeng Gao, and Weizhu Chen. 2023. Debertav3: Improving deberta using electra-style pre-training with gradient-disentangled embedding sharing.

Yiğit Bekir Kaya and A. Cüneyd Tantuğ. 2024. Effect of tokenization granularity for turkish large language models. *Intelligent Systems with Applications*, 21:200335.

Yinhan Liu, Myle Ott, Naman Goyal, Jingfei Du, Mandar Joshi, Danqi Chen, Omer Levy, Mike Lewis, Luke Zettlemoyer, and Veselin Stoyanov. 2019. Roberta: A robustly optimized bert pretraining approach.

LocalDoc. 2024. Ldquad (revision e082d87).

Tomáš Mikolov, Martin Karafiát, Lukáš Burget, Jan Černocký, and Sanjeev Khudanpur. 2010. Recurrent neural network based language model. In *Proc. Interspeech 2010*, pages 1045–1048.

Shervin Minaee, Tomas Mikolov, Narjes Nikzad, Meysam Asgari Chenaghlu, Richard Socher, Xavier Amatriain, and Jianfeng Gao. 2024. Large language models: A survey. *ArXiv*, abs/2402.06196.

Pedro Javier Ortiz Suárez, Laurent Romary, and Benoît Sagot. 2020. A monolingual approach to contextualized word embeddings for mid-resource languages. In *Proceedings of the 58th Annual Meeting of the Association for Computational Linguistics*, pages 1703–1714, Online. Association for Computational Linguistics.

Xiaoman Pan, Boliang Zhang, Jonathan May, Joel Nothman, Kevin Knight, and Heng Ji. 2017. Cross-lingual name tagging and linking for 282 languages. In *Proceedings of the 55th Annual Meeting of the Association for Computational Linguistics (Volume 1: Long Papers)*, pages 1946–1958, Vancouver, Canada. Association for Computational Linguistics.

Alec Radford and Karthik Narasimhan. 2018. Improving language understanding by generative pretraining.

Alec Radford, Jeff Wu, Rewon Child, David Luan, Dario Amodei, and Ilya Sutskever. 2019. Language models are unsupervised multitask learners.

Colin Raffel, Noam Shazeer, Adam Roberts, Katherine Lee, Sharan Narang, Michael Matena, Yanqi Zhou, Wei Li, and Peter J. Liu. 2020. Exploring the limits of transfer learning with a unified text-to-text transformer. *The Journal of Machine Learning Research*, 21(1).

Colin Raffel, Noam M. Shazeer, Adam Roberts, Katherine Lee, Sharan Narang, Michael Matena, Yanqi Zhou, Wei Li, and Peter J. Liu. 2019. Exploring the limits of transfer learning with a unified text-to-text transformer. *J. Mach. Learn. Res.*, 21:140:1–140:67.

Mohammad Salehi and Aydin Neysani. 2017. Receptive intelligibility of turkish to iranian-azerbaijani speakers. *Cogent Education*, 4(1):1326653.

Holger Schwenk, Daniel Dechelotte, and Jean-Luc Gauvain. 2006. Continuous space language models for statistical machine translation. In *Proceedings of the COLING/ACL 2006 Main Conference Poster Sessions*, pages 723–730, Sydney, Australia. Association for Computational Linguistics.

Oleh Shliazhko, Alena Fenogenova, Maria Tikhonova, Vladislav Mikhailov, Anastasia Kozlova, and Tatiana Shavrina. 2023. mgpt: Few-shot learners go multilingual.

R. Smith. 2007. An overview of the tesseract ocr engine. In *Ninth International Conference on Document Analysis and Recognition (ICDAR 2007)*, volume 2, pages 629–633.

Hugo Touvron, Thibaut Lavril, Gautier Izacard, Xavier Martinet, Marie-Anne Lachaux, Timothée Lacroix, Baptiste Rozière, Naman Goyal, Eric Hambro, Faisal Azhar, Aurelien Rodriguez, Armand Joulin, Edouard Grave, and Guillaume Lample. 2023. Llama: Open and efficient foundation language models.

Ashish Vaswani, Noam Shazeer, Niki Parmar, Jakob Uszkoreit, Llion Jones, Aidan N Gomez, Ł ukasz Kaiser, and Illia Polosukhin. 2017. Attention is all you need. In *Advances in Neural Information Processing Systems*, volume 30. Curran Associates, Inc.

Atabay Ziyaden, Amir Yelenov, Fuad Hajiyev, Samir Rustamov, and Alexandr Pak. 2024. Text data augmentation and pre-trained language model for enhancing text classification of low-resource languages. *PeerJ Computer Science*, 10:e1974.

ImplicaTR: A Granular Dataset for Natural Language Inference and Pragmatic Reasoning in Turkish

Mustafa Kürşat Halat
Boğaziçi University, İstanbul
kursathalat@gmail.com

Ümit Atlamaz
Boğaziçi University, İstanbul
umit.atlamaz@bogazici.edu.tr

Abstract

We introduce ImplicaTR, a linguistically informed diagnostic dataset designed to evaluate semantic and pragmatic reasoning capabilities of Natural Language Inference (NLI) models in Turkish. Existing Turkish NLI datasets treat NLI as determining whether a sentence pair represents *entailment*, *contradiction*, or a *neutral* relation. Such datasets do not distinguish between *semantic entailment* and *pragmatic implicature*, which linguists have long recognized as separate inferences types. ImplicaTR addresses this by testing NLI models' ability to differentiate between *entailment* and *implicature*, thus assessing their pragmatic reasoning skills. The dataset consists of 19,350 semi-automatically generated sentence pairs covering *implicature, entailment, contradiction,* and *neutral* relations. We evaluated various models (BERT, Gemma, Llama-2, and Mistral) on ImplicaTR and found out that these models can reach up to 98% accuracy on semantic and pragmatic reasoning. We also fine tuned various models on subsets of ImplicaTR to test the abilities of NLI models to generalize across unseen implicature contexts. Our results indicate that model performance is highly dependent on the diversity of linguistic expressions within each subset, highlighting a weakness in the abstract generalization capabilities of large language models regarding pragmatic reasoning. We share all the code, models, and the dataset.[1]

1 Introduction

Natural Language Inference (NLI) tasks are generally designed as three-way classification problems between sentence pairs (Gubelmann et al., 2023). Given a sentence pair consisting of a premise (P) and a hypothesis (H), the task is to classify the relation between P and H as one of *entailment, contradiction,* or *neutral.* Some of the most commonly used NLI datasets such as SNLI (Bowman et al., 2015) and MNLI (Williams et al., 2018) contain three way annotations of sentence pairs and recently Budur et al. (2020) translated both datasets into Turkish to create the combined NLI-TR dataset. Although these NLI datasets have been useful in testing the sentential understanding and reasoning capabilities of language models, they fall short of detecting the precise nature of reasoning, i.e. semantic vs. pragmatic, due to the coarseness of their labeling schemas. In particular, these datasets conflate various implicational relations such as *entailment, implicature,* and *presupposition* under the same label i.e. *entailment.* However, linguists have long observed that entailments differ from implicatures and presuppositions specifically in terms of what kind of reasoning mechanisms underlie such implicational relations (Grice, 1975; Horn, 2006, 1972; Levinson, 2000; Sauerland, 2012).

A key distinction between entailments and implicatures is that of reasoning over *what is said* and *what is not said.* Entailment relations are inferences based on *what is said* and they arise as a consequence of the meanings of expressions in a sentence and the general laws of logic. The defining characteristic of an entailment relation between a premise (P) and a hyopthesis (H) is Truth. P entails H if and only iff whenever P is True H must be True as well. The P-H pair in (1) illustrates entailment. This is a logical corollary of the subset-superset relation between *fluffy cats* and *cats.*

(1) P *entails* H
P: Garfield is a fluffy cat.
H: Garfield is a cat.

Implicatures on the other hand are inferences based on what is not said and they follow from general cooperativeness principles of conversation (Grice, 1975, 1989). In (2), the relation between P and H is *implicature* but not *entailment.*

[1] https://github.com/kursathalat/ImplicaTR

Proceedings of the First Workshop on Natural Language Processing for Turkic Languages (SIGTURK 2024), pages 29–41
August 15, 2024 ©2024 Association for Computational Linguistics

(2) P *implicates* H
Q: Is he handsome?
P: He is smart.
H: He is not handsome.

Unlike entailments, implicatures are not logical consequences of their premises. Instead, they arise through pragmatic reasoning. Implicatures can be distinguished from ordinary entailments by means of various tests such as *cancellation*, *suspension*, and *reinforcement*. For example, implicatures can be cancelled without leading to a contradiction but entailments cannot as illustrated in (3) and (4).

(3) **Entailment cancelled, contradiction**
P: Garfield is a fluffy cat.
H': Garfield is not a cat.

(4) **Implicature cancelled, no contradiction**
Q: Is he handsome?
P: He is smart... (H':) And handsome.

To test the pragmatic reasoning capabilities of language models in Turkish, we introduce ImplicaTR, the first fine-grained Turkish NLI dataset consisting of Premise-Hypothesis pairs containing *entailment, implicature, contradiction,* and *neutral* labels. We test various types of large language models (LLMs) using ImplicaTR and observe that LLMs are capable of carrying out both semantic and pragmatic reasoning with success rates of up to 98% accuracy. Despite their high levels of success, our ablation studies reveal that LLMs do not form a high level abstraction for pragmatic reasoning as they *cannot generalize* across various types of implicature contexts.

2 Related Work

NLI, a subset of the broader task known as Natural Language Reasoning (Yu et al., 2023), has been extensively researched within the context of textual entailment. Research in NLI led to the creation of numerous benchmark datasets aimed at training and evaluating the inferencing capabilities of language models. Major NLI datasets such as SNLI (Bowman et al., 2015) and (Williams et al., 2018) focused on three-way (entailment, contradiction, neutral) classification of inferential relations. Although these benchmark datasets have been widely adopted, they have also been noted to have some issues such as the predictability of the inference between premise and hypothesis due to repeating patterns within the hypothesis like negation (Gururangan et al., 2018; Poliak, 2020) or the overwhelming majority of upward entailing contexts leading the models to make errors in downward entailing contexts (Yanaka et al., 2019a). To overcome some of these challenges various NLI datasets have been created. (Yanaka et al., 2019b) created the HELP dataset to overcome the issues with downward entailment contexts. (Conneau et al., 2018) created the XNLI dataset to expand the NLI research into languages other than English. The availability of NLI datasets in Turkish is limited with NLI-TR (Budur et al., 2020), which presents an automatic translation of SNLI and MNLI combined, and with STSb-TR (Fikri et al., 2021) for semantic textual similarity.

Recent NLI research started to pay attention to more granular inference types that can help evaluate the precise reasoning capabilities of language models by distinguishing inference types such as *implicature, entailment, presupposition*. Implicature (George and Mamidi, 2020) and BIG-Bench (Srivastava and others, 2022) datasets were created for *particulatized implicatures*. Similarly, GRICE (Zheng et al., 2021) offers conversational reasoning and implicature data in the form of open dialogues devised by an automated grammar. The IMPPRESsive dataset (Jeretic et al., 2020) consists of semi-automatically generated *scalar implicatures* and *presuppositions* as Premise-Hypothesis pairs, where authors show that models can do pragmatic reasoning for some types of scales in their dataset.

This brief review of the literature reveals that the NLI literature needs more work in the areas of pragmatic reasoning and we aim to help fill this gap by investigating implicatures, which present a distinct line of work for the NLI research with its more granular comprehension of the pragmatic inferences. In addition, NLI research in Turkish has a limited scope, totally lacking an investigation into implicatures to the best of our knowledge. With its rich morphology and agglutinative nature especially reflected on the verbs, Turkish presents a peculiar case for probing into how implicatures are handled by NLI models.

3 Dataset: ImplicaTR

ImplicaTR is a semi-automatically generated Turkish NLI dataset annotated with a granular classification of sentential inference types covering *scalar implicatures* in addition to the conventional three-

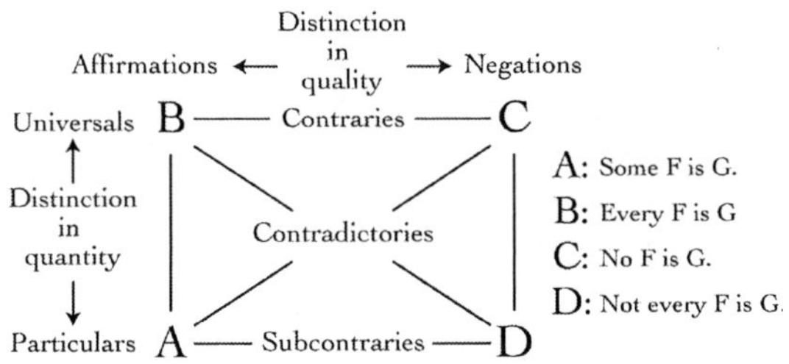

Figure 1: Square of Opposition

way NLI classes (*entailment, contradiction, neutral*). The dataset comprises five different linguistic categories (quantifiers, adjectives, verbs, modals, and numerals) with varying number of scalar pairs for each category.

3.1 Scalar Pairs

A scale (or a Horn Scale) (Horn, 1972) is a set of two or more lexemes that are in a relationship of strength or intensity. For instance, the scalar pair $\langle some, all \rangle$ contains the weaker term $some$ and the stronger term all, between which there is a quantificational difference. Horn (2006) observed a set of logical relations between scalar elements (e.g. *some - all*) and their negations (*none - not all*) which he represented as quadruplets on a square of opposition shown in Figure 1.

In Figure 1, the universals B and C *entail* A and D, respectively, while B and C logically *contradict* each other. The particulars A and D are in a *neutral* relationship with their universal counterparts B and C. Notably, utterance of A or D *implicate* the truthfulness of one another. Thus, we obtain the conventional NLI classes along with the *implicature* inference from a quadruplet of sentences stemming from a scalar pair and their negation.

We created ImplicaTR by using a variety of scalar pairs and their negations as captured by the Square of Opposition. To ensure wide coverage, we covered a total of 44 scalar pairs from give distinct linguistics categories consisting of *adjectives, verbs, quantificational determiners, modal expressions*, and *numerals*. Some scalar pairs, as those in De Melo and Bansal (2013), were excluded as their scalar interpretations are highly contextual and impossible to control without further context.

3.2 Linguistic Categories

Scalar meanings in natural languages can be expressed by different lexical categories (e.g. adjectives, verbs, etc.) and yet the logical relations among scalar pairs are constant as noticed by linguists (Horn, 2006; Kennedy and McNally, 2005; Kennedy, 1999) and illustrated on the Square of Opposition in Figure 1. This indicates that humans are able to make abstract generalizations regarding the logical relations among scalar expressions regardless of their lexical categories or linguistic expression. To evaluate the abstract generalization capabilities of language models across different lexical categories, we used scalar pairs from five different categories: *adjectives, verbs numerals, modals* and *quantificational determiners.*

Adjectives and *verbs* form open-class categories. Open-class categories permit new members and cover a wider range of linguistic expressions compared to closed-class categories. Usually, this translates lower relative frequency per lexeme in a corpus compared to closed class categories. We used a total of 46 open-class words (28 adjectives and 18 verbs). Adjectival pairs include examples such as ⟨*benzer,aynı*⟩ ('similar-same'), ⟨*yakın, bitişik*⟩ ('close-adjacent'), whereas verbal pairs include instances such as ⟨*başla, bitir*⟩ ('start - finish') (following Jackendoff (1996); Pedersen (2014)).

Quantificational determiners, modals, and numerals form closed-class categories. Quantificational determiners are naturally scalar as they denote degrees of quantification. We used seven quantificational determiners to form various scalar pairs such as ⟨*birkaç, bütün*⟩ ('a few'- 'all'). Modal expressions also encode quantificational force (Hacquard, 2010) and thus create scalar pairs. Modal expressions come in various flavors such as *epistemic*, referring to the certainty of knowledge (Kaufmann et al., 2006), and *deontic*, referring to the cases of obligation or permission (Johanson, 2009). We have only used four epistemic modal expressions as deontic modals in Turkish usually result in ambiguity which makes it hard to evaluate the success of language models.

The last type of scalar expressions in the dataset are numerals. Numerals belong to closed-class words consisting of a finite number of lexical items yet they require particular attention for two key reasons. Numerals are by definition ordered and they form an infinite scale ($\langle 0, 1, 2, 3, 4, ... \rangle$ or ⟨*bir, iki, üç, dört, ...*⟩. This makes their distribution in any given dataset quite unbalanced. While some common numerals such as *bir, iki, beş, on* can be very frequent in a corpus, complex numeral expressions such as *üç yüz elli yedi* (357) or *on iki bin sekizyüz otuz üç* (12833) will be rare if present at all. To alleviate the sparsity issue, we have limited the number of unique numerals in the dataset to 18 and we opted for relatively common numerals such as *bir, iki, beş, otuz, altmış, ...* (1,2,5,30,60,...) The second point to note is that numerals behave differently from other scalar expressions when they are combined with negation. In general, negation of a stronger value on a scalar pair implicates the weaker term. *"Not all chairs are dirty."* implicates *"Some chairs are dirty."* With numerals, negation of a stronger value raises two additional implicatures besides the implicature of the weaker value. These are *at-most* (Papafragou and Schwarz, 2005) and the *existential* implicatures as illustrated in (5).

(5) A: You need five apples for this dessert.
P: Oh, we don't have four apples.
H1: We have at most four apples.
H2: We have at least one apple.

3.3 Data Generation

ImplicaTR was built semi-automatically through an iterative process. For each scalar pair (<bazı, tüm> <some, all>), we manually created a few sample quadruplets of sentences ⟨A,B,C,D⟩, where sentence A contains the weaker term (bazı), B the stronger term (tüm), C negation of the weaker term (hiç), and D negation of the stronger term (tümü değil) as illustrated in Figure 2. A sample quadruplet is given in Table 1.

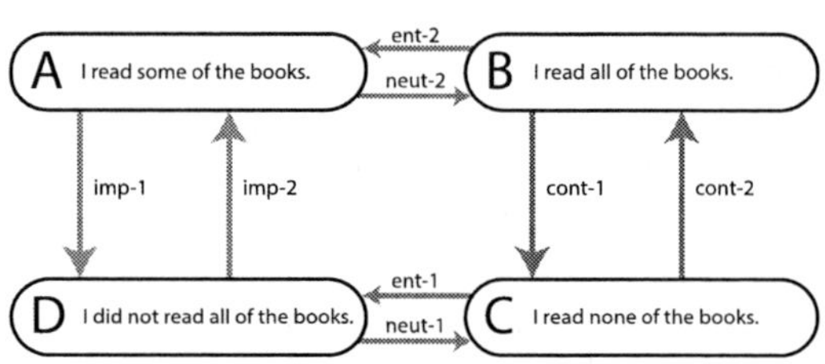

Figure 2: Quadruplets and inference relations

Table 1: A Sample Quadruplet

Sentence ID	Scalar Item	Sentence
A	bazı	Kitapların bazısını okudum.
B	tüm	Kitapların tümünü okudum.
C	hiç	Kitapların hiçbirini okumadım.
D	tümü değil	Kitapların tümünü okumadım.

In addition, we manually created a set of A sentences for each scalar pair that covers a wide range of linguistic structures. By using the manually created quadruplets as few-shot examples, we employed GPT-4 (OpenAI, 2024) to autogenerate the B, C, and D sentences for the remaining A sentences. At each iterative step, two expert linguists reviewed the autogenerated quadruplets to verify their grammaticality and the accuracy of the inference relations among the quadruplets. Scalar pairs that led to ambiguities and linguistic structures that disrupted the inference relations were removed after each iteration until we reached a reliable set of scalar pairs and linguistic structures. See Table 2 for a complete set of inferences obtained from a quadruplet.

In the final iteration, we created 19,350 sentence pairs covering the four types of inference types *entailment, implicature, contradiction* and *neutral.* The quality of the dataset was verified by randomly sampling 2,137 sentence pairs, ensuring a 95% confidence interval and a 2% margin of error. An expert linguist reviewed these sentence pairs, revealing that 97.89% of the data had correct inference labels. See Appendix A for the distribution of scalar pairs and other descriptive statistics about the dataset.

4 Experiment 1

Experiment 1 aims to explore whether LLMs exhibit pragmatic reasoning, specifically in scalar implicature resolution. We fine-tuned a series of models on ImplicaTR and observed that language models can successfully identify implicatures.

4.1 Experimental Setup

4.2 Data

We split the dataset into train (12,309 items), validation (3,153 items), and test (3,888 items) sets via stratified sampling to ensure that the model can see examples from each category and scalar pair and that a single quadruplet is included in only and only one of the splits.

4.3 Models

For this experiment, we used two different sets of models: Masked Language Models (e.g. BERT-family models) and generative models. BERT (Devlin et al., 2019) is an encoder-decoder model based on the transformers architecture (Vaswani et al., 2017). With their bidirectional architecture, BERT-family models take into account the left and the right context of a masked element within a sentence. On the other hand, generative LLMs based on transformers are trained on seq2seq tasks, where they take the input sequence and generate an out-

Table 2: A Sample Set of Inferences out of a Quadruplet

Premise Type	Hypothesis Type	Premise Example	Hypothesis Example	Inference Type/Label
A	D	Kitapların bazısını okudum.	Kitapların tümünü okumadım.	implicature
D	A	Kitapların tümünü okumadım.	Kitapların bazısını okudum.	implicature
C	D	Kitapların hiçbirini okumadım.	Kitapların tümünü okumadım.	entailment
B	A	Kitapların tümünü okudum.	Kitapların bazısını okudum.	entailment
D	C	Kitapların tümünü okumadım.	Kitapların hiçbirini okumadım.	neutral
A	B	Kitapların bazısını okudum.	Kitapların tümünü okudum.	neutral
B	C	Kitapların tümünü okudum.	Kitapların hiçbirini okumadım.	contradiction
C	B	Kitapların hiçbirini okumadım.	Kitapların tümünü okudum.	contradiction

put sequence; thus, these models learn and generate output by performing next-word prediction. We selected these two types of models as BERTs have been shown to demonstrate superior comprehension of language (Cho et al., 2021), while generative models are in widespread use in spite of their relatively poorer grasp of the linguistic insights (Fu et al., 2023; Raffel et al., 2023).

BERT-family models employed in this experiment are bert-base-uncased, BERT-NLI (Laurer et al., 2023), and BERTurk (Schweter, 2020). BERT-NLI is the DeBERTaV3-based zero-shot model and was trained on XNLI and MNLI datasets, which we expect would show greater performance on NLI tasks. BERTurk is a Turkish model and was trained on Turkish Wikipedia dumps, which allows us to compare the cross-task ability of this model against the cross-lingual ability of BERT-NLI. As for generative models, we fine-tuned the 7B parameter versions of Llama-2 (Touvron et al., 2023), Gemma (Team et al., 2024), and Mistral (Jiang et al., 2023). Training was done via prompting for generative models, for which a sample training item is given in Appendix B.

The training hyperparameters used for the BERT models are as given below.

Table 3: Training Hyperparameters for BERT Models

Hyperparameter	Value
hidden dropout value	0.3
attention dropout prob	0.25
number of epochs	10
gradient accumulation steps	2
warmup ratio	0.01
batch size	64
weight decay	0.05
learning rate	0.00001
lr reduction factor	0.5
lr reduction threshold	0.2

4.4 Results

We fine tuned the models on the training datasets and evaluated their success on the test sets. Figure 3 presents the accuracy scores of the fine-tuned models as well as the base models (before fine tuning). We observe that the base models are not biased towards any of the inference classes.

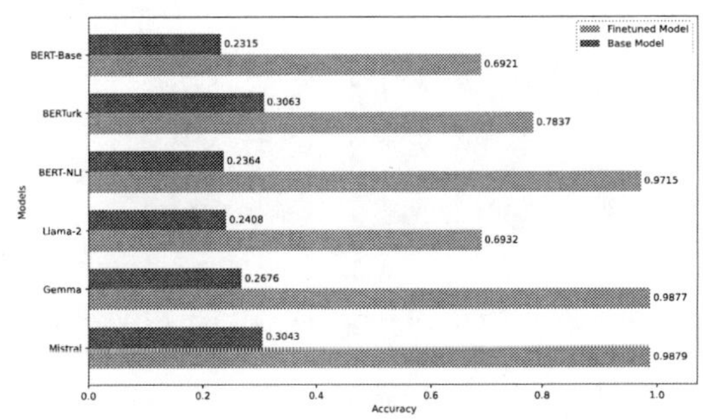

Figure 3: Accuracy scores from Experiment 1

Within the BERT family, BERT-NLI excelled the task with 0.97 while BERTurk achieves a higher score than the base model. This shows that the NLI training of BERT-NLI increased the ability of the model to recognize textual entailment even though we introduced a new class, *implicature*. Generative models demonstrated parallel results, where Gemma and Mistral reached accuracy scores of 0.98. These results suggest that generative models can handle pragmatic reasoning tasks such as detecting scalar implicatures. Llama-2 showed a poorer performance with 0.69, which we think is due to the the size the of the training data. Llama-2 was trained on 2T tokens whereas this number is 6T for Gemma and probably a similarly high number for Mistral. Therefore, models seem to learn the pragmatic contributions of words when they are exposed to them more during training.

4.5 Benchmark on XNLI and MNLI

In order to evaluate the performance of our fine-tuned models, we tested our fine-tuned BERT-NLI model on the XNLI and MNLI test sets as it was the best performing BERT model in our experiments. The original BERT-NLI model as well as XNLI and MNLI offers a three-way classification whereas our fine-tuned BERT-NLI model does more granular classification by predicting *implicature* as well. Thus, to evaluate the performance, we employed four different strategies in mapping our 4-way classification onto the 3-way classes of XNLI and MNLI test sets. First, without any alteration, we calculated the accuracy score by comparing predictions against ground labels as is. Then, we converted the implicature predictions to entailment, neutral and contradiction, and we calculated the accuracy score accordingly to see how the accuracy scores change per label.

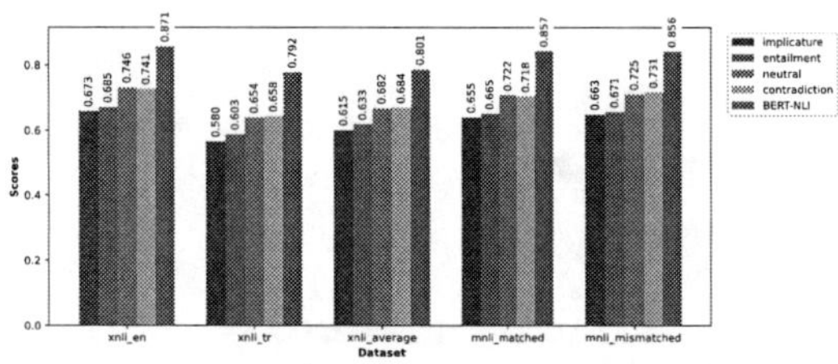

Figure 4: Accuracies of Finetuned BERT-NLI with Different Labeling on selected XNLI and MNLI sets, and Original BERT-NLI Score

The original *implicature* case has the lowest score in all sets while converting the predicted label to *neutral* or *contradiction* yielded the best scores. This is in line with the argument that NLI models are positively biased towards the *contradiction* and *neutral* classes because of the existence of negation words like *not* and superlative expressions denoting the maximal values (Gururangan et al., 2018). Compared to the base BERT-NLI model, our model's accuracy score is lower by 12%, which is expected due to the granularity of our labels and the smaller size of the implicature data.

5 Experiment 2

Upon observing that LLMs are capable of learning pragmatic inferences in the form of scalar implicatures, we conducted a second experiment where we perform an ablation study to test the generalization abilities of LLMs with respect to pragmatic reasoning in a supervised fashion. This experiment consists of two phases. In the first phase, we train five models by eliminating one of the linguistic categories entirely from training split in each model training and then test the model on the eliminated linguistic category. The goal is to test whether LLMs can create a sufficiently abstract generalization of scalar implicatures that can be used independent of the linguistic structures. In the second phase, we develop a sixth model by eliminating some scalar pairs from each linguistic category and test the model on the eliminated pairs. The goal in this second phase is to test the generalization abilities of LLMs within each category. The ablation study is followed by a feature analysis to inspect which linguistic features are influential in LLM performance in textual entailment and implicature reasoning.

5.1 Data Preparation

For the ablation study, we created five different splits. Table 4 presents the training and test categories for each model. We used stratified sampling to create training and validation splits to ensure that the model does not encounter any particular sentence in more than one split.

Table 4: Linguistic Categories Used for Training and Testing for Each Model

	Train	Test
Model-NUM	Adjectives Verbs Quantifiers Modals	Numerals
Model-MOD	Adjectives Verbs Quantifiers Numerals	Modals
Model-QUA	Adjectives Verbs Modals Numerals	Quantifiers
Model-VER	Adjectives Quantifiers Modals Numerals	Verbs
Model-ADJ	Verbs Quantifiers Modals Numerals	Adjectives

The second phase of the experiment involves MODEL-ALL, where some of the scalar pairs from

Table 5: Split sizes of models in Experiment 2

	Each Model in Phase 1	MODEL-ALL
	N of pairs	N of pairs
Train	11520	10560
Validation	2880	2640
Test	3600	4800
Total	**18000**	**18000**

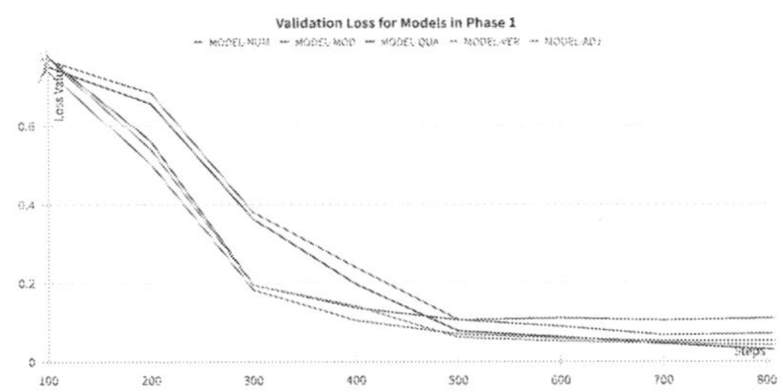

Figure 5: Validation Loss of Models in Phase 1

each category are removed from the training set (except for modals since the total number of pairs is very low). For example, all 30 quadruplets of <harmful, lethal> are left out in training and they are included in the test set of MODEL-ALL with a view to test whether the model can generalize what it learns for a specific linguistic category to the unseen scalar pairs within the same category. Data split sizes for all models are given in Table 5.

5.2 Ablation Study

We conducted Experiment 2 with the BERT-NLI model as it achieved the best performance in the Experiment 1 among the BERT models. Losses on validation set are plotted in Figure 5. While the elimination of *adjectives*, *verbs*, or *numerals* from the training data exhibits similar decrease patterns in loss, MODEL-MOD and MODEL-QUA values indicate that the absence of *modals* or *quantificational determiners* introduce a slight challenge for the model to learn the patterns but the models converge eventually.

Table 6: Chi-Square and Cramer's V Results

Pearson Chi-Square	p-value	Cramer's V
1256.2951	<0.0001	0.1525

5.3 Results

We evaluated each model on their respective test datasets and conducted a chi-square test to determine whether differences between categories are significant or not. The results indicated a significant differences between category results with a p-value <0.0001. Table 6 presents the results of the chi-square test and Table 7 reports the test scores for each model.

The results indicate that the models can successfully generalize to the categories of *modals* and *quantificational determiners* while we see moderate accuracy scores for *verbs* and *adjectives* and relatively low scores for *numerals*. We believe that these results are due to the distribution of scalar items in the pre-training data. *Modals* and *quantificational determiners are* closed-class expressions with relatively lower type frequencies (and thus higher token frequencies for each type). On the other hand, *adjectives* and *verbs* are members of open-class categories with relatively higher type frequencies (and thus lower token frequencies for each type). Finally, numerals have the largest type frequencies (theoretically infinite) despite being members of a closed-class category. Thus, the number of scalar relationships that a particular numeral can establish is also large (theoretically infinite), majority of which are unknown to the model or not reinforced in pre-training, which possibly decreases the model performance for numerals. These results suggest that the token frequency of a lexical item in the pre-training data is an important factor in a model's ability to execute pragmatic reasoning over expressions involving that lexical item. The results suggest that the tested LLMs may lack the ability to create sufficiently abstract generalizations for pragmatic reasoning that transcend particular linguistic structures.

In the second phase, we trained and evaluated MODEL-ALL in order to test the performance of the fine tuned NLI model on unseen scalar pairs within a previously trained category. The results are presented in Table 7.

MODEL-ALL suggests that the scalar reasoning exists within the linguistic categories for *adjectives* and *numerals*. Training on similar structures helped the model gain pragmatic reasoning capabilities to identify implicatures. Quantificational determiners also showed similarly accuracy scores. However, the model did not achieve high scores within the category of *verbs*. We believe that this

Table 7: Test results of models in Phase 1 and of respective linguistic categories in MODEL-ALL, where MODEL-ALL Accuracy scores specifically refer to the accuracy score of the linguistic category tested in the respective model from Phase 1. No score for modals as they are not tested in MODEL-ALL.

Model	Test Loss	Accuracy	F1	Precision	Recall	MODEL-ALL Accuracy
MODEL-NUM	1.5592	0.6036	0.5506	0.6723	0.6036	0.8541
MODEL-MOD	0.1416	0.9622	0.9621	0.9644	0.9622	-
MODEL-QUA	0.286	0.9336	0.934	0.9396	0.9336	0.9866
MODEL-VER	0.7137	0.7969	0.7948	0.8153	0.7969	0.6625
MODEL-ADJ	1.3374	0.7152	0.715	0.7169	0.7152	0.9733

might be due to the agglutinating nature of Turkish verbs (verbs usually occur with various suffixes on them) leading to a sparsity in the training data and impeding its generalization abilities.

5.4 Featural Significance Analysis

We followed up the ablation study with a featural significance analysis in order to unveil the potential linguistic triggers in our dataset that lead to the correct or incorrect classification of the premise-hypothesis pairs. For this, we first extracted a set of linguistic features and then fit logistic regression and random forest models to measure their impact on model performance.

In the NLI literature, various linguistic features have been argued to affect the model performance (Miaschi et al., 2020; Kriz et al., 2015; Talman et al., 2021; Wendland et al., 2021). Accordingly, we have included various features such as counts and lengths of certain tokens, predicate type, polarity, the word similarity within sentence, the similarity between premise and hypothesis, TF-IDF scores of the scalar items, the position of scalar item, and NER tags and sentiments in our analysis. The full list of features extracted is given in Appendix C . In a preliminary regression test, we observed that the NER and sentiment features had no impact on model performance; therefore, we excluded them from further analysis.

5.5 Logistic Regression

We fit a linear regression model with predictors as our extracted features and the outcomes as the prediction accuracy of the model. The linear regression model achieved an accuracy score of 0.80, which, we believe, makes the model appropriate for featural significance analysis. Figure 6 below presents the features with the most effect along with their coefficient scores.

The results suggest that the similarity between

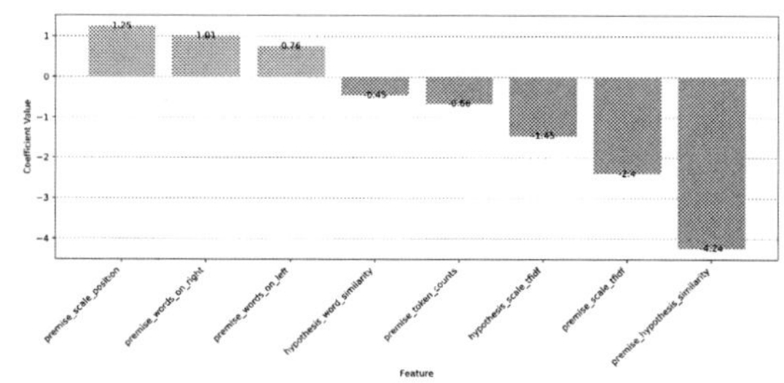

Figure 6: Feature coefficients of logistic regression model

a premise and a hypothesis and the high TF-IDF score of the scalar item in the premise sentence lowered the model performance. The feature 'premise_scale_position' refers to the position of the scalar item in the sentence. Given that Turkish is an SOV language and our dataset does not contain any word order inversions, we observe that closeness of the scalar item to the main verb improves the accuracy of the model. Although it goes beyond the scope of our current study to explain this observation properly, we speculate that this might be due to the pre-verbal position in Turkish being associated with new information focus (Göksel and Özsoy, 2000). In general, this position is reserved for new information in Turkish and new information is usually more attended to by speech participants. If LLMs are capable of associating the pre-verbal position with new information focus, they might be paying more attention to the scalar items in this position, leading to an increased accuracy.

5.6 Random Forest Model

We also fit a random forest model to further verify the effects of the features on the model prediction accuracy. For this model, we eliminated the features with low effect size and only used the continuous variables as predictors. The random forest model achieved 0.79 accuracy and the coefficient results are in Figure 7.

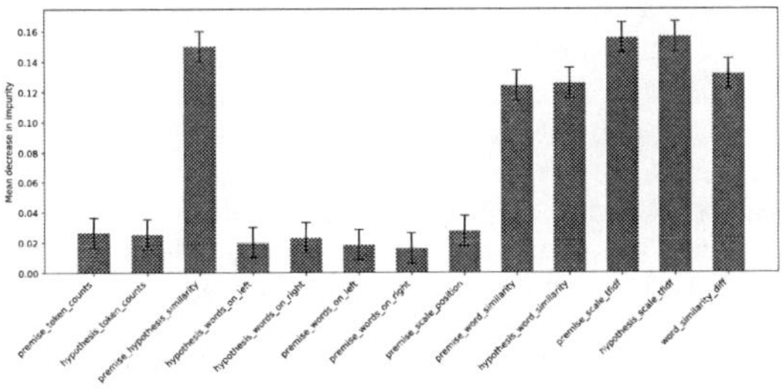

Figure 7: Feature importance of random forest model

We see that the results of the random forest model are in line with the regression analysis we did. In this model, where the coefficients are calculated by the decrease they cause in the mean accuracy (MDI), the features with the highest decrease are TF-IDF scores of the scalar items within the sentence. This is valid for both premise and hypothesis sentences, as the values of both are the highest. The similarities of the embeddings of the premise-hypothesis pair can be seen to have a negative effect on the correctness of the model prediction. Additionally, the average similarity scores of the words within a sentence are again one of the factors that decrease the score.

6 Conclusion

We presented ImplicaTR, a diagnostic dataset to test the pragmatic reasoning abilities of language models. ImplicaTR contains NLI-style sentence pairs with four distinct inference types, *entailment, contradiction, neutral* and *implicature*. We evaluated various LLMs and showed that they are capable of doing pragmatic reasoning and distinguishing *entailments* from *implicatures* with a high degree of accuracy. Our results also indicated that the models we tested cannot make sufficiently abstract generalizations across various linguistic structures for pragmatic reasoning and the type frequency of the scalar items is inversely correlated with the model success.

7 Limitations

This study introduces ImplicaTR and conducts two experiments on it to investigate the pragmatic capabilities of LLMs, but it also comes with a couple of limitations. First, while ImplicaTR is a diagnosis dataset, it is not a large one considering that it introduces a new class. Second, the genre and style of the items are not versatile, which might hinder the generalization capabilities of models. While the linguistic inquiry in Experiment 2 offers an insight into how models execute reasoning over implicatures, the features extracted can be extended to account for other syntactic and semantic phenomena.

8 Ethical Considerations

All sentence pairs used in ImplicaTR were generated synthetically, and no personal or sensitive information was used in order to ensure compliance with privacy standards and data protection regulations. Besides, efforts were made to minimize bias in the dataset by including a diverse range of linguistic expressions and contexts. We have made all code, models, and the dataset publicly available to promote transparency and reproducibility.

Acknowledgments

We thank Ömer Demirok, Cem Bozşahin, and an anonymous SIGTURK reviewer for their insightful comments at various stages of this work.

References

Samuel R. Bowman, Gabor Angeli, Christopher Potts, and Christopher D. Manning. 2015. A large annotated corpus for learning natural language inference. In *Proceedings of the 2015 Conference on Empirical Methods in Natural Language Processing*, pages 632–642, Lisbon, Portugal. Association for Computational Linguistics.

Emrah Budur, Rıza Özçelik, Tunga Gungor, and Christopher Potts. 2020. Data and Representation for Turkish Natural Language Inference. In *Proceedings of the 2020 Conference on Empirical Methods in Natural Language Processing (EMNLP)*, pages 8253–8267, Online. Association for Computational Linguistics.

Won Ik Cho, Emmanuele Chersoni, Yu-Yin Hsu, and Chu-Ren Huang. 2021. Modeling the Influence of Verb Aspect on the Activation of Typical Event Locations with BERT. In *Findings of the Association for Computational Linguistics: ACL-IJCNLP 2021*, pages 2922–2929, Online. Association for Computational Linguistics.

Alexis Conneau, Guillaume Lample, Ruty Rinott, Adina Williams, Samuel R. Bowman, Holger Schwenk, and Veselin Stoyanov. 2018. XNLI: Evaluating Cross-lingual Sentence Representations. *arXiv preprint*. ArXiv:1809.05053 [cs].

Gerard De Melo and Mohit Bansal. 2013. Good, Great, Excellent: Global Inference of Semantic Intensities.

Transactions of the Association for Computational Linguistics, 1:279–290.

Jacob Devlin, Ming-Wei Chang, Kenton Lee, and Kristina Toutanova. 2019. BERT: Pre-training of Deep Bidirectional Transformers for Language Understanding. *arXiv preprint*. ArXiv:1810.04805 [cs].

Figen Beken Fikri, Kemal Oflazer, and Berrin Yanıkoğlu. 2021. Turkish dataset for semantic textual similarity. In *2021 29th Signal Processing and Communications Applications Conference (SIU)*, pages 1–4.

Zihao Fu, Wai Lam, Qian Yu, Anthony Man-Cho So, Shengding Hu, Zhiyuan Liu, and Nigel Collier. 2023. Decoder-Only or Encoder-Decoder? Interpreting Language Model as a Regularized Encoder-Decoder. *arXiv preprint*. ArXiv:2304.04052 [cs].

Elizabeth Jasmi George and Radhika Mamidi. 2020. Conversational implicatures in English dialogue: Annotated dataset. *Procedia Computer Science*, 171:2316–2323.

Aslı Göksel and A Sumru Özsoy. 2000. Is there a focus position in turkish. *Studies on Turkish and Turkic languages*, 107:119–228.

H. P. Grice. 1975. Logic and Conversation. In Donald Davidson and Gilbert Harman, editors, *The Logic of Grammar*, pages 64–75.

H. P. Grice. 1989. *Studies in the way of words*. Harvard University Press, Cambridge, Mass.

Reto Gubelmann, Ioannis Katis, Christina Niklaus, and Siegfried Handschuh. 2023. Capturing the Varieties of Natural Language Inference: A Systematic Survey of Existing Datasets and Two Novel Benchmarks. *Journal of Logic, Language and Information*, 33(1):21–48.

Suchin Gururangan, Swabha Swayamdipta, Omer Levy, Roy Schwartz, Samuel Bowman, and Noah A. Smith. 2018. Annotation Artifacts in Natural Language Inference Data. In *Proceedings of the 2018 Conference of the North American Chapter of the Association for Computational Linguistics: Human Language Technologies, Volume 2 (Short Papers)*, pages 107–112, New Orleans, Louisiana. Association for Computational Linguistics.

Valentine Hacquard. 2010. Modality. *Language*, 86(3):739–741.

Laurence R. Horn. 2006. Implicature. In Laurence R. Horn and Gregory Ward, editors, *The Handbook of Pragmatics*, 1 edition, pages 2–28. Wiley.

Laurence Robert Horn. 1972. *On the Semantic Properties of Logical Operators in English*. Ph.D. thesis, University of California, California.

Ray Jackendoff. 1996. The proper treatment of measuring out, telicity, and perhaps even quantification in english. *Natural Language and Linguistic Theory*, 14(2):305–354.

Paloma Jeretic, Alex Warstadt, Suvrat Bhooshan, and Adina Williams. 2020. Are Natural Language Inference Models IMPPRESsive? Learning IMPlicature and PRESupposition. In *Proceedings of the 58th Annual Meeting of the Association for Computational Linguistics*, pages 8690–8705, Online. Association for Computational Linguistics.

Albert Q. Jiang, Alexandre Sablayrolles, Arthur Mensch, Chris Bamford, Devendra Singh Chaplot, Diego de las Casas, Florian Bressand, Gianna Lengyel, Guillaume Lample, Lucile Saulnier, Lélio Renard Lavaud, Marie-Anne Lachaux, Pierre Stock, Teven Le Scao, Thibaut Lavril, Thomas Wang, Timothée Lacroix, and William El Sayed. 2023. Mistral 7B. *arXiv preprint*. ArXiv:2310.06825 [cs].

Lars Johanson. 2009. 15. Modals in Turkic. In Björn Hansen and Ferdinand De Haan, editors, *Modals in the Languages of Europe*, pages 487–510. Mouton de Gruyter.

Stefan Kaufmann, Cleo Condoravdi, and Valentina Harizanov. 2006. Formal approaches to modality. In William Frawley, Erin Eschenroede, Sarah Mills, and Thao Nguyen, editors, *The Expression of Modality*, pages 71–106. Mouton de Gruyter.

Christopher Kennedy. 1999. GRADABLE ADJECTIVES DENOTE MEASURE FUNCTIONS, NOT PARTIAL FUNCTIONS.

Christopher Kennedy and Louise McNally. 2005. Scale Structure, Degree Modification, and the Semantics of Gradable Predicates. *Language*, 81(2):345–381.

Vincent Kriz, Martin Holub, and Pavel Pecina. 2015. Feature Extraction for Native Language Identification Using Language Modeling.

Moritz Laurer, Wouter Van Atteveldt, Andreu Casas, and Kasper Welbers. 2023. Less Annotating, More Classifying: Addressing the Data Scarcity Issue of Supervised Machine Learning with Deep Transfer Learning and BERT-NLI. *Political Analysis*, 32(1):84–100.

Stephen C. Levinson. 2000. *Presumptive Meanings: The Theory of Generalized Conversational Implicature*. The MIT Press.

Alessio Miaschi, Dominique Brunato, Felice Dell'Orletta, and Giulia Venturi. 2020. Linguistic Profiling of a Neural Language Model. In *Proceedings of the 28th International Conference on Computational Linguistics*, pages 745–756. ArXiv:2010.01869 [cs].

OpenAI. 2024. GPT-4 Technical Report. *arXiv preprint*. ArXiv:2303.08774 [cs].

Anna Papafragou and Naomi Schwarz. 2005. Most Wanted. *Language Acquisition*, 13(3):207–251. Publisher: Taylor & Francis, Ltd.

Walter A Pedersen. 2014. *Inchoative verbs and adverbial modification: Decompositional and scalar approaches*. Ph.D. thesis, McGill University, Montreal.

Adam Poliak. 2020. A Survey on Recognizing Textual Entailment as an NLP Evaluation. *arXiv preprint*. ArXiv:2010.03061 [cs].

Colin Raffel, Noam Shazeer, Adam Roberts, Katherine Lee, Sharan Narang, Michael Matena, Yanqi Zhou, Wei Li, and Peter J. Liu. 2023. Exploring the Limits of Transfer Learning with a Unified Text-to-Text Transformer. *arXiv preprint*. ArXiv:1910.10683 [cs, stat].

Uli Sauerland. 2012. The Computation of Scalar Implicatures: Pragmatic, Lexical or Grammatical? *Language and Linguistics Compass*, 6(1):36–49.

Stefan Schweter. 2020. BERTurk - BERT models for Turkish.

Aarohi Srivastava et al. 2022. Beyond the Imitation Game: Quantifying and extrapolating the capabilities of language models. *arXiv preprint*. ArXiv:2206.04615 [cs, stat].

Aarne Talman, Marianna Apidianaki, Stergios Chatzikyriakidis, and Jörg Tiedemann. 2021. NLI Data Sanity Check: Assessing the Effect of Data Corruption on Model Performance. *arXiv preprint*. ArXiv:2104.04751 [cs].

Gemma Team, Thomas Mesnard, Cassidy Hardin, Robert Dadashi, Surya Bhupatiraju, Shreya Pathak, Laurent Sifre, Morgane Rivière, Mihir Sanjay Kale, Juliette Love, Pouya Tafti, Léonard Hussenot, Aakanksha Chowdhery, Adam Roberts, Aditya Barua, Alex Botev, Alex Castro-Ros, Ambrose Slone, Amélie Héliou, Andrea Tacchetti, and et al. Bulanova. 2024. Gemma: Open Models Based on Gemini Research and Technology. *arXiv preprint*. ArXiv:2403.08295 [cs].

Hugo Touvron, Louis Martin, Kevin Stone, Peter Albert, Amjad Almahairi, Yasmine Babaei, Nikolay Bashlykov, Soumya Batra, Prajjwal Bhargava, Shruti Bhosale, Dan Bikel, Lukas Blecher, Cristian Canton Ferrer, Moya Chen, Guillem Cucurull, David Esiobu, Jude Fernandes, Jeremy Fu, Wenyin Fu, and et al. Fuller. 2023. Llama 2: Open Foundation and Fine-Tuned Chat Models. *arXiv preprint*. ArXiv:2307.09288 [cs].

Ashish Vaswani, Noam Shazeer, Niki Parmar, Jakob Uszkoreit, Llion Jones, Aidan N. Gomez, Lukasz Kaiser, and Illia Polosukhin. 2017. Attention Is All You Need. *arXiv preprint*. ArXiv:1706.03762 [cs].

André Wendland, Marco Zenere, and Jörg Niemann. 2021. Introduction to Text Classification: Impact of Stemming and Comparing TF-IDF and Count Vectorization as Feature Extraction Technique. In Murat Yilmaz, Paul Clarke, Richard Messnarz, and Michael Reiner, editors, *Systems, Software and Services Process Improvement*, volume 1442, pages 289–300. Springer International Publishing, Cham. Series Title: Communications in Computer and Information Science.

Adina Williams, Nikita Nangia, and Samuel Bowman. 2018. A Broad-Coverage Challenge Corpus for Sentence Understanding through Inference. In *Proceedings of the 2018 Conference of the North American Chapter of the Association for Computational Linguistics: Human Language Technologies, Volume 1 (Long Papers)*, pages 1112–1122, New Orleans, Louisiana. Association for Computational Linguistics.

Hitomi Yanaka, Koji Mineshima, Daisuke Bekki, Kentaro Inui, Satoshi Sekine, Lasha Abzianidze, and Johan Bos. 2019a. Can neural networks understand monotonicity reasoning? *arXiv preprint*. ArXiv:1906.06448 [cs].

Hitomi Yanaka, Koji Mineshima, Daisuke Bekki, Kentaro Inui, Satoshi Sekine, Lasha Abzianidze, and Johan Bos. 2019b. HELP: A dataset for identifying shortcomings of neural models in monotonicity reasoning. In *Proceedings of the Eighth Joint Conference on Lexical and Computational Semantics (*SEM 2019)*, pages 250–255, Minneapolis, Minnesota. Association for Computational Linguistics.

Fei Yu, Hongbo Zhang, Prayag Tiwari, and Benyou Wang. 2023. Natural Language Reasoning, A Survey. *arXiv preprint*. ArXiv:2303.14725 [cs].

Zilong Zheng, Shuwen Qiu, Lifeng Fan, Yixin Zhu, and Song-Chun Zhu. 2021. GRICE: A Grammar-based Dataset for Recovering Implicature and Conversational rEasoning. In *Findings of the Association for Computational Linguistics: ACL-IJCNLP 2021*, pages 2074–2085, Online. Association for Computational Linguistics.

A Appendix A: Data Distribution

Table 8: ImplicaTR: Data Distribution

	N of scales	N of distinct terms	N of quadruplets per scale	N of sentences per quadruplet	Total N of Quadruplets	Total Pairs
Adjectives	15	28	30	8	450	3600
Verbs	9	18	50	8	450	3600
Quantifiers	9	7	50	8	450	3600
Modals	2	4	225	8	450	3600
Numerals	9	18	50	11	450	4950
Total					2250	19350

B Appendix B: Prompt Example

Below is an instruction that describes a classification task. Give a label in your response that appropriately completes the request.
You will give only the label.
Instruction:
The labels are:
Labels: entailment, neutral, contradiction, implicature
The two sentences that you will classify are:
Sentences: A: *Yeni kullanmaya başladığı ilaçlar zararlı değil.* B: *Yeni kullanmaya başladığı ilaçlar ölümcül.* **Question:** What is the correct label that describes the relationship of B to A?
Response:
contradiction

C Appendix C: Features

Group	Description	Names of Variables
Counts and Lengths	The counts of nouns and tokens, and average length of each token per premise-hypothesis	premise_noun_counts hypothesis_noun_counts premise_token_counts hypothesis_token_counts avg_premise_token_length avg_hypothesis_token_length
Verb	Whether the predicate is nominal or verbal	premise_is_root_verb hypothesis_is_root_verb
Polarity and Negation	The polarity of the sentence as obtained from the morphological markers on the root for premise and hypothesis. Also, the possible combinations between premise-hypothesis	premise_polarity hypothesis_polarity isPol_PosPos isPol_PosNeg isPol_NegPos isPol_NegNeg
NER	The NER tags obtained from both premise and hypothesis	CARDINAL, GPE, PERCENT, ORG, NORP, LOC, MONEY, QUANTITY, DATE, TIME, PERSON, LANGUAGE, EVENT, WORK_OF_ART, FAC, TITLE, ORDINAL
Sentiment	The sentiment as predicted by zero-shot as one of positive, negative, or neutral	sentiment_premise_negative sentiment_premise_neutral sentiment_premise_positive sentiment_hypothesis_negative sentiment_hypothesis_neutral sentiment_hypothesis_positive
Word Similarity	The average word similarity for each premise and hypothesis obtained from fastText and the difference between the two	premise_word_similarity hypothesis_word_similarity word_similarity_diff
Sentence Similarity	The similarity score premise-hypothesis pair calculated by the embeddings	premise_hypothesis_similarity
TF-IDF	TF-IDF score of the scalar item in each sentence for premises and hypotheses	premise_scale_tfidf hypothesis_scale_tfidf
Scalar Position	The respective position of the scalar item within a sentence along with the number of tokens to left and to the right for both premise and hypothesis	premise_scale_position premise_words_on_right premise_words_on_left hypothesis_scale_position hypothesis_words_on_right hypothesis_words_on_left

A coreference corpus of Turkish situated dialogs

Faruk Büyüktekin and **Umut Özge**
Informatics Institute, Department of Cognitive Science,
Middle East Technical University
faruk.buyuktekin@metu.edu.tr, umozge@metu.edu.tr

Abstract

The paper introduces a publicly available corpus of Turkish situated dialogs annotated for coreference. We developed an annotation scheme for coreference annotation in Turkish, a language with pro-drop and rich agglutinating morphology. The annotation scheme is tailored for these aspects of the language, making it potentially applicable to similar languages. The corpus comprises 60 dialogs containing in total 3900 sentences, 18360 words, and 6120 mentions.

1 Introduction

Coreference annotation and corpus research have attracted significant attention among NLP researchers, cognitive scientists, and linguists, as understanding referring expressions and the relations between them is fundamental to natural language understanding. Numerous NLP tasks, including information retrieval, question answering, and summarization, require coreference resolution for effective performance. This need has resulted in an increase in the number of corpora annotated for coreference relations in recent decades, particularly with the success of data-driven techniques, especially for widely-studied languages like English (Weischedel et al., 2011; Zeldes, 2017; Uryupina et al., 2020) and German (Lapshinova-Koltunski and Ferreira, 2022; Bourgonje and Stede, 2020).

However, the majority of languages still remain low-resourced in this respect. Turkish, a member of the Turkic language family, is among these low-resourced languages, facing a scarcity of coreference-annotated datasets. The available annotation schemes, predominantly designed for languages like English, fall short when applied to morphologically rich and pro-drop languages like Turkish. Such languages exhibit complex inflectional morphemes and allow reduced or null forms when the referents are pragmatically inferable or morphologically cued by agreement.

In this connection, adapting existing annotation schemes to Turkish poses numerous challenges and it is particularly challenging to offer a universal scheme for all languages when the complexity of the anaphoric phenomena is taken into consideration as stated by Poesio (2004). For instance, the treatment of morphological information, such as suffixes that carry referential information, is often overlooked. Similarly, the handling of phonologically null elements, which are pervasive in Turkish, is not sufficiently addressed. This inadequacy can lead to a loss of critical information necessary for accurate coreference resolution. As a result, there is a need for developing a specialized annotation scheme that can accommodate the unique features of Turkish and similar languages, ensuring more robust and reliable coreference annotation.

This study is driven by the necessity to develop a coreference dataset in Turkish, a language with relatively limited resources. It proposes a novel annotation scheme for coreference annotation, addressing the challenges encountered when adapting existing schemes designed for languages such as English. The paper is organized as follows: Sections 2 outlines the basic terminology related to coreference. Section 3 reviews the related work in coreference corpora. Section 4 describes the initial steps in corpus development. Section 5 introduces the proposed annotation scheme. Section 6 provides descriptive statistics of the resulting corpus. Section 7 ends with a summary and outlines future research directions.

2 Basic terminology

Coreference can be better understood within the larger picture of cohesion and concepts related to it. Cohesion itself is based on the idea that the spoken or written communication is usually a united whole rather than unrelated utterances or sentences. For cohesion to occur, the interpretation of some

Proceedings of the First Workshop on Natural Language Processing for Turkic Languages (SIGTURK 2024), pages 42–52
August 15, 2024 ©2024 Association for Computational Linguistics

linguistic element in the discourse sometimes depends on previously mentioned items in the text (Halliday and Hasan, 1976). A closely related notion to cohesion is reference. It is the relationship between a linguistic expression and an entity in the world. There are two main types of reference. Exophoric reference refers to an entity which is outside the text. On the contrary, endophoric reference refers to another expression in the preceding discourse segment. Endophora is further divided into two types. Anaphora can be described as an item which relates back to a previous item in some way. The element which is referring back is called anaphor and the previously mentioned entity which then anaphor refers to or is related to is its antecedent. The process of linking the anaphor with its antecedent is called anaphora resolution. Cataphora, on the other hand, points to an item in the following discourse segment.

There are a variety of anaphora which are observed in written or oral language based on the form of the anaphor (Mitkov, 2014). Lexical noun phrase anaphora could appear as proper names and definite descriptions. Pronominal anaphora is one of the most studied and therefore understood type of anaphora in the literature. Anaphors in this type can be in the form of personal pronouns, possessive pronouns, reflexive pronouns, and demonstrative pronouns. Another type of anaphora is zero anaphora. It is considered to be one of the most challenging types of anaphora to resolve since they are not physically realized at the surface level. Although they are invisible, they do not damage the cohesion of the discourse but strengthen it. They are decoded by the reader or hearer without any loss during the comprehension of the discourse. If the anaphor and antecedent refer to the same entity, they are thought to be coreferential. This relation is also called identity anaphora, as in (1).

(1) A man came. **He** brought a book.

An anaphor can be preceded by a number of expressions referring to the same entity and therefore they are said to form a coreference chain. Such theoretical work on reference and anaphora has become the foundation of the guidelines which have been prepared to create coreference corpora.

3 Related work

The earliest attempts to develop annotation schemes for coreference annotation could be traced back to the Message Understanding Conference (MUC) information extraction tasks (Hirschman et al., 1997). The task was created to group all the mentions of an entity together and the scheme specified the basic task criteria, the markables to be annotated and the relations to be established in English. The task evolved with Automatic Content Extraction (ACE) Program (Doddington et al., 2004) enriching the coverage with entity, relation, and event annotation in English, Chinese and Arabic. The MATE/GNOME proposals (Poesio, 2004) were geared towards being more linguistically oriented than previous schemes, making a discourse model assumption. It also included bridging anaphora in addition to identity relations.

The PoCoS – Potsdam Coreference Scheme (Krasavina and Chiarcos, 2007) claimed to adopt language independent principles during markable annotation. The scheme applied to German, English and Russian. The OntoNotes guidelines (Weischedel et al., 2011) includes several layers, one of which is coreference layer. It aimed to include all coreferential relations and specifically focuses on how to handle identity relations and appositives. Like the ACE scheme, it was applied to English, Arabic and Chinese. The later schemes have become more comprehensive, including different kinds of anaphora in addition to coreference and more fine grained subcategories like ARRAU (Uryupina et al., 2020).

However, some guidelines took a more psychological approach and considered coreference as part of information structure annotation. Nissim et al. (2004) developed a scheme to annotate coreference and information status relations in English dialogs. Götze et al. (2007) prepared guidelines for information status, topic, and focus annotation. They aimed for language independence, theory neutrality, reliable marking, and framed coreference under information status annotation in terms of givenness. The RefLex scheme (Riester and Baumann, 2017) was developed for referential and lexical analysis of spoken and written text. Coreferentiality has been at the referential level along with bridging relations in the scheme.

The development of annotation schemes have paved the way for the construction of many corpora in different languages. The initial products were naturally produced in the languages of the schemes mentioned above. One of the well-known and largest coreference corpora is the OntoNotes project (Weischedel et al., 2013). It consists of various genres such as news, conversational telephone speech, weblogs, usenet newsgroups, broadcast, talk shows. It was annotated for syntax and predicate argument structure and word sense and coreference in English, Chinese, and Arabic. ARRAU (Uryupina et al., 2020) is another multi-genre corpus which contains around 350K tokens. Unlike many corpora, it accepts nonreferential NPs and singletons as markable. It was annotated for different kinds of anaphoric relations including coreference, bridging anaphora and discourse deixis.

Similar to OntoNotes, AnCora (Taulé et al., 2008) is also a multilingual corpus. It consists of 500k tokens of newspaper texts in Spanish and Catalan. The texts were annotated for morphological information, syntactic phrases, grammatical functions relations. ParCorFull (Lapshinova-Koltunski and Ferreira, 2022) is a parallel corpus of English and German with a total of 160K tokens. It was only annotated for coreference relations. The growing interest and need in coreference datasets triggered corpus development in other languages such as Czech (Nedoluzhko et al., 2016), Hungarian (Vincze et al., 2018), Polish (Ogrodniczuk et al., 2016), Dutch and (Hendrickx et al., 2008).

However, to the best of our knowledge, the only coreference corpus developed in Turkish was Marmara Turkish Coreference Corpus (Schüller et al., 2017). It is an annotation layer on top of the METU-Sabancı Treebank, which consists of 33 documents from various genres with 53925 tokens in total. The scheme prepared for corpus includes noun phrases, pronouns, and nominalized adjectives as markables, but it does not consider the role of morphological information and null elements in Turkish. The gold data obtained from several annotators resulted in 5170 mentions and 944 coreference chains. Arslan and Eryiğit (2023) reannotated the corpus to handle the dropped pronouns with the data representation scheme they proposed. However, their scheme only deals with how to represent third person singular agreement makers and possessive pronouns for dropped pronouns.

Due to this limited availability of Turkish coreference data, the computational work on coreference in Turkish is also rather limited and mostly have exploited rule-based and classical machine learning methods. Yıldırım et al. (2004) developed a rule-based system for anaphora resolution in Turkish. Their model depends on the theoretical framework of the Centering Theory. In a later study, Tüfekçi and Kılıçaslan (2007) presented a computational model for resolving pronominal anaphora. It is based on Hobbs' naïve algorithm (Hobbs, 1978), which traverses a parse tree to find the antecedent of a pronominal anaphora. The first learning-based approach to anaphora resolution is limited to pronoun resolution (Yıldırım and Kılıçaslan, 2006). They trained a decision tree on a corpus of popular child stories. Pamay and Eryiğit (2018) proposed the first coreference resolution system, which uses support vector machines with a mention-pair model. There are recent attempts to use deep learning methods for Turkish coreference resolution. Demir (2023) presented the first neural coreference resolution system and Arslan et al. (2023) introduced a neural multilingual coreference resolution model which makes use of morphological information. However, they remain limited due to data sparsity.

4 Corpus creation

4.1 Genre selection

We selected situated dialogs as the genre for our corpus. Most coreference corpora started with texts like news, and continued with articles, and stories (Uryupina et al., 2020). However, we chose to annotate situated dialogs with spontaneous speech. The language in this genre exhibit certain features. The utterances/sentences are relatively short compared to the genres like news and articles and therefore grammatically less complicated. Speakers might often produce ungrammatical forms and add disfluencies, which is associated with cognitive load and planning.

Our decision to use situated dialogs as our texts has several reasons. Firstly, situated dialogs provide rich contextual information, including the nature of the task, the setting, the discourse participants, the entities in the physical context, and the shared knowledge among participants. Additionally, situated dialogs possess the spontaneity and complexity of natural language interaction absent in experimental stimuli or controlled experiments. This makes them valuable for testing cognitive and linguistic theories and hypotheses. Moreover, they offer diverse linguistic structures since they are produced in a situated context. Analyzing them can help investigate how these forms evolve throughout the text.

4.2 The source of our texts

Our dialogs were taken from an experimental setting where pairs were expected to solve tangram

Entities	Anchors
Presenter	presenter
Operator	operator
Pink triangle	pinktr
Green triangle	greentr
Yellow triangle	yellowtr
Red triangle	redtr
Blue triangle	bluetr
Black square	blacksq
Grey parallelgram	greyp

Table 1: Anchors for the entities

puzzles (Mançe-Çalışır, 2018). The task requires them to build a target shape by manipulating seven geometric shapes through a computer simulator. They are seated face to face and perform the tasks through shared screens. The separator between the tables prevents them from seeing each other. They are assigned specific roles, which aims to promote real-life language production. The presenter has access to the target shape and is expected to give instructions to the other participant about how to build the shape and the operator cannot see the shape but has control over the mouse to manipulate the geometric shapes to achieve the goal.

4.3 Text preparation

We firstly transcribed the speech between the participants in the form of dialogs, indicating the roles of the pairs (ie. presenter and operator). Then, we manually split them into sentences and added punctuation where necessary. We added anchors for the entities available in the physical context at the beginning of each dialog. These are discourse participants and seven geometric including shapes two small triangles, one middle triangle, and two big triangles, small square, small parallelogram (see Table 1). We then encoded the dialogs in JSON format.

4.4 Tool choice

As a result of our evaluation of various annotation tools, we decided to use Labelbox (2024). It offers inherent templates for conversational texts, relatively easy annotation, and most importantly allows morpheme and character selection to capture morphological and null elements. It was also the most suitable tool to work with dyadic dialog data (see Figure 1 for a sample annotation).

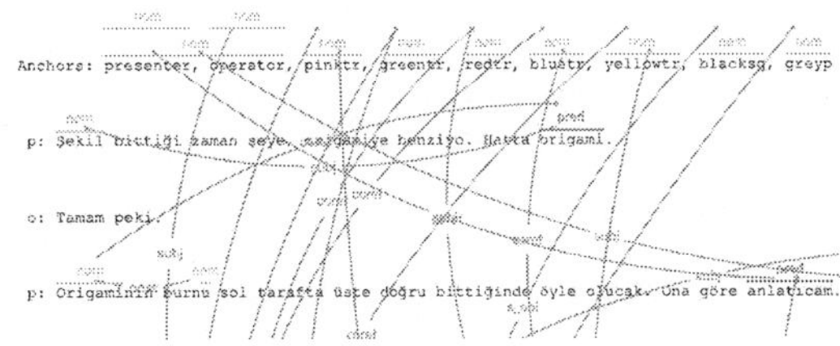

Figure 1: Annotation sample from the annotation tool

4.5 Training the annotators

We hired three graduate students, all native speakers of Turkish with the necessary linguistic background. We conducted training sessions with materials that were not included in the corpus to familiarize them with the coreference task and test our annotation scheme. We detected the challenging issues and specified how to handle them.

5 Annotation scheme development

We evaluated available schemes mentioned above and found that they were lacking the devices that are required for the annotation of sub-word morphological units and null elements. Therefore, we developed a scheme which is comprehensive enough to handle all realizations of mentions at different levels of Turkish structure. In this way, the scheme could be a model for morphologically rich low-resourced Turkic languages which frequently utilize null elements.

5.1 Scope

Our annotation scheme mainly focuses on how to annotate co-referring expressions. Our definition of coreference follows Deemter and Kibble (2000): "α_1 and α_2 corefer if and only if Referent(α_1) = Referent(α_2)"

However, certain anaphoric relations fall beyond the scope of this work. Discourse deixis (Webber, 1988) can be associated with coreference but discourse deictic expressions may refer to preceding or succeeding discourse segments, such as clauses or sentences. Given that the antecedents in these cases are non-nominal expressions (Çallı, 2012), we do not include them in our dataset. Additionally, there exists another type of relationship between an anaphor and its antecedent beyond identity relations. Bridging anaphora (Clark, 1975), also known as associative anaphora (Hawkins, 2015), requires the hearer or reader to establish an indirect connection between the anaphor and its antecedent, drawing on their world knowledge. In sentence (2), the cover functions as the anaphor and *a book* as its antecedent. The reader infers the relationship because it is commonly understood that covers are parts of books.

(2) The man brought a book. **The cover** has a nice illustration.

This brings us to the central aspects of the present study:

- referentiality
- strict coreference.

The present work is limited to the annotation of referential noun phrases. The operational test we employ for referentiality is case-marking. In this regard, we ignore all the nominal expressions that come in non-case-marked positions (see below for examples and exceptions).

We limit ourselves to strict coreference between referents, leaving out looser linking relations like discourse deixis and bridging anaphora.

Our scheme also involves annotating the grammatical roles of the mentions with the embedding level (matrix or subordinate) of their occurrences.

5.2 Markables

Our scheme restricts the class of mentions which are to be annotated as referential noun phrases and their manifestations as agreement markers on predicates, possessive suffixes, and null elements. We correlate referentiality of a referring expression with case-marking (Ozturk, 2004). Although it is problematic at times especially at the conceptual level, it provides a strong basis for decision-making during annotation. The other condition is that the noun phrase should refer to another expression with an identity relation either anaphorically or cataphorically. Therefore, a mention qualifies as a markable only if it is case-marked and part of a coreferential chain. We annotate the full span of the overt entities due to maximal projection principle, which is established in most schemes. This choice enables us to annotate noun phrases of varying complexity in a uniform way. Here are the major types of Turkish markables included in the present work:
Overt nominals:

(3) **Bir kitap** okuyorum. (Indefinite NP)
a book read.PROG.1sg
'I am reading **a book**.'

(4) **Kitap** okuyorum. (Bare noun)
book read.PROG.1sg
'I am reading.'

(5) **Kitabı** okuyorum. (Definite NP)
book.Acc read.PROG.1sg
'I am reading **the book**.'

(6) Adamın okuduğu kitap (modified NPs)
man.Gen read.Rel.Agr book
'The book that the man read'

(7) Adamın okuduğu (Headless relative)
man.Gen read.Rel.Agr
'The one that the man read'

(8) Masa-da-ki (kitap) (Pron. locative)
table-Loc-Rel book
'The book/one on the table.'

(9) Proper names, pronouns and demonstratives and demonstrative NPs.

Null nominals:

(10) Kitap geldi. **ø** Eskiydi. (Subject drop)
book.Nom came **it** old.Past.3sg
'The book came. **It** was old.'

(11) Elma vardı. Ali **ø** yedi. (Object drop)
apple.Nom existed Ali **it** eat.Past.3sg
'There was an apple. Ali ate **it**.'

(12) ø ev-**i** güzel. (Possessor drop)
his/her house-Poss beautiful.Cop
'**His/her** house is beautiful.'

(13) Ben ø **okurken** uyudum. (Converbs)
I I/she read.Conv slept
'I fell asleep, while I/she was reading.'

5.3 Non-markables

We did not annotate the following categories:

Singletons: We left out mentions that occur only once throughout the text and therefore do not take part in a coreferential chain. Zhu et al. (2023) showed that incorporating singleton information along with entity type and information status could help coreference models generalize better. We are planning to enrich our dataset with singletons in the future.

Predicatives: Predicatives are usually complements of a linking verb or a copula and state a property of the subject. Some schemes accept them as markables such as the Gum corpus (Zeldes, 2017), but we do not annotate them because they are not discourse entities themselves but properties so they cannot pass our referentiality criterion.

(14) Ali **öğretmen** oldu.
Ali **teacher** become.Past.3sg

'Ali became **teacher**.'

Abstract Entities: We left out reference to abstract objects like propositions, state-of-affairs, and other sort of such entities discussed by (Asher, 1993), as their inclusion immensely complicates the annotation task when handled along with conceptually simpler type of referents we aimed to capture in the present study. (See Zeyrek et al. (2010) for abstract object annotation in Turkish Discourse Bank (Zeyrek et al., 2013)).

Local adverbial and verbal demonstratives: We annotated only the nominal type out of the three major types of demonstratives There are three types of demonstratives (Dixon, 2003), leaving local adverbial and verbal demonstratives out. because they constitute either a reference to an abstract entity or are not referential.

5.4 Various issues in coreference annotation

The annotation process revealed a number of issues and challenges that, in our opinion, might be of help for researchers planning to build similar corpora for languages like Turkish.

5.4.1 Embedded mentions

One issue that complicated the annotation process was the annotation of embedded mentions. As a principle stated above, we annotate the whole noun phrase but sometimes the phrase can consist of other mentions. For instance in a form like in (15), the markable *the book* is embedded in *the man who brough the book*. We annotated the embedded mention along with the larger one, in cases where there is a reference back to the embedded markable in the text.

(15) [[Kitabı]$_{M2}$ getiren adam]$_{M1}$ gitti.
book-Acc bring.Rel man.Nom left
'**The man** who brought **the book left.**'

A similar issue arose with coordinated noun phrases where there are separate references to both the entire NP and individually to its components.

5.4.2 Appositives

We include the appositives like *Istanbul, Turkey's most crowded city* in the markable of the nominal expression they attach to. Our rationale for doing this is the possible significance of this modification type for modelling efforts of coreference phenomena which might be conducted on the corpus in the future (See also Weischedel et al. (2011) and Hirschman et al. (1997) for discussion of appositives).

5.4.3 Genitive-possessive constructions

Turkish makes extensive use of genitive-possessive agreement both on a type and a token basis. There are 3 major constructions that depend on the agreement of a genitive marked noun phrase and a possessive marked head: Genitive-possesive NPs, object relative clauses, and subordinate clauses. The genitive marked possessor can be dropped in all these constructions. Therefore, it is imperative for a coreference corpus to systematically handle these constructions. In this regard, we annotated all the possessive suffixes as markables and linked them to their null and overt possessors.

5.4.4 Grammatical coreference

We left out all coreference relations that are governed by syntax rather than discourse, such as control structures, Turkish versions of *want*-type constructions, reflexive binding, and so on. Our aim here was to simplify the annotation process, as the mentioned dependencies can be automatically discovered by accurate syntactic parsing in the future.

5.4.5 Split anaphora

In split anaphora, which is a rather rare case of anaphora slightly more complex than standard anaphora (Yu et al., 2021), the antecedent of the anaphor can be the addition of previous discourse entities, which is also called aggregation. These cases are included in our dataset.

(16) Ali Ayşe'yi bekliyor. **Onlar** birlikte gelecek.
'Ali is waiting for Ayşe. **They** will come together.'

5.4.6 Null elements

Turkish is a pro drop language, where zero pronouns are abundant in both spoken and written text, and get involved in coreference chains (see Section 6. In cases where a null markable has an overt morphosyntactic agreement like a verbal inflection or a possessive suffix, we annotated the corresponding suffix in lieu of the markable itself. However, when it comes to null objects there is no overt agreement correlate. It is still a matter of discussion how to treat such cases in annotation. For instance, Pradhan et al. (2012) inserted a small *pro* into the place the null element is omitted, but the detection of the correct place is also problematic on its own. We employed a convention of marking the space character just before the head predicate to represent a dropped object. The information concerning both types of null anaphora is recovered during post-processing, abstracting away from the conventions we employed in the annotation process.

5.5 Annotation procedure

Our scheme basically requires detecting a mention, assigning a grammatical role to it, and establishing a link with its antecedent. Although it might look complicated, we clearly defined the steps which our annotators need to follow.

1. Identify the markable.
2. Check whether it is a referential phrase or not. Case marking is an important indicator here.
3. Check whether it is a singleton or not.
4. Check whether it is realized at the subordinate or matrix clause level.
5. Assign its grammatical role accordingly.
6. Connect the markable with its closest antecedent.

6 Analysis

Each text in the corpus has been independently annotated by two annotators. They identified the mentions in the texts and established the identity relations between them. This provided us with the unique entities and their realizations in the texts, in other words, their mentions. They labeled these mentions with the grammatical information with the categories subject, object, and other.

We built a custom tool in Python that (i) exported the annotated texts from LabelBox, (ii) compared the annotations and calculated inter-coder agreement, (iii) extracted a graph representation of the coreference patterns of the dialogs, and (iv) performed basic statistics.

6.1 Inter-Annotator Agreement

Coreference annotation has been traditionally associated with two subtasks. Mention annotation involves detecting the mentions and their boundaries and relation annotation requires creating a link between an anaphor and its antecedent. Our annotation workflow also involves detecting mentions and establishing relations. Cohen's κ (Cohen, 1960) and Krippendorf's α (Krippendorff, 1970) are two widely used coefficients to measure inter-annotator agreement reliability in NLP annotation tasks (Artstein and Poesio, 2008). Cohen's κ has been developed to measure inter-annotator reliability between two annotators for nominal data taking chance factor into account. Fleiss κ (Fleiss, 1971) is an extension which can measure the agreement between two or more coders. Similarly, Krippendorf's α can measure the agreement between two or more coders, but can be applied to different metrics (eg. nominal, ordinal, interval, and etc.).

However, these coefficients are not the best candidates for coreference annotation because mentions and relations are not fixed and the negative cases are unknown (Deleger et al., 2012). Under such circumstances, it has been shown that the agreement between annotators can be measured with standard measures like precision, recall, and F-score (Brants, 2000; Hripcsak and Rothschild, 2005). We took one of the annotations to be predictions and the other one to be our gold standard to calculate F1 score to measure the agreement between our annotators for each text using the formulae below. We adopted the basic metrics introduced in Sang and De Meulder (2003) and implemented a strict evaluation based on the exact matches between both mentions and relations.

$$\text{Precision} = \frac{\text{True Positives}}{\text{True Positives} + \text{False Positives}} \tag{1}$$

$$\text{Recall} = \frac{\text{True Positives}}{\text{True Positives} + \text{False Negatives}} \tag{2}$$

$$F_1 = 2 \cdot \frac{\text{Precision} \cdot \text{Recall}}{\text{Precision} + \text{Recall}} \tag{3}$$

Our annotators achieved high precision, recall and F1 scores (0.96) for mentions and (0.90) for relations on average, which is quite satisfactory for corefererence annotation task (See Table 2 for interannotator agreement scores).

	Precision	**Recall**	**F1**
Mentions	0.96	0.96	096
Relations	0.90	090	0.90

Table 2: Interannotator agreement scores

6.2 Corpus statistics

We annotated 60 situated dialogues of participants solving a puzzle. Our dialogues have an average of 306 tokens. The dialogue with minimum number of words has 127 words and the one with maximum number of words has 961 (See Table 3 for average number of words in our dialogues).

	tokens	mentions	entities
mean	306	102	12
min	127	43	7
max	961	280	19
std	167	48	2.5
total	18360	6120	720

Table 3: Counts of the corpus. Statistics are per dialog.

Our analysis indicated that there is an average of 12.3 entities and 102.4 mentions per dialogue, which means that each entity is mentioned approximately 8.2 times on average throughout a dialog.

We also looked at the grammatical functions of the mentions. We found out that 50.5% of the mentions occupy a subject position in a sentence. 49.5% of the mentions occupy an object position or part of a genitive possessive construction. (See Table 4 for the percentage of grammatical roles of mentions)

%subject	%non-subject
50.5	49.5

Table 4: Percentage of the grammatical roles of mentions

We also analyzed the form of our referring expressions. We observed a relatively close distribution of null and overt form in our mentions. The percentage of mentions which have overt forms is 57.3% while the percentage of null forms is 42.7% (See Table 5 for the percentage of forms of the mentions).

%overt	%null
57.7	42.7

Table 5: Percentage of linguistic forms of mentions

We aligned the grammatical function of the referring expressions along with their forms to see if the grammatical function has a relation with the form. When we looked at the mentions which occupy the subject position, we observed that 61.91% of the expressions have null forms. However, when we looked at the non-subject positions including objects and all other positions, our analysis showed that only 23.34% of referring expressions have null forms (See Table 6 for null forms in subject and non-subject positions). Consequently, our data indicated that there can be a strong relationship between subjecthood and linguistic form of the mentions.

	subj	nonsubj
null	62.1	23.3
overt	37.9	76,7

Table 6: Distribution of linguistic forms according to function

7 Conclusion and future work

We introduced a new publicly available[1] corpus of situated dialogs manually annotated for mentions and coreference relations. Our work has made novel contributions in a number of ways. Our dataset comprises 60 conversational texts. To our knowledge, it has been the first dialog corpus, which has been annotated for mentions and coreference relations in Turkish. Another significant contribution is that it includes null elements, agreement markers, and possessive suffixes as realizations of entities in text in addition to overt noun phrases and pronouns.

We also proposed an annotation scheme about how to annotate coreferential phenomena including both overt and null mentions in a morphologically rich and pro drop Turkic language. The high inter-annotator agreement shows that our scheme can be reliably applied to languages similar to Turkish in the relevant respects.

We believe that our corpus and scheme can serve as a resource for researchers working in different fields such as linguists, computational linguists, and cognitive scientists. The scheme can be a model for researchers who want do develop an annotation scheme and create a coreference corpus in other Turkic languages and similar low resourced languages.

The corpus can be improved in various ways. The most critical is the accumulation of more annotations. Another direction for improvement would

[1]Please contact the corresponding author to obtain the corpus for research purposes.

be to enrich the corpus with further grammatical information.

Acknowledgements

This work was supported by the Middle East Technical University Scientific Research Projects Coordination Unit under the grant number GAP-704-2023-11066. The first author acknowledges the financial support by The Scientific and the Technological Research Council of Türkiye (TÜBİTAK) under the 2214-A International Research Fellowship Programme for a research stay at the University of Cologne. We would like to thank our annotators Derin Dinçer, Batuhan Karataş and Anıl Öğdül for their meticulous work during scheme development and corpus creation. We are grateful to Klaus von Heusinger and his team at the Collaborative Research Centre (CRC 1252) at the University of Cologne, İsmail Sengör Altıngövde, Murat Perit Çakır, and Asiye Tuba Özge for their valuable feedback during annotation scheme development. We are also thankful to the anonymous reviewers for their helpful comments and suggestions to improve our work.

References

Tuğba Pamay Arslan, Kutay Acar, and Gülşen Eryiğit. 2023. Neural end-to-end coreference resolution using morphological information. In *Proceedings of the CRAC 2023 Shared Task on Multilingual Coreference Resolution*, pages 34–40.

Tuğba Pamay Arslan and Gülşen Eryiğit. 2023. Incorporating dropped pronouns into coreference resolution: the case for turkish. In *Proceedings of the 17th Conference of the European Chapter of the Association for Computational Linguistics: Student Research Workshop*, pages 14–25.

Ron Artstein and Massimo Poesio. 2008. Inter-coder agreement for computational linguistics. *Computational linguistics*, 34(4):555–596.

Nicholas Asher. 1993. *Reference to Abstract Objects in Discourse*. Springer, Dordrecht, Holland.

Peter Bourgonje and Manfred Stede. 2020. The potsdam commentary corpus 2.2: Extending annotations for shallow discourse parsing. In *Proceedings of the Twelfth Language Resources and Evaluation Conference*, pages 1061–1066.

Thorsten Brants. 2000. Inter-annotator agreement for a german newspaper corpus. In *LREC*. Citeseer.

Ayışığı B Sevdik Çallı. 2012. Demonstrative anaphora in turkish: A corpus based analysis. In *First workshop on language resources and technologies for turkic languages*, page 33. Citeseer.

Herbert H Clark. 1975. Bridging. In *Theoretical issues in natural language processing*.

Jacob Cohen. 1960. A coefficient of agreement for nominal scales. *Educational and Psychological Measurement*, 20:37–46.

Kees van Deemter and Rodger Kibble. 2000. On coreferring: Coreference in muc and related annotation schemes. *Computational linguistics*, 26(4):629–637.

Louise Deleger, Qi Li, Todd Lingren, Megan Kaiser, Katalin Molnar, Laura Stoutenborough, Michal Kouril, Keith Marsolo, Imre Solti, et al. 2012. Building gold standard corpora for medical natural language processing tasks. In *AMIA Annual Symposium Proceedings*, volume 2012, page 144. American Medical Informatics Association.

Şeniz Demir. 2023. Neural coreference resolution for turkish. *Journal of Intelligent Systems: Theory and Applications*, 6(1):85–95.

Robert MW Dixon. 2003. Demonstratives: A cross-linguistic typology. *Studies in Language. International Journal sponsored by the Foundation "Foundations of Language"*, 27(1):61–112.

George R Doddington, Alexis Mitchell, Mark A Przybocki, Lance A Ramshaw, Stephanie M Strassel, and Ralph M Weischedel. 2004. The automatic content extraction (ace) program-tasks, data, and evaluation. In *Lrec*, volume 2, pages 837–840. Lisbon.

Joseph L Fleiss. 1971. Measuring nominal scale agreement among many raters. *Psychological bulletin*, 76(5):378.

Michael Götze, Thomas Weskott, Cornelia Endriss, Ines Fiedler, Stefan Hinterwimmer, Svetlana Petrova, Anne Schwarz, Stavros Skopeteas, and Ruben Stoel. 2007. Information structure. *Interdisciplinary studies on information structure: ISIS*, (7):147–187.

M. A. K. Halliday and Ruqaiya Hasan. 1976. *Cohesion in English*, 1st edition. Routledge.

John Hawkins. 2015. *Definiteness and indefiniteness: A study in reference and grammaticality prediction*. Routledge.

Iris Hendrickx, Gosse Bouma, Frederik Coppens, Walter Daelemans, Veronique Hoste, Geert Kloosterman, Anne-Marie Mineur, Joeri Van Der Vloet, and Jean-Luc Verschelde. 2008. A coreference corpus and resolution system for dutch. In *LREC*.

Lynette Hirschman, Patricia Robinson, John Burger, and Marc Vilain. 1997. Automating coreference: The role of annotated training data. In *Proceedings of the AAAI Spring Symposium on Applying Machine Learning to Discourse Processing*, pages 118–121.

Jerry R Hobbs. 1978. Resolving pronoun references. *Lingua*, 44(4):311–338.

George Hripcsak and Adam S Rothschild. 2005. Agreement, the f-measure, and reliability in information retrieval. *Journal of the American medical informatics association*, 12(3):296–298.

Olga Krasavina and Christian Chiarcos. 2007. Pocos–potsdam coreference scheme.

Klaus Krippendorff. 1970. Estimating the reliability, systematic error and random error of interval data. *Educational and Psychological Measurement*, 30:61–70.

Labelbox. 2024. Labelbox. `https://labelbox.com`. Online; accessed 2024.

Ekaterina Lapshinova-Koltunski and Pedro Augusto Ferreira. 2022. *ParCorFull2. 0: A parallel corpus annotated with full coreference*. Saarländische Universitäts-und Landesbibliothek.

Özge Mançe-Çalışır. 2018. *Geniş Otizm Fenotipi Gösteren Erişkinlerde Sosyal Biliş: Bir Göz İzleme Çalışması [Social Cognition in Adults with Broad Autism Phenotype: An Eye-Tracking Study]*. Ph.D. thesis, Ankara University, Ankara.

Ruslan Mitkov. 2014. *Anaphora resolution*. Routledge.

Anna Nedoluzhko, Michal Novák, Silvie Cinková, Marie Mikulová, and Jiří Mírovský. 2016. Coreference in prague czech-english dependency treebank. In *Proceedings of the Tenth International Conference on Language Resources and Evaluation (LREC'16)*, pages 169–176.

Malvina Nissim, Shipra Dingare, Jean Carletta, Mark Steedman, et al. 2004. An annotation scheme for information status in dialogue. In *LREC*. Citeseer.

Maciej Ogrodniczuk, Katarzyna Głowińska, Mateusz Kopeć, Agata Savary, and Magdalena Zawisławska. 2016. Polish coreference corpus. In *Human Language Technology. Challenges for Computer Science and Linguistics: 6th Language and Technology Conference, LTC 2013, Poznań, Poland, December 7-9, 2013. Revised Selected Papers 6*, pages 215–226. Springer.

Balkiz Ozturk. 2004. *Case, referentiality and phrase structure*. Harvard University.

Tuğba Pamay and Gülşen Eryiğit. 2018. Turkish coreference resolution. In *2018 Innovations in Intelligent Systems and Applications (INISTA)*, pages 1–7. IEEE.

Massimo Poesio. 2004. The mate/gnome proposals for anaphoric annotation, revisited. In *Proceedings of the 5th SIGdial Workshop on Discourse and Dialogue at HLT-NAACL 2004*, pages 154–162.

Sameer Pradhan, Alessandro Moschitti, Nianwen Xue, Olga Uryupina, and Yuchen Zhang. 2012. CoNLL-2012 shared task: Modeling multilingual unrestricted coreference in OntoNotes. In *Joint Conference on EMNLP and CoNLL - Shared Task*, pages 1–40, Jeju Island, Korea. Association for Computational Linguistics.

Arndt Riester and Stefan Baumann. 2017. The reflex scheme-annotation guidelines.

Erik F Sang and Fien De Meulder. 2003. Introduction to the conll-2003 shared task: Language-independent named entity recognition. *arXiv preprint cs/0306050*.

Peter Schüller, Kübra Cıngıllı, Ferit Tunçer, Barış Gün Sürmeli, Ayşegül Pekel, Ayşe Hande Karatay, and Hacer Ezgi Karakaş. 2017. Marmara turkish coreference corpus and coreference resolution baseline. *arXiv preprint arXiv:1706.01863*.

Mariona Taulé, Maria Antònia Martí, and Marta Recasens. 2008. Ancora: Multilevel annotated corpora for catalan and spanish. In *Lrec*, volume 2008, pages 96–101.

Pınar Tüfekçi and Yılmaz Kılıçaslan. 2007. A computational model for resolving pronominal anaphora in turkish using hobbs-naïve algorithm. *International Journal of Computer and Information Engineering*, 1(5):1402–1405.

Olga Uryupina, Ron Artstein, Antonella Bristot, Federica Cavicchio, Francesca Delogu, Kepa J Rodriguez, and Massimo Poesio. 2020. Annotating a broad range of anaphoric phenomena, in a variety of genres: the arrau corpus. *Natural Language Engineering*, 26(1):95–128.

Veronika Vincze, Klára Hegedűs, Alex Sliz-Nagy, and Richárd Farkas. 2018. Szegedkoref: A hungarian coreference corpus. In *Proceedings of the Eleventh International Conference on Language Resources and Evaluation (LREC 2018)*.

Bonnie Webber. 1988. Discourse deixis: Reference to discourse segments. In *26th Annual Meeting of the Association for Computational Linguistics*, pages 113–122.

Ralph Weischedel, Martha Palmer, Mitchell Marcus, Eduard Hovy, Sameer Pradhan, Lance Ramshaw, Nianwen Xue, Ann Taylor, Jeff Kaufman, Michelle Franchini, et al. 2013. Ontonotes release 5.0 ldc2013t19. *Linguistic Data Consortium, Philadelphia, PA*, 23:170.

Ralph Weischedel, Sameer Pradhan, Lance Ramshaw, Martha Palmer, Nianwen Xue, Mitchell Marcus, Ann Taylor, Craig Greenberg, Eduard Hovy, Robert Belvin, et al. 2011. Ontonotes release 4.0. *LDC2011T03, Philadelphia, Penn.: Linguistic Data Consortium*, 17.

Savaş Yıldırım and Yılmaz Kılıçaslan. 2006. A machine learning approach to personal pronoun resolution in turkish. *Computational Linguistics*, 27(4):521–544.

Savaş Yıldırım, Yılmaz Kılıçaslan, and R Erman Aykaç. 2004. A computational model for anaphora resolution in turkish via centering theory: an initial approach. In *International Conference on Computational Intelligence*, pages 124–128.

Juntao Yu, Nafise Sadat Moosavi, Silviu Paun, and Massimo Poesio. 2021. Stay together: A system for single and split-antecedent anaphora resolution. *arXiv preprint arXiv:2104.05320*.

Amir Zeldes. 2017. The gum corpus: Creating multilayer resources in the classroom. *Language Resources and Evaluation*, 51(3):581–612.

Deniz Zeyrek, Işın Demirşahin, and Ayışığı B Sevdik Çallı. 2013. Turkish discourse bank: Porting a discourse annotation style to a morphologically rich language. *Dialogue & Discourse*, 4(2):174–184.

Deniz Zeyrek, Isin Demirsahin, Ayisigi B Sevdik-Calli, Hale Ögel Balaban, İhsan Yalçinkaya, and Umit Deniz Turan. 2010. The annotation scheme of the turkish discourse bank and an evaluation of inconsistent annotations. In *Proceedings of the fourth linguistic annotation workshop*, pages 282–289.

Yilun Zhu, Siyao Peng, Sameer Pradhan, and Amir Zeldes. 2023. Incorporating singletons and mention-based features in coreference resolution via multi-task learning for better generalization. *arXiv preprint arXiv:2309.11582*.

Do LLMs Recognize *me*, When *I* is not *me*: Assessment of LLMs Understanding of Turkish Indexical Pronouns in Indexical Shift Contexts

Metehan Oğuz*
USC
moguz@usc.edu

Yusuf Umut Ciftci*
USC
yciftci@usc.edu

Yavuz Faruk Bakman*
USC
ybakman@usc.edu

Abstract

Large language models (LLMs) have shown impressive capabilities in tasks such as machine translation, text summarization, question answering, and solving complex mathematical problems. However, their primary training on data-rich languages like English limits their performance in low-resource languages. This study addresses this gap by focusing on the Indexical Shift problem in Turkish. The Indexical Shift problem involves resolving pronouns in indexical shift contexts, a grammatical challenge not present in high-resource languages like English. We present the first study examining indexical shift in any language, releasing a Turkish dataset specifically designed for this purpose. Our Indexical Shift Dataset consists of 156 multiple-choice questions, each annotated with necessary linguistic details, to evaluate LLMs in a few-shot setting. We evaluate recent multilingual LLMs, including GPT-4, GPT-3.5, Cohere-AYA, Trendyol-LLM, and Turkcell-LLM, using this dataset. Our analysis reveals that even advanced models like GPT-4 struggle with the grammatical nuances of indexical shift in Turkish, achieving only moderate performance. These findings underscore the need for focused research on the grammatical challenges posed by low-resource languages. We released the dataset and code here.

1 Introduction

Large language models demonstrate remarkable capabilities in zero-shot and few-shot learning, excelling across a diverse range of tasks such as machine translation, text summarization, question answering, and solving complex mathematical problems (Ye et al., 2023; OpenAI, 2024; Touvron et al., 2023). However, most large language models (LLMs) are primarily trained on data-rich languages like English, and their performance evaluations are also conducted in these languages (Üstün et al., 2024). Consequently, this focus on data-rich languages may lead to the under-exploration of challenges unique to low-resource languages.

Recent studies have evaluated the performance of large language models on linguistic tasks such as coreference resolution to examine their ability to match expressions referring to the same entity (Gan et al., 2024; Le and Ritter, 2023; Brown et al., 2020a; Yang et al., 2022; Agrawal et al., 2022). In this study, we investigate LLMs' performance on interpreting indexical pronouns, with a focus on the Indexical Shift problem, a unique linguistic challenge related to but distinct from pronoun resolution, primarily encountered in low-resource languages like Turkish (Şener and Şener, 2011), Amharic (Schlenker, 1999), Zazaki (Anand and Nevins, 2004), Uyghur (Shklovsky and Sudo, 2014), Nez Perce (Deal, 2020) and Japanese (Sudo, 2012).

Indexical elements like *I* and *here* refer to the referents of the speech context such as the speaker or location of utterance. In most languages, these elements must be interpreted within the actual speech context, referring to the actual speaker or location of utterance. However, indexical shift occurs in some languages, like Turkish, where an indexical element can refer to the referents of the reported context, rather than the actual speech context (see Section 2 for details).

Indexical elements are substantially different from pronouns regarding what antecedents they can refer to and what factors restrict their interpretations. For example, while pronouns are almost always ambiguous and can refer to a wide range of entities, first person indexical unambiguously refers to the speaker of the utterance. Even in languages that allow indexical shift, the first person indexical is ambiguous between only two possible referents (the speaker vs the attitude holder), being interpreted based on contex/world knowledge. Moreover, Turkish allows indexical shift

*Equal Contribution

Proceedings of the First Workshop on Natural Language Processing for Turkic Languages (SIGTURK 2024), pages 53–61
August 15, 2024 ©2024 Association for Computational Linguistics

only in some syntactic structures (finite embedded clauses) but not in others (e.g. nominalized embedded clauses), which makes indexical shift a unique challenge, requiring attention to specific syntactic rules and context (see Section 3 for a detailed comparison of indexical elements and pronouns regarding coreference resolution).

We investigate the capability of multilingual large language models to handle pronoun resolution within the context of indexical shift in Turkish. To the best of our knowledge, this is the first study examining indexical shift in any language. Therefore, we have released a Turkish dataset specifically designed to evaluate LLMs on the indexical shift problem. Our contributions in this work are as follows:

- We released the Indexical Shift Dataset in Turkish, comprising 156 multiple-choice questions to evaluate LLMs on the indexical shift problem in few-shot setting. Each sample in this dataset includes the necessary linguistic details.

- We evaluate recent multilingual LLMs, including GPT-4, GPT-3.5 (OpenAI, 2024), Cohere-AYA (Üstün et al., 2024), Trendyol-LLM (Trendyol, 2023), and Turkcell-LLM (Turkcell, 2023), using our dataset. We statistically analyze the factors that influence these models' decisions.

- We conclude that even advanced models like GPT-4 struggle to grasp the grammatical nuances of indexical shift in Turkish, showing only moderate performance at best. These findings highlight the need for a special focus on the grammatical challenges of low-resource languages.

2 Indexical Shift in Turkish

Indexical elements. Indexical elements such as English *I, you, here* and *yesterday* are used to refer to referents of the speech-act coordinates (Kaplan, 1977; Schlenker, 2003; Anand and Nevins, 2004; Deal, 2020). For example, *I* is used to refer to *author* (speaker) of the utterance, while *here* is used to refer to the *location* where the utterance was made, and thus sentences like (1) mean different things if uttered by different people and/or in different locations. If (1-a) is uttered by *John* in *Los Angeles*, it means that John was born in Los Angeles, but if it is uttered by *Mary* in *Boston* it means that Mary was born in Boston.

(1) a. **I** was born **here**.
b. Peter thinks that **I** went to Atlanta.

In most languages, including English, indexical elements must always be interpreted inside the actual speech context, referring to actual speech-act coordinates (e.g. author, location).[1] So, if (1-b) is uttered by *John*, the indexical *I* can only be interpreted as referring to John (e.g. John is believed to have gone to Atlanta) but nobody else. Importantly, even though Peter's beliefs are reported in (1-b), the indexical element *I* cannot be interpreted as referring to Peter (author of the reported belief), but must be interpreted as referring to John (author of the actual sentence).

Indexical Shift. Turkish allows indexical shift (e.g. Şener and Şener, 2011), a situation where an indexical element gets its referent from the reported context, rather than the actual context of utterance. For instance, the Turkish first person indexical *ben* in (2) can refer to the attitude holder *Burak*, who is the author of the reported belief, or to the author/speaker of the actual sentence.[2]

(2) Burak yine [(**ben**) mezun ol-du-m]
Burak again 1SG graduate be-PST-1SG
san-ıyor.
think-PROG
'Burak thinks again that {he/*speaker*} graduated.'

In this regard, sentences like (2) are ambiguous between readings where first person indexical *ben* is shifted (referring to the attitude holder *Burak*) or non-shifted (referring to actual speaker), and Turkish speakers interpret such sentences based on previous context or upcoming sentences (Kuram, 2020). For example, in a context where the actual speaker is the conversation topic, (2) would naturally be interpreted in the non-shifted reading (I = speaker), but if the conversation is about *Burak*, the sentence would be naturally interpreted in the

[1] One exception for this generalization is direct quotation (e.g. Peter said/thought, 'I went to Atlanta'.), where quoted material is interpreted as verbatim utterance/thought produced by its owner. Direct quotation is out of the scope of this paper.

[2] Turkish is a *pro*-drop language, meaning that the subject of the clause can be dropped (phonologically null). In this example, and henceforth, parentheses indicate that the subject can optionally be dropped. When subject is dropped, its person features are indicated by the agreement marker on the verb.

shifted reading (I = Burak).[3]

Syntactic Restrictions on Indexical Shift. Indexical shift is a quite rare syntactic/grammatical property, observed in a small set of languages like Amharic (Schlenker, 1999), Zazaki (Anand and Nevins, 2004), Uyghur (Shklovsky and Sudo, 2014), Nez Perce (Deal, 2020). These languages are different from others (e.g. English) in that their syntax possesses the necessary machinery to allow indexical shift (see Deal (2020) for theoretical details and a comprehensive list of languages that allow indexical shift). Moreover, even within a language, indexical shift might be allowed or disallowed depending on the syntactic structure of a sentence. For example, indexical shift in Turkish is observed only with finite embedded clauses like (2), but is not allowed in other grammatical structures such as nominalized embedded clauses like (3), formed by the nominalizer suffix *-DIK* on the embedded verb.

(3) Burak yine [(**ben**-im) mezun ol-duğ-um-u] san-ıyor.
Burak again 1SG-GEN graduate be-NMLZ-1SG-ACC think-PROG
'Burak thinks again that {*he/*speaker*} graduated.'

Different from (2), the first person indexical *ben* in (3) can only refer to the actual speaker of the sentence (similar to English), regardless of the context it is uttered in (e.g. it cannot undergo indexical shift and refer to the attitude holder Burak). This contrast between (2) and (3) is due to the syntactic/grammatical properties of the finite and nominalized embedded clauses in Turkish, which are acquired by the native speakers of the language (see Şener and Şener (2011) and Oğuz et al. (2020) for syntactic details).

In this study, we aim to test whether LLMs are able to capture this grammatical contrast between two embedded clause types and successfully interpret indexical elements in syntactic environments that allow (e.g. finite embedded clauses) or block indexical shift (e.g. nominalized embedded clauses).

[3]Some readers may wonder if embedded material in sentences like (2) is direct quotation (e.g. *Peter thinks, 'I am smart.'*, in English). Özyıldız (2012) and Oğuz et al. (2020) use linguistic diagnostics to show that these are not instances of direct quotation but are true instances of indexical shift.

3 Related Work

There are substantial differences between pronouns and indexical elements. To begin with, even though syntactic/semantic factors can influence pronoun resolution by making some nouns more likely antecedents of pronouns (e.g. subject bias), they do not totally rule out other nouns as possible referents.[4] For example, previous work suggests that speakers mostly interpret the third person pronoun *he* in (4) as referring to the subject *John* (for syntactic or contextual reasons), but the object *Bill* is still a possible antecedent, meaning that the sentence is ambiguous (e.g. Crawley et al., 1990; Stewart and Pickering, 1998; Pickering and Majid, 2007).

(4) John hit Bill and **he** ran away.

Moreover, pronouns can refer to nouns that are contextually salient, but not present in the sentence. For example, the third person pronoun *he* can be interpreted as referring to a contextually salient person named *Peter*. As a result, context plays a crucial role in how speakers interpret pronouns. Previous work in the field (cited above) show that LLMs are able to use contextual information during coreference resolution and show good performance.

Indexical elements, on the other hand, must unambiguously refer to the discourse coordinates (e.g. speaker), except for indexical shifting environments. In syntactic contexts where indexical shift is allowed (e.g. Turkish finite embedded clauses), indexical elements are similar to pronouns in that their referent can be ambiguous. However, indexical elements are still different from pronouns in that they are ambiguous between only two referents (speaker vs attitude holder), while pronouns are technically free to refer to an unlimited amount of antecedents (that can be salient in context).

In summary, indexical elements are restricted by different syntactic factors than pronouns (e.g. clause type) and are usually unambiguous. Moreover, even in contexts where indexical shift is possible, indexical elements are restricted to two possible referents, depending on whether indexical shift takes place or not, while pronouns are free to refer to a wide range of entities. Thus, indexical elements and indexical shift create a unique challenge for LLMs, requiring to take into account the syntactic constraints regarding indexical shift while also

[4]Except for ones that violate syntactic principles like the Binding Theory (Chomsky, 1981).

				Question NAMENull kimin Almanca bildiğini sanıyor?
Context	**Context prime**	**Sentence type**	**Sentence**	**Ground truth**
Merhaba, ben SPEAKER. Ankara'da yaşayan bir öğrenciyim. NAMENull diye bir arkadaşım var. On tane Almanca kelime öğrenmiş. "Hi, my name is SPEAKER. I am a student living in Ankara. I have a friend named NAMENull. He learned ten German words."	Shifted	Finite	NAMENull Almanca biliyorum sanıyor. "NAMEnull thinks he knows German."	Shifted
		Nominalized	NAMENull Almanca bildiğimi sanıyor. "NAMEnull thinks I know German."	Speaker
Merhaba, ben SPEAKER. Ankara'da yaşayan bir öğrenciyim. NAMENull diye bir arkadaşım var. NAMENull söylediklerini havaalanındaki turistler için Almanca'ya çevirmemi istedi. "Hello, I'm SPEAKER. I am a student living in Ankara. I have a friend named NAMEnull. NAMEnull asked me to translate what he said into German for the tourists at the airport."	Speaker	Finite	NAMENull Almanca biliyorum sanıyor. "NAMEnull thinks I know German."	Speaker
		Nominalized	NAMENull Almanca bildiğimi sanıyor. "NAMEnull thinks I know German."	Speaker

Table 1: An example four context-sentence pairs from the dataset.

employing general coreference resolution strategies like contextual information.

4 Turkish Indexical Shift Dataset

To test LLMs' ability to understand indexical shift in Turkish, we created a dataset containing 156 entries with sentences containing the Turkish first person indexical (silent/dropped) that could potentially refer to the speaker (non-shifted) or to the attitude holder of the clause (shifted).

Since the interpretation of indexical elements in Turkish (shifted vs non-shifted) depend on the context they appear in, we created two contexts for each experimental sentence: one priming the shifted reading, the other priming the non-shifted reading of the first-person indexical. Moreover, for each context, we created a version of the sentence with a nominalized embedded clause like (3) (rather than finite embedded clause like (2)), where indexical shift is not allowed by the grammar (e.g. the indexical must refer to the speaker even if the reported context priming otherwise). Together, this four context-sentence pairs lead to four different classes as summarized in Table 1.

We used sentences with three different verbs that allow indexical shift in Turkish: *iste* 'to want', *san* 'to think/believe', *düşün* 'to think'. These verbs trigger specific morphosyntactic requirements in Turkish. For example, *iste* 'to want' requires a subjunctive marker on the embedded verb, while *san* 'to think/believe' and *düşün* 'to think' require regular tense morphology. Also, *düşün* 'to think' requires the complementizer *diye* while the other two does not require/allow *diye*.

Each entry in the dataset have the following information:

- The embedding verb used in the sentence.
- The context first person indexical meaning that the context encourages (context prime).
- Ground truth entity that the indexical is referring to (SPEAKER or SHIFTED).
- The sentence.
- Sentence type (Nominalized or Finite).
- Question to reveal the LLM's interpretation of the indexical.

In order to augment our dataset with different name pairs for testing, SPEAKER and NAMENull placeholders are used instead of the speaker name and the reported third party with NAME-ACC, NAME-GEN, NAME-DAT, NAME-LOC, NAME-COM were used for the accusative, genitive, dative, locative, and comitative forms of the third person subject's name.

The Turkish language indexical shift test dataset is open sourced along with the associated source code, here.

5 Experiments

In this section, we explain our experimental setup, results, and discussion of the results.

5.1 Experimental Design

Models. We assess the performance of five language models: GPT-4 (OpenAI, 2024), GPT-3.5 (Brown et al., 2020b), Cohere-AYA (Üstün et al., 2024), Trendyol-LLM (Trendyol, 2023), and Turkcell-LLM (Turkcell, 2023). Both GPT-4 and GPT-3.5 are closed-source, advanced multilingual models. Cohere-AYA, a 13-billion parameter model, is trained in 101 languages and is built by fine-tuning the mT5 model (Xue et al., 2021). Trendyol-LLM is based on the LLama-2 7-billion model and fine-tuned on both Turkish and English data. Lastly, Turkcell-LLM is a fine-tuned version of the Mistral 7-billion model, specifically adapted for Turkish data.

Evaluation Strategy. We evaluate the performance of models using a multiple-choice question-answer format similar to the Massive Multitask Language Understanding benchmark (MMLU) (Hendrycks et al., 2021) with a 5-shot setting. The

Table 2: Precision, recall, and f1 performances of each model for each class and their macro averages.

	Speaker			Shifted			Macro Average		
Model	Precision	Recall	F1	Precision	Recall	F1	Precision	Recall	F1
GPT-4	**0.91**	0.69	0.78	0.46	**0.79**	**0.58**	**0.68**	**0.74**	**0.68**
GPT-3.5	0.77	0.59	0.67	0.28	0.47	0.35	0.53	0.53	0.51
Cohere-AYA	0.83	**0.84**	**0.84**	**0.51**	0.50	0.51	**0.67**	0.67	**0.67**
Trendyol-LLM	0.71	0.49	0.58	0.22	0.42	0.29	0.47	0.45	0.43
Turkcell-LLM	0.88	0.12	0.22	0.27	0.95	0.42	0.57	0.54	0.32

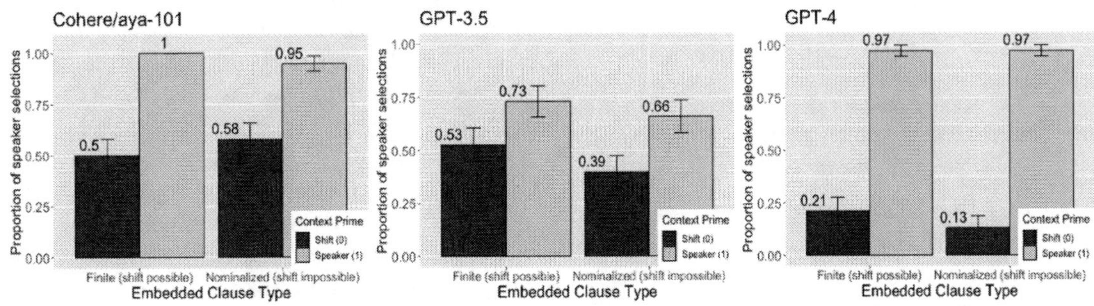

Figure 1: Selection analysis plot of GPT-4, GPT-3.5 and Cohere-AYA models. Their outputs are significantly influenced by the context prime, indicating the context's meaning toward either the speaker or the shifted class. No other significant factors were observed.

questions are presented in Turkish, following this template:

```
{in_context_learning_examples}
Soru: {context} {question}?

Seçenekler:
A. {choice_a}
B. {choice_b}

Doğru cevap:
```

where Soru means "question", Seçenekler means "choices", and Doğru cevap means "correct answer". We select five random examples from our dataset as in-context examples and evaluate the remainder. For open-source models, we calculate the probabilities of the tokens "A" and "B" to determine the most likely answer. For closed-source models, we modify the prompt by adding: *"Aşağıdaki soruları cevapla. Sadece cevap olarak A veya B yazman lazım."*[5] to ensure accurate response generation. Both GPT models comply strictly with this rule, generating only the letters A or B as responses.

Our dataset originally contains placeholders such as "NAMENull" and "SPEAKER" instead of real names. We replace these placeholders with actual random Turkish names to provide more natural linguistic contexts. To decrease the effect of potential gender biases within the models, we uniformly use either female or male names for all placeholders within a single question.

Lastly, to address the choice bias demonstrated in prior studies (Zheng et al., 2024), we implement random assignment of choice options in both the question prompts and in-context examples. Additionally, for open-source models, we enhance reliability by presenting each question twice with the order of choices reversed. We then aggregate the probabilities assigned by the model to each option across these iterations to determine the most likely choice. This method helps to mitigate any inherent preference the model may have towards the position of the answer choices.

Table 3: Accuracy results for each clause type: finite and nominalized. All models except Cohere-AYA shows worse performance in nominalized sentences.

Model	Finite	Nominalized	Average
GPT-4	**0.88**	0.55	0.72
GPT-3.5	0.60	0.53	0.57
Cohere-AYA	0.75	**0.76**	**0.76**
Trendyol-LLM	0.50	0.50	0.50
Turkcell-LLM	0.57	0.09	0.33

[5] In English: Answer the following questions. You need to write only A or B as your answer.

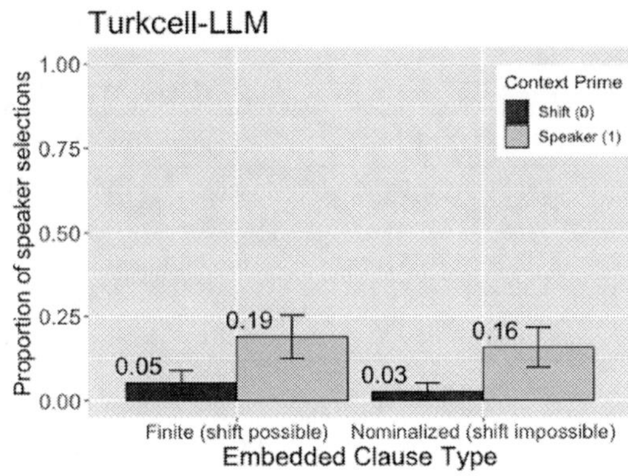

Figure 2: Selection analysis plot of Turkcell-LLM. Neither clause type nor context prime has a statistically significant effect.

Metrics. Our dataset exhibits a class imbalance, with 75% of the ground truth labeled as SPEAKER and the remaining 25% as SHIFTED. Given this imbalance, accuracy alone would not provide a comprehensive measure of model performance; a trivial model that consistently outputs "SPEAKER" could achieve 75% accuracy without truly understanding the data. To address this, we follow the common practice in the literature (Branco et al., 2015) and report precision, recall, and F1 scores for both the SPEAKER and SHIFTED classes. We also compute the macro precision, recall and F1 score to summarize overall performance. Moreover, to see the performance of the models in different clause types (finite or nominalized), we provide the accuracy of all models in different clause types and average accuracy as well. Lastly, analyze factors influencing an LLM's decision-making on a given question, using R Software (R Core Team, 2013) to build the best fitting Linear Mixed-Effect Regression (LMER) model (Bates et al., 2015) with item as the random factor and model selection as the dependent variable. The findings of our statistical analyses are discussed in detail in Section 5.3.

5.2 Main Results

The performance of all models is presented in Table 2. For the Speaker class, GPT-4 achieves the highest precision, while Cohere-AYA consistently delivers high precision and recall, resulting in the highest F1 score for this class. For the Shifted class, GPT-4 attains a maximum F1 score of 0.58, significantly lower than its performance for the Speaker class. All models, except Turkcell-LLM, exhibit lower performance for the Shifted class, indicating a tendency to make mistakes when either the ground truth or the model output is the class Shifted (low precision and low recall).

Examining the macro average results, we observe that GPT-4 and Cohere-AYA have comparable and highest F1 performance, whereas other models are behind of them with a significant margin. This performance gap for GPT-4 can be attributed to its advanced capabilities, likely due to a large training corpus and model size (OpenAI, 2024). Similarly, the performance gap for Cohere-AYA may be due to its training data, which includes many Turkish samples (Üstün et al., 2024). However, even the performance of GPT-4 and Cohere-AYA is far from optimal. Lastly, as shown in Table 3, GPT-4 and Cohere-AYA perform relatively well at predicting indexical shift in sentences with finite clauses, where shift is possible. However, in sentences with nominalized clauses, where shift is not possible, the performance of all models drops significantly. Among them, only the Cohere-AYA model demonstrates a significantly better prediction accuracy than random guessing (50%). This finding highlights the need for greater attention to the grammatical challenges in low-resource languages.

5.3 Which Factors Effect LLMs' Decision?

In this section, we employ Linear Mixed-Effect Regression (LMER) models to measure the impact of various factors in the dataset on LLM decisions. These factors include sentence type (*finite* vs *nominalized*), gender, and context prime (priming *shifted* vs *non-shifted* readings). Through this analysis, we observe that LLM behaviors can be clustered based on their responses to our task. Below, we examine each LLM cluster and their behavior patterns in detail.

GPT Family and Cohere-AYA. The decisions of these three models are influenced by the context prime, indicating that the context's meaning leans towards either the speaker or shifted class. This effect is statistically significant (p's < 0.001). As illustrated in Figure 1, the models' decisions change significantly when the context prime is altered (represented by dark blue and blue colors). For instance, Cohere-AYA selects the speaker class 100% of the time when the context prime indicates the speaker in finite sentences, but this proportion drops to 50% when the context prime indicates the shifted class. This substantial difference in selection proportions highlights the significant impact

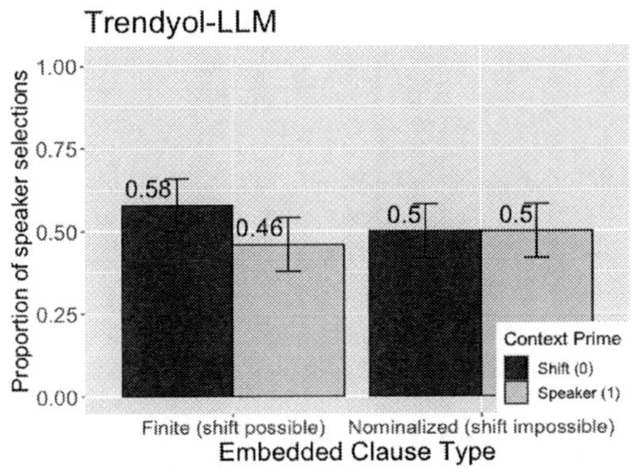

Figure 3: Selection analysis plot of Trendyol-LLM. Neither clause type nor context prime has a statistically significant effect.

of the context prime, an effect that is also observed in GPT models across different sentence types.

Aside from the effect of context prime, all other factors have a statistically non-significant impact on the models' decisions (p's > .05). This is interesting because, for a native speaker, the clause type (finite or nominalized) directly influences the interpretation of the sentences, allowing indexical shift in finite embedded clauses (2) but not in nominalized embedded clauses (3).

Trendyol-LLM and Turkcell-LLM. Figures 2 and 3 illustrate the mean decisions of these models in each item class. Our analyses show that the decisions of these models are not influenced by either context prime or clause type (p's > .05). Specifically, no factors significantly affect the decisions of Turkcell-LLM, while the only factor that affects the decisions of Trendyol-LLM is interestingly gender (p < .001). Furthermore, Turkcell-LLM almost consistently outputs the shifted class, as seen in Figure 2. Given their comparatively low performance, we interpret these results to mean that these two models lack the reasoning capability to understand the indexical shift problem in Turkish and produce reasonable outputs.

Summary. Overall, none of the models tested in this study are sensitive to clause type, showing that all of these models fail to learn the grammatical grounds where indexical shift is possible (finite embedded clauses) or not (nominalized embedded clauses). Trendyol-LLM and Turkcell-LLM struggle significantly with interpreting the task. The decisions of the other models are primarily affected by the context prime, mimicking native speaker behavior with finite embedded clauses, but overgeneralizing this behavior with nominalized embedded clauses, where context prime does not play a role for native speakers (since indexical shift is not available).

6 Conclusion

In this study, we assess large language models (LLMs) on pronoun resolution tasks within indexical shift contexts, focusing specifically on a low-resource language, Turkish. To facilitate this evaluation, we release a Turkish indexical shift dataset comprising 156 samples. We test recent multilingual models on this dataset and find their performance lacking. Additionally, we observe that none of the LLMs' decisions are influenced by grammatical nuances, such as finite versus nominalized clauses, which contrasts with the behavior of native speakers. Our findings highlight the need for greater attention to the grammatical challenges of low-resource languages in the development and evaluation of LLMs.

7 Limitations

One limitation of the current study is that it concentrated solely on the first person indexical in Turkish, which was due to linguistic limitations regarding indexical shift in Turkish. As explained in detail by Deal (2020), indexical elements within a language do not need to show a uniform behavior, and can have different properties than one another. For example, in Turkish, the person indexicals *ben* 'I' and *sen* 'you' and the temporal indexical *yarın* 'tomorrow' allow indexical shift, while the locative indexical *bura* 'here' does not allow indexical shift (Oğuz et al., 2020). In other words, the locative indexical *bura* 'here' cannot undergo indexical shift, and it must always be interpreted as the location where the sentence was uttered (similar to English *here*). Considering this, the locative indexical *bura* 'here' could not be included in our study. Moreover, the second person indexical *sen* can only shift under the verb *de* 'to say', and cannot shift under other verbs like *san* 'to think' or *iste* 'to want' (because they cannot take an addressee). In the current study, we aimed to observe LLMs' performance under various types of embedding verbs, while keeping our experimental sentences maximally consistent. For this reason, we could not investigate the second person indexical *sen*, which does not allow indexical shift in any other verb than *de* 'to say'. Future work can extend our findings by investigating LLMs' performance with other indexical elements than the first person *ben*.

References

Monica Agrawal, Stefan Hegselmann, Hunter Lang, Yoon Kim, and David A. Sontag. 2022. Large language models are few-shot clinical information extractors. In *Conference on Empirical Methods in Natural Language Processing*.

Pranav Anand and Andrew Nevins. 2004. Shifty operators in changing contexts. In *Proceedings of SALT XIV*, pages 20–37, Cornell University, Ithaca. CLC Publications.

Douglas Bates, Martin Maechler, Ben Bolker, Steven Walker, Rune Haubo Bojesen Christensen, Henrik Singmann, Bin Dai, and Gabor Grothendieck. 2015. Package 'lme4'. *Convergence*, 12.

Paula Branco, Luis Torgo, and Rita Ribeiro. 2015. A survey of predictive modelling under imbalanced distributions. *Preprint*, arXiv:1505.01658.

Tom B. Brown, Benjamin Mann, Nick Ryder, Melanie Subbiah, Jared Kaplan, Prafulla Dhariwal, Arvind Neelakantan, Pranav Shyam, Girish Sastry, Amanda Askell, Sandhini Agarwal, Ariel Herbert-Voss, Gretchen Krueger, Tom Henighan, Rewon Child, Aditya Ramesh, Daniel M. Ziegler, Jeff Wu, Clemens Winter, Christopher Hesse, Mark Chen, Eric Sigler, Mateusz Litwin, Scott Gray, Benjamin Chess, Jack Clark, Christopher Berner, Sam McCandlish, Alec Radford, Ilya Sutskever, and Dario Amodei. 2020a. Language models are few-shot learners. *ArXiv*, abs/2005.14165.

Tom B. Brown, Benjamin Mann, Nick Ryder, Melanie Subbiah, Jared Kaplan, Prafulla Dhariwal, Arvind Neelakantan, Pranav Shyam, Girish Sastry, Amanda Askell, Sandhini Agarwal, Ariel Herbert-Voss, Gretchen Krueger, Tom Henighan, Rewon Child, Aditya Ramesh, Daniel M. Ziegler, Jeffrey Wu, Clemens Winter, Christopher Hesse, Mark Chen, Eric Sigler, Mateusz Litwin, Scott Gray, Benjamin Chess, Jack Clark, Christopher Berner, Sam McCandlish, Alec Radford, Ilya Sutskever, and Dario Amodei. 2020b. Language models are few-shot learners. *Preprint*, arXiv:2005.14165.

Noam Chomsky. 1981. *Lectures on government and binding*. Dordrecht, Holland: Foris.

Rosalind A. Crawley, Rosemary J. Stevenson, and David Kleinman. 1990. The use of heuristic strategies in the interpretation of pronouns. *Journal of Psycholinguistic Research*, 14.

Amy Rose Deal. 2020. *A theory of indexical shift: meaning, grammar, and crosslinguistic variation*. MIT Press, Boston, MA.

Yujian Gan, Massimo Poesio, and Juntao Yu. 2024. Assessing the capabilities of large language models in coreference: An evaluation. In *International Conference on Language Resources and Evaluation*.

Dan Hendrycks, Collin Burns, Steven Basart, Andy Zou, Mantas Mazeika, Dawn Song, and Jacob Steinhardt. 2021. Measuring massive multitask language understanding. *Preprint*, arXiv:2009.03300.

David Kaplan. 1977. Demonstratives: An essay on the semantics, logic, metaphysics, and epistemology of demonstratives and other indexicals. *Themes from Kaplan*, pages 565–614.

Kadri Kuram. 2020. L2 Acquisition of the Indexical Shift Parameter in Turkish. *Dilbilim Araştırmaları Dergisi*, 2:231–263.

Nghia T. Le and Alan Ritter. 2023. Are large language models robust coreference resolvers?

OpenAI. 2024. Gpt-4 technical report. *Preprint*, arXiv:2303.08774.

Metehan Oğuz, Burak Öney, and Dennis Ryan Storoshenko. 2020. Obligatory indexical shift in Turkish. In *Proceedings of Canadian Linguistic Association (CLA)*, Western University, London, ON, Canada.

Martin Pickering and Asifa Majid. 2007. What are implicit causality and consequentiality? *Language & Cognitive Processes*, 22.

R Core Team. 2013. *R: A Language and Environment for Statistical Computing*. R Foundation for Statistical Computing, Vienna, Austria.

Philippe Schlenker. 1999. *Propositional attitudes and indexicality*. Ph.D. thesis, Massachussetts Institute of Technology.

Philippe Schlenker. 2003. A plea for monsters. *Linguistics and Philosophy*, 26:29–120.

Kirill Shklovsky and Yasutada Sudo. 2014. The syntax of monsters. *Linguistic Inquiry*, 45:381–402.

Andrew J. Stewart and Martin Pickering. 1998. Implicit consequentiality. In *Proceedings of the 20th Annual Conference of the Cognitive Science Society*.

Yasutada Sudo. 2012. *On the Semantics of Phi Features on Pronouns*. Ph.D. thesis, Massachussetts Institute of Technology.

Hugo Touvron, Louis Martin, Kevin Stone, Peter Albert, Amjad Almahairi, Yasmine Babaei, Nikolay Bashlykov, Soumya Batra, Prajjwal Bhargava, Shruti Bhosale, Dan Bikel, Lukas Blecher, Cristian Canton Ferrer, Moya Chen, Guillem Cucurull, David Esiobu, Jude Fernandes, Jeremy Fu, Wenyin Fu, Brian Fuller, Cynthia Gao, Vedanuj Goswami, Naman Goyal, Anthony Hartshorn, Saghar Hosseini, Rui Hou, Hakan Inan, Marcin Kardas, Viktor Kerkez, Madian Khabsa, Isabel Kloumann, Artem Korenev, Punit Singh Koura,

Marie-Anne Lachaux, Thibaut Lavril, Jenya Lee, Diana Liskovich, Yinghai Lu, Yuning Mao, Xavier Martinet, Todor Mihaylov, Pushkar Mishra, Igor Molybog, Yixin Nie, Andrew Poulton, Jeremy Reizenstein, Rashi Rungta, Kalyan Saladi, Alan Schelten, Ruan Silva, Eric Michael Smith, Ranjan Subramanian, Xiaoqing Ellen Tan, Binh Tang, Ross Taylor, Adina Williams, Jian Xiang Kuan, Puxin Xu, Zheng Yan, Iliyan Zarov, Yuchen Zhang, Angela Fan, Melanie Kambadur, Sharan Narang, Aurelien Rodriguez, Robert Stojnic, Sergey Edunov, and Thomas Scialom. 2023. Llama 2: Open foundation and fine-tuned chat models. *Preprint*, arXiv:2307.09288.

Trendyol. 2023. Trendyol LLM 7B Base v0.1. `https://huggingface.co/Trendyol/Trendyol-LLM-7b-base-v0.1`. Accessed: 2024-05-20.

Turkcell. 2023. Turkcell LLM 7B v1. `https://huggingface.co/TURKCELL/Turkcell-LLM-7b-v1`. Accessed: 2024-05-20.

Linting Xue, Noah Constant, Adam Roberts, Mihir Kale, Rami Al-Rfou, Aditya Siddhant, Aditya Barua, and Colin Raffel. 2021. mt5: A massively multilingual pre-trained text-to-text transformer. *Preprint*, arXiv:2010.11934.

Xiaohan Yang, Eduardo Peynetti, Vasco Meerman, and Christy Tanner. 2022. What gpt knows about who is who. In *First Workshop on Insights from Negative Results in NLP*.

Junjie Ye, Xuanting Chen, Nuo Xu, Can Zu, Zekai Shao, Shichun Liu, Yuhan Cui, Zeyang Zhou, Chao Gong, Yang Shen, Jie Zhou, Siming Chen, Tao Gui, Qi Zhang, and Xuanjing Huang. 2023. A comprehensive capability analysis of GPT-3 and GPT-3.5 series models. *Preprint*, arXiv:2303.10420.

Chujie Zheng, Hao Zhou, Fandong Meng, Jie Zhou, and Minlie Huang. 2024. Large language models are not robust multiple choice selectors. *Preprint*, arXiv:2309.03882.

Deniz Özyıldız. 2012. When I is not me: A preliminary case study of shifted indexicals in Turkish. Unpublished ms.

Ahmet Üstün, Viraat Aryabumi, Zheng-Xin Yong, Wei-Yin Ko, Daniel D'souza, Gbemileke Onilude, Neel Bhandari, Shivalika Singh, Hui-Lee Ooi, Amr Kayid, Freddie Vargus, Phil Blunsom, Shayne Longpre, Niklas Muennighoff, Marzieh Fadaee, Julia Kreutzer, and Sara Hooker. 2024. Aya model: An instruction finetuned open-access multilingual language model. *Preprint*, arXiv:2402.07827.

Nilüfer Gültekin Şener and Serkan Şener. 2011. Null subjects and indexicality in Turkish and Uyghur. In *Proceedings of the 7th Workshop on Altaic Formal Linguistics (WAFL7)*, pages 269–284.

Towards a Clean Text Corpus for Ottoman Turkish

Fatih Burak Karagöz and **Berat Doğan** and **Şaziye Betül Özateş**
Boğaziçi University, Turkey

{fatih.karagoz,berat.dogan}@std.bogazici.edu.tr, saziye.ozates@bogazici.edu.tr

Abstract

Ottoman Turkish, as a historical variant of modern Turkish, suffers from a scarcity of available corpora and NLP models. This paper outlines our pioneering endeavors to address this gap by constructing a clean text corpus of Ottoman Turkish materials. We detail the challenges encountered in this process and offer potential solutions. Additionally, we present a case study wherein the created corpus is employed in continual pre-training of BERTurk, followed by evaluation of the model's performance on the named entity recognition task for Ottoman Turkish. Preliminary experimental results suggest the effectiveness of our corpus in adapting existing models developed for modern Turkish to historical Turkish.

1 Introduction

Natural Language Processing (NLP) has been extensively facilitated through widely spoken modern languages. These models cover various fields, from sentiment analysis to medical assessments and question-answering. Such applications require extensive data sources, which are relatively more straightforward to collect and optimize for modern languages due to the abundance of digitized documents available on the Internet. However, integrating such applications into historical and less commonly spoken languages presents significant challenges due to the need for more available resources in these languages. Collecting and optimizing documents in these languages is more complex, necessitating more efficient data extraction methods to achieve comparable performance levels.

The development of software tools and the application of automation for historical languages are crucial for scholarly research, offering invaluable insights into political, sociological, and historical contexts. Among these languages, Ottoman Turkish has a significant legacy in history, literature, culture, and science, influencing three continents over 600 years. This extensive historical impact highlights the importance of applications and studies involving Ottoman Turkish, as they can generate profound value across various fields.

One of the pathways to such value creation is through the use of pre-trained language models (PLMs), which have revolutionized natural language processing by achieving state-of-the-art performance across many tasks. However, the availability of clean text corpora is essential for the automation of any language, as it is necessary for training algorithms to perform tasks such as text analysis (Agarwal et al., 2007), language modeling (Snæbjarnarson et al., 2022), and information extraction (Hamdi et al., 2020; Li et al., 2020). This is particularly important for pre-training language models, which require a comprehensive understanding of a language's statistical properties and intricate patterns. Therefore, our study aims to create a clean data corpus for the natural language processing of Ottoman Turkish. Despite its importance, integrating Ottoman Turkish into modern Natural Language Processing (NLP) frameworks presents significant challenges. Ottoman texts' unique linguistic and structural characteristics require specialized approaches for effective digitization, standardization, and analysis. Leveraging advanced NLP techniques, such as pre-training BERT models, has the potential to scale these studies and meet the growing demand for research in this area.

While striving to create a clean corpus for Ottoman Turkish texts, we faced several challenges that impeded effective data collection. These challenges were addressed in four phases: (i) Converting PDF documents into clean text files, (ii) normalizing unique characters, (iii) handling intertwined bidirectional text in Arabic and Latinized Turkish, and (iv) minimizing the impact of decorative textures. The solutions needed to be simple and cost-efficient in terms of computational power allocation, adhering to the philosophical principle of

Proceedings of the First Workshop on Natural Language Processing for Turkic Languages (SIGTURK 2024), pages 62–70
August 15, 2024 ©2024 Association for Computational Linguistics

Occam's Razor (Bowen and Breuer, 1992), which advocates simplicity. We chose Regular Expression (Regex) methods over competing hypotheses and sophisticated machine learning techniques because Regex requires minimal additional memory, in which optimizing computational overhead, and allows for immediate application through modes of Non-deterministic Finite Automata (NFA).

This paper summarizes our initial efforts to create a clean text corpus of Ottoman Turkish texts that can be used for various purposes including automatic processing of Ottoman Turkish. We mention some related work on data cleaning and extraction in Section 2. We explain the methodology followed to create the intended corpus of Ottoman Turkish texts and state the main challenges faced and possible solutions to them in Section 3. Then we provide a case study in Section 4 where we further pre-train the BERTurk (Schweter, 2020) model using our corpus to adapt it to Ottoman Turkish texts and fine-tune the model on a named entity recognition (NER) dataset for NER tagging of Ottoman Turkish. The preliminary experiment results suggest that further pre-training the BERTurk model, initially designed for modern Turkish, with Ottoman Turkish data is effective for Ottoman NER tagging. We conclude the paper and state future directions of this study in Section 5. To the best of our knowledge, this study represents the first attempt to provide language resources and models for state-of-the-art natural language processing of Ottoman Turkish.

2 Related Work

Modern languages provide relatively clean corpora when obtained from web text sources (Sharoff, 2006). In contrast, historical languages require a different approach due to the variety of digitization methods used by various institutions (Piotrowski, 2012). Unique challenges, such as non-standard orthography, mixed scripts, and the scarcity of digitized texts, necessitate specialized approaches. This section reviews several studies that have addressed these challenges and contributed to developing effective methods for language processing, which can be utilized in historical document automation.

The Impresso project (Ehrmann et al., 2020) focuses on the semantic indexing of a multilingual corpus of digitized historical newspapers. This interdisciplinary research involves computational linguists, designers, and historians collaborating to transform noisy and unstructured textual content into semantically indexed, structured, and linked data. The authors highlight the challenges posed by large-scale collections of digitized newspapers, including incomplete collections, extensive and messy data, noisy historical text, and the need for robust system architecture. The project emphasizes the importance of transparency and critical assessment of inherent biases in exploratory tools, digitized sources, and annotations.

Piotrowski (2012) highlights the importance of text normalization in processing historical languages. The study presents various techniques for handling non-standard orthography, including using historical dictionaries and context-based normalization algorithms. These methods help standardize the text, making it more suitable for NLP tasks. The challenges of interpreting private use area (PUA)[1] characters and integrating Arabic sentences within Ottoman Turkish texts are addressed through mapping systems and regular expressions.

Jain et al. (2021) propose an extensible parsing pipeline to process unstructured data, particularly within network monitoring and diagnostics. Their methodology employs rule-based extraction techniques to transform unstructured data into structured formats, utilizing pattern mining strategies and heuristics-based analysis. This approach demonstrates resilience to changes in data structure and effectively filters out extraneous information. Notably, the use of regular expressions for pattern recognition and data extraction mirrors the techniques employed in our study for processing Ottoman Turkish texts. The pipeline's capability to handle diverse data structures without necessitating labeled training data or manual intervention underscores its robustness and efficiency in data extraction tasks.

Nundloll et al. (2021) discuss the automation of information extraction from historical texts using the Journal of Botany as a case study. They document the use of OCR-based software for digitization and the subsequent application of NLP frameworks to customize entity recognition models. Tools like Prodigy and Spacy were employed to identify specific entities such as plant names, observers, locations, and attributes. The authors em-

[1]The code points in these regions are not standardized characters within Unicode. They remain intentionally undefined, enabling third parties to create their own characters without clashing with the assignments made by the Unicode Consortium.

phasize the importance of creating training and test datasets to evaluate the accuracy of the entity recognition models, highlighting the iterative process of model training, error-checking, and annotation.

3 Methods, Challenges, and Solutions

This study employs a systematic methodology to extract, standardize, and analyze Ottoman Turkish texts from historical documents. The process involves several key steps and leverages various tools and libraries to ensure efficient and accurate data handling. In the following subsections, we first explain the source of data and then give the two main steps of our method[2] for creating a clean corpus of Ottoman Turkish texts. For each step, we state the challenges faced and explain our solutions to them.

3.1 Data

There are two primary Ottoman periodicals used as data source: Sebilürreşad and Sırat-ı Müstakim magazines.

Sırat-ı Müstakim was a prominent Ottoman Turkish magazine that was first published on 1908. During the period of the Second Constitutional Monarchy, Mehmed Akif, a famous Turkish writer at the time, took the position of editorial writer for this magazine. Published weekly, the magazine included written texts about various topics, including religious, national, literary, and political issues (Gündoğdu, 2008). The periodical was published under the same name until 1912, and from issue 183 it continued to be published under the name Sebilürreşad until 1925. Sebilürreşad had to suspend its publication starting from its 641st issue on 1925. Later, it resumed publication in May 1948, until March 1965, during which it released 359 issues (Ceyhan, 1991). These periodicals, first published as Sırat-ı Müstakim and later as Sebilürreşad, contributed to Turkish culture, art, literature, and intellectual life for a total of thirty-four years (Çakır, 2014).

In our study, the issues of both periodicals published between 1908-1925 have been taken into account. These issues have been collected as twenty five volumes (seven of them under the name Sırat-ı Müstakim and remaining eighteen as Sebilürreşad) and made publicly available as images by National Library of Turkey[3] and as PDF documents in Latin script by Bağcılar Municipality.[4] Figure 1 shows example segments from each periodical.

3.2 Step 1: Data Extraction

The two periodicals used as our data source were in PDF format. These PDF documents were created using OCR systems and have a complex structure due to the usage of both Latinized Turkish and Arabic letters, recursive polluted texts such as dates, page numbers, prices of the magazine, and illustrations used in Ottoman textures. Also, the source documents followed inconsistent margin formats and illustrations. These inconsistencies varied from document to document and page to page within the same file. Variation in calligraphy, irrelevant notes, and irregular design further exacerbating these challenges. These elements often led to misconducting of text and incorrect character recognition, leading to a poor corpus cleaning. Such variations posed significant challenges for accurate text extraction and processing.

Given these complexities, using multiple post-OCR approaches could have been a more optimal strategy for document assembly modeling (Lopresti and Jiangying, 1997; D'hondt et al., 2017; Schulz and Kuhn, 2017). However, OCR performance heavily depends on image quality, and implementing document-specific OCR solutions would be computationally intensive and inefficient. Also, most of these approaches require labeled training data for post-OCR correction. Hence, we opted not to use these supervised approaches in the data extraction phase.

In order to represent the text data in a simpler and cleaner format, we convert PDFs into TXT format while maximizing text extraction accuracy. The goal is to ensure that the resulting text files represent the original content of the historical documents. For this purpose, we utilize a range of Python tools and libraries.

Initially, we utilized Pdfplumber, a Python library known for its effective text extraction capabilities. Our first attempt was defining rigid constraints on page margins to capture central text bodies, excluding footnotes, repetitive dates, and titles outside of these margins. However, these constraints were less effective when the text alignment varied. Some documents started with wider margins in a single column and changed arbitrarily. Consequently, margin framing failed to extract

[2] The code is available under `https://github.com/Ottoman-NLP/Ottoman_LLM_Repos`.

[3] Milli Kütüphane. https://www.millikutuphane.gov.tr/

[4] Bağcılar Belediyesi. https://www.bagcilar.bel.tr/

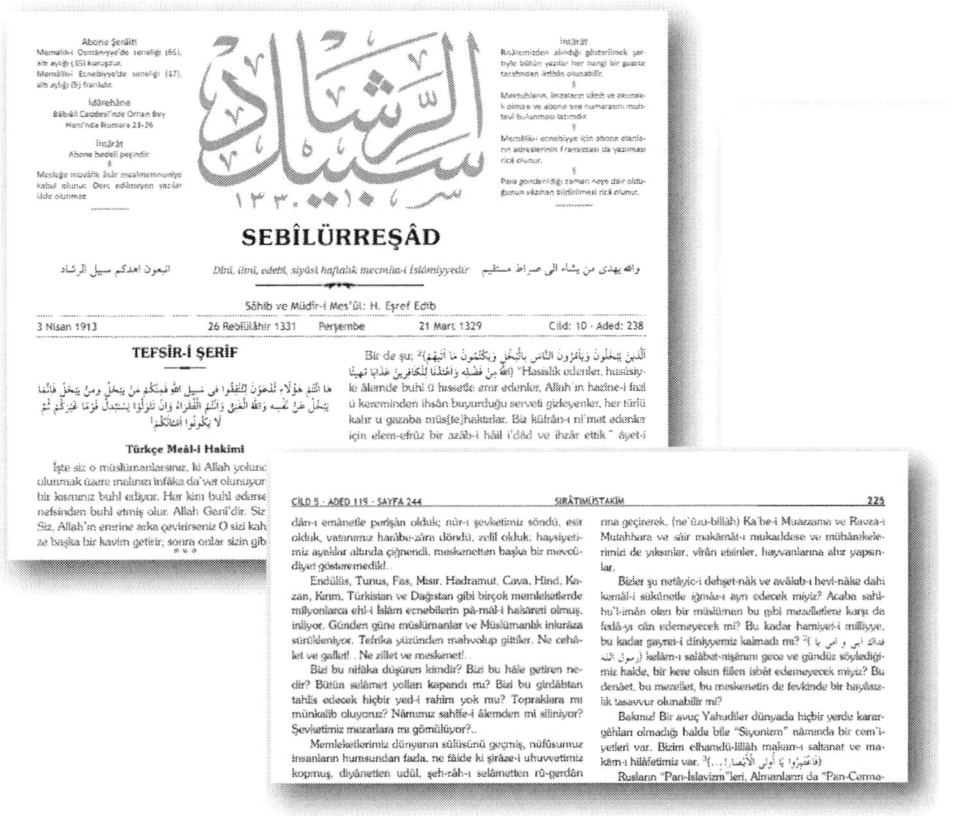
SEBÎLÜRREŞÂD

Dînî, ilmî, edebî, siyâsî haftalık mecmûa-i İslâmiyyedir

Sâhib ve Müdîr-i Mes'ûl: H. Eşref Edib

3 Nisan 1913 26 Rebîülâhir 1331 Perşembe 21 Mart 1329 Cild: 10 - Aded: 238

TEFSÎR-İ ŞERÎF

Türkçe Meâl-i Hakimi

CİLD 5 - ADED 119 - SAYFA 244 SIRÂTIMÜSTAKÎM 225

Figure 1: Segments of two randomly selected pages from the magazines Sebilürreşad (back) and Sırat-ı Müstakim (front).

text from documents that did not adhere to defined rules.

After the unsuccessful trial in setting up one script to extract all varied documents, we consider another scheme where each document should have a unique margin frame sets handling the extraction processes. However, as discussed earlier, any given document might not consistently follow the same format, as the format occasionally changes from page to page as well. Furthermore, creating scripts for each document is an energy deterrent process and disfavors automation extraction for later models.

For these reasons, the library used for PDF conversion was later changed to PyMuPDF, a high performance Python library for data extraction and analysis for PDF documents, to ensure the expected extraction of documents. In this alternative script, the PDFs are converted without applying any margin rules into plain texts, and documents are subsequently reformatted using regular expression rules during the text manipulation. By removing margin constraints and employing direct text extraction, the processing time for each document is significantly reduced. This improvement in throughput enables the handling of larger datasets within shorter time-frames. We then utilized regular expressions to define a regular pattern recognition module. The illustrations are ignored and remaining Arabic sentences did not require any intelligent character recognition. This proved to be a computationally efficient and time-effective method, allowing us to have a more robust and efficient text processing pipeline by addressing the specific challenges posed by the unique characteristics of Ottoman Turkish documents without using post-OCR techniques.

3.3 Step 2: Text Standardization

Standardizing the extracted text is crucial for proponent analysis. Regular Expressions (Regex) are employed to normalize the text, addressing inconsistencies such as varying orthographic representations and diacritics. This step ensures a uniform text format, facilitating more reliable processing and analysis.

We utilize various techniques for noise filtering, which involves removing non-essential components, segmenting relevant categories, and cleansing the data. In this step, pattern recognition is integral in identifying and extracting specific patterns within the text, such as dates, names, or other structured information. In the following subsections we discuss the challenges we faced in the text standardization step and explain how we overcome these challenges.

3.3.1 Normalization and Mapping

Some Arabic characters in the documents are occasionally interpreted as Private Use Area (PUA) characters (Unicode Consortium, 2021), as well as some Latinized Turkish words loaned from Arabic. This misinterpretation leads to poor identification of Arabic text using standard Unicode ranges. Initially, a function was used to eliminate characters with ordinals above 128; however, this approach inadvertently removed both standard Arabic and PUA characters, resulting in incomplete and inaccurate text standardization.

In historical documents, it is plausible for PUA characters to appear due to various factors such as font issues, scanning techniques, OCR software limitations or non-standard encoding. This is where character normalization technique plays a pivotal role as it standardizes various representations of characters to ensure document uniformity. This hurdle is overcome through normalization process where different forms of the same letter, such as accented characters, are converted to a common form. We developed a mapping system to identify and replace PUA characters with their equivalent standard Arabic variations. If a character had no equivalent, it was removed. As character normalization applied the text, UNICODE range matching for character level precision became operable. Figure 2 depicts this process on example words.

Original Word (PUA)		Normalized Word
تِجَارَةً	→	تجارة
لَهْوًا	→	لهوا
انْفَضُّوا	→	انفضوا

Figure 2: Normalization process of PUA characters by mapping.

In addition to the normalization of Arabic characters, we also mapped accented Latin letters that are no longer present in the current Turkish alphabet to their equivalents. This is for reducing the number of unknown words due to the accented letters when adapting a model developed for modern Turkish to Ottoman Turkish. The outcome of this operation is visible in Figure 3 which shows a segment from the Sebilürreşad magazine and its processed version.

3.3.2 Right-to-Left Scripts (RTL)

Arabic sentences posed another significant challenge for regex patterns, as well. Since Arabic is written from right to left, sentences containing both Latinized Turkish and Arabic text intertwined causing data-pollution as can be seen in the example in Figure 4a. We debated whether to filter out Arabic sentences altogether. However, Arabic texts often provide relevant references, adding potential contextual value to the documents. Therefore, it is concluded that more viable options should be employed by preserving Arabic sentences to increase document enhancement.

Therefore, we implemented a method to move Arabic sentences to a new line and separate them from Turkish sentences. The effect of this method is visible in Figure 4b. This approach ensures that each language maintains its correct orientation and readability in different lines. Additionally, this separation makes it easier to define pattern rules for different orthographies between Turkish and Arabic. By segmenting Arabic characters, we effectively isolated the two languages, preserving regex pattern functionality.

3.3.3 Optional Translation Feature

After this segmentation process, Arabic sentences were intended to be translated through an API to enhance the contextual information of the main text. However, directly integrating the translated Arabic sentences within the main document proved to be resource-intensive and time-consuming. Prior to API translation, the script needed to encapsulate Arabic sentences individually to flag their positions for replacing the original text with the translations. While processing the document in chunks helped manage memory and reduce complexity, the NFA-like backtracking and segmentation functionality increased inefficiency, led to incorrect translations, and caused frequent hits to the API rate limit.

Consequently, we proposed a new method: segmenting Arabic sentences into a separate text doc-

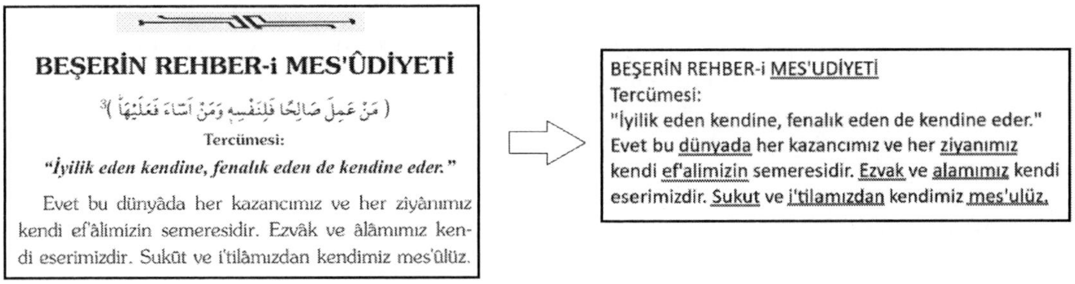

Figure 3: A segment from the PDF document of the 628th issue, 25th volume of Sebilürreşad magazine (on the left) and its processed version (on the right). Note the omission of the Arabic sentence and normalization of accented letters (in underlined words) in the processed version.

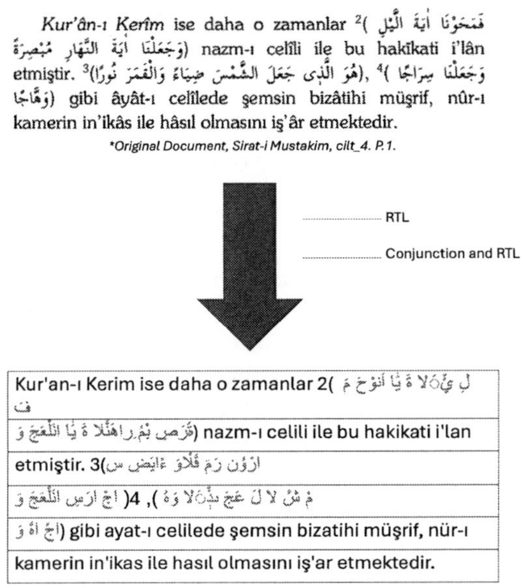

(a) PDF extraction by non-RTL formatting causes divergence.

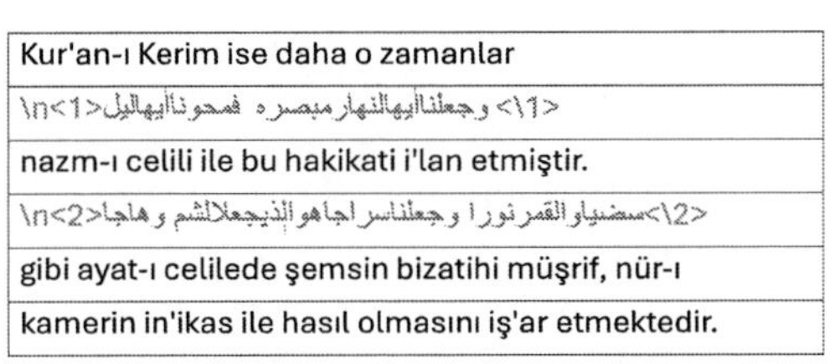

(b) Expected format for the text in Figure 4a.

Figure 4: The effect of RTL formatting.

ument and removing them from the primary text documents. These sentences' line order and text positions were mapped back to the main text separately. This segmentation allowed Arabic sentences to be translated independently, ensuring that contextual information relevant to the corresponding Turkish sentences was preserved without requiring complex filtering over the primary text documents. This approach significantly enhanced performance and simplified the rule-setting process for text manipulation. In the current version of the corpus however, we do not use this feature. Hence, the corpus does not include the translations of the Arabic sentences in it. At present, we exclude all Arabic texts from the corpus and only include Latinized Ottoman Turkish texts in it for the sake of simplification.

4 Evaluation on the Named Entity Recognition Task

As the result of the data extraction and cleaning steps explained in Section 3, we created a 17M-token corpus of Ottoman Turkish texts. In its current version, this corpus is too small to pre-train a transformer-based language model from scratch. Hence, in order to see its effect on a downstream NLP task, we further pre-train a PLM which was already pre-trained on various modern Turkish corpora. Further or continual pre-training is a common approach to train language models for low-resource languages (Liu et al., 2021; Micallef et al., 2022). By this way, we hope to benefit from the PLM's prior knowledge on Turkish words and grammatical structures that are common in modern Turkish and Ottoman Turkish.

In our preliminary experiments, we observed that among different architectures and models, BERTurk (Schweter, 2020), a Turkish language model utilizing the BERT architecture and pre-trained on modern Turkish text, reached the highest F1 scores on several NLP tasks. Hence, we chose to utilize BERTurk for our experiments. As in the architecture of the original BERT base model,

BERTurk has 12 transformer layers. Each transformer layer consists of 12 attention heads and the number of hidden units is 768. The model includes a total of 110 million parameters that are fine-tuned during the pre-training phase on a large corpus of Turkish text data.

4.1 Continual Pre-training

We further pre-trained the BERTurk model with sentences from our corpus (885K sentences in total) to adapt it to the Ottoman Turkish context using Masked Language Modelling with 15% masking probability. We used Adam optimizer with the learning rate of 5e-5 and the batch size is 32. The training was performed on NVIDIA L4 accelerator with 22.5 GB of GPU RAM and a system RAM of 62.8 GB.

4.2 Fine-tuning on the Named Entity Recognition Task

As an extrinsic evaluation of our further pre-trained BERTurk model, we utilize the model for the task of named entity recognition (NER) on an Ottoman Turkish NER dataset. The main reason behind this choice is Ottoman Turkish being extremely low-resource in terms of labeled datasets and we have a newly annotated NER dataset for Ottoman Turkish, albeit small. This dataset contains 462 training, 200 validation, and 200 test sentences sourced from Servet-i Fünun journal. Due to the very rare occurrence of other entity types, annotation has been performed only for `PERSON` and `LOCATION` entities. The total number of `PERSON` entities in the dataset is 386 while the number of `LOCATION` entities is 794. The inter annotator agreement (IAA) between the two annotators of the dataset is measured as 0.82.

To observe the performance of our pre-trained model on the NER task, we fine-tuned the model on the mentioned Ottoman Turkish NER dataset for 10 epochs using Adam optimizer with 5e-5 learning rate. We chose the batch size to be 32. Table 1 shows the entity-level precision, recall and F1 scores of BERTurk with and without the further pre-training step on the test set of our NER dataset. We see that there is only a slight improvement in the performance when the model is further pretrained on Ottoman Turkish texts.

4.3 Ablation Study

In order to analyze this outcome more deeply, we performed an ablation study. Here, we further pre-trained the model by incrementally increasing the pre-training data, and at each stage, we fine-tuned it on the NER data to test its performance on this task. Figure 5 depicts the results of this study. We observe that the model reached its peak performance after training with around 50% of the pre-training corpus and started to decrease afterwards. Only at the end of the pre-training we see a significant increase in the performance. Table 2 shows the exact scores in this case.

Models	Precision	Recall	F1
BERTurk + PT	0.820	**0.9**	**0.858**
BERTurk	**0.829**	0.872	0.850

Table 1: Performance of the models on the test split of the NER dataset.

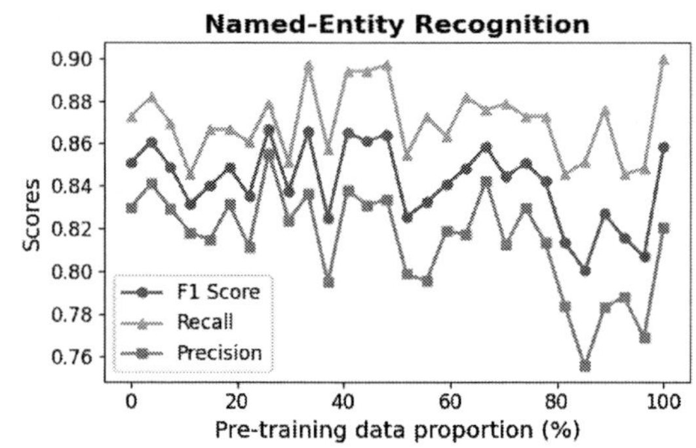

Figure 5: NER task performance as the pre-training data size grows

One possible reason for this mixed performance might be our current approach to the inline Arabic sentences or sentence parts in the corpus texts. At present, we exclude all Arabic texts from the main text as they are not relevant in a Turkish corpus. Yet, deleting them might lead to gaps in the meaning of text. We detect some cases in the corpus where omitting Arabic phrases embedded in Turkish sentences resulted in meaningless sentence parts in the text. We believe dealing with the Arabic parts of the corpus in a way that will not distort the context will result in a cleaner corpus and better pre-training performance.

One way of dealing with the Arabic parts in the sentences could be facilitating machine translation in reconstructing fragmented sentences and filling in missing alphanumeric characters as proposed in Section 3.3.3. However, the application of such models is deterred by the intensive computational resources required. Our preliminary analysis indicated that approximately 8% of our data contains Arabic sentences or sentence parts, with less than .9% of it is being completely unusable. Thus, although employing generative models to predict and reconstruct the semantics and pragmatics of corrupted Arabic sentences is highly beneficial, the costs associated with this approach are outweighed by the potential benefits, especially considering the significant yet smaller proportion of Arabic sentences compared to Turkish.

Models	Precision	Recall	F1
BERTurk + 50% PT	**0.833**	0.896	**0.864**
BERTurk + 100% PT	0.820	**0.9**	0.858
BERTurk	0.829	0.872	0.850

Table 2: Performance of BERTurk when further pretrained on the half of the corpus and on the whole corpus.

5 Conclusion

In this study, we presented the first foundations of a clean Ottoman Turkish text corpus. We discussed the challenges faced in extracting clean text data from documents with complex structures and explained our approaches in handling these challenges. By domain adapting a PLM initially created for modern Turkish to Ottoman Turkish using our corpus, we demonstrated the potential to bridge the gap between historical languages and modern NLP frameworks. The preliminary experimental findings highlight the effectiveness of our corpus in enhancing NER tagging for Ottoman Turkish, showcasing its utility for various NLP applications.

Our study takes one of the first steps towards providing comprehensive resources for the state-of-the-art natural language processing of Ottoman Turkish. Future research directions may involve expanding the corpus, refining preprocessing techniques, and exploring additional NLP tasks to further enrich the resources available in this historical language.

Limitations

There are certain limitations of our study. Firstly, the reliance on periodicals from a specific time frame may introduce biases in the diversity of language usage and topics covered. Additionally, while efforts were made to ensure accuracy and completeness, there may exist inherent errors or omissions in the preprocessing step of the documents. Moreover, the current size of the corpus might be too small to properly pre-train a BERT model, so careful consideration should be given to the scalability and generalizability of the model.

Ethics Statement

The source of text data used to create the corpus are periodicals published between 1908 and 1925. As these periodicals are publicly available and there are no copyright restrictions associated with them, we adhered to ethical guidelines in utilizing the data for research purposes. In addition, Ottoman Turkish is an extremely understudied language in natural language processing. So, there is no risk of exposure for our case.

References

Sumeet Agarwal, Shantanu Godbole, Diwakar Punjani, and Shourya Roy. 2007. How much noise is too much: A study in automatic text classification. In *Seventh IEEE International Conference on Data Mining (ICDM 2007)*, pages 3–12. IEEE.

Jonathan P Bowen and Peter T Breuer. 1992. Occam's razor: The cutting edge of parser technology. *Proc. TOULOUSE*, 92.

Ömer Çakır. 2014. II. Meşrutiyet Dönemi'nde Sırat-ı Müstakîm ve Sebilürreşad dergilerine Türk dünyasından gönderilen bazı mektuplar. *Çankırı Karatekin Üniversitesi Sosyal Bilimler Enstitüsü Dergisi*, 5(1):237–246.

Abdullah Ceyhan. 1991. *Sırat-ı müstakim ve Sebilürreşad mecmuaları fihristi*, volume 55. Diyanet İşleri Başkanlığı Yayınları.

Eva D'hondt, Cyril Grouin, and Brigitte Grau. 2017. Generating a training corpus for ocr post-correction using encoder-decoder model. In *Proceedings of the Eighth International Joint Conference on Natural Language Processing (Volume 1: Long Papers)*, pages 1006–1014.

Maud Ehrmann, Matteo Romanello, Simon Clematide, Phillip Benjamin Ströbel, and Raphaël Barman. 2020. Language resources for historical newspapers: the impresso collection. In *Proceedings of the Twelfth Language Resources and Evaluation Conference*, pages 958–968, Marseille, France. European Language Resources Association.

Abdullah Gündoğdu. 2008. Sırat-ı Müstakim (later, Sebilürreşad) and the origin of the Japanese image in Turkish intellectuals. *Annals of Japan Association for Middle East Studies*, 23(2):245–259.

Ahmed Hamdi, Axel Jean-Caurant, Nicolas Sidère, Mickaël Coustaty, and Antoine Doucet. 2020. Assessing and minimizing the impact of OCR quality on named entity recognition. In *Digital Libraries for Open Knowledge: 24th International Conference on Theory and Practice of Digital Libraries, TPDL 2020, Lyon, France, August 25–27, 2020, Proceedings 24*, pages 87–101. Springer.

Rakesh Jain et al. 2021. Rule-based and relationship-based extraction in network monitoring. *International Journal of Data Processing*, 18(3):121–139.

Lin Li, Tiong-Thye Goh, and Dawei Jin. 2020. How textual quality of online reviews affect classification performance: A case of deep learning sentiment analysis. *Neural Computing and Applications*, 32:4387–4415.

Zihan Liu, Genta Indra Winata, and Pascale Fung. 2021. Continual mixed-language pre-training for extremely low-resource neural machine translation. In *Findings of the Association for Computational Linguistics: ACL-IJCNLP 2021*, pages 2706–2718, Online. Association for Computational Linguistics.

Daniel Lopresti and Zhou Jiangying. 1997. Using consensus sequence voting to correct ocr errors. *Computer Vision and Image Understanding*, 67(1):39–47. Cited on p. 34.

Kurt Micallef, Albert Gatt, Marc Tanti, Lonneke van der Plas, and Claudia Borg. 2022. Pre-training data quality and quantity for a low-resource language: New corpus and BERT models for Maltese. In *Proceedings of the Third Workshop on Deep Learning for Low-Resource Natural Language Processing*, pages 90–101, Hybrid. Association for Computational Linguistics.

Vinay Nundloll, Koichi Watanabe, and Alan Cohen. 2021. Automating information extraction: Case study of the Journal of Botany. *Journal of Heliyon*, pages 4–6.

Michael Piotrowski. 2012. *Natural Language Processing for Historical Texts*, volume 17 of *Synthesis Lectures on Human Language Technologies*. Morgan & Claypool.

Sarah Schulz and Jonas Kuhn. 2017. Multi-modular domain-tailored ocr post-correction. In *Proceedings of the 2017 Conference on Empirical Methods in Natural Language Processing*, pages 2716–2726.

Stefan Schweter. 2020. BERTurk - BERT models for Turkish.

Serge Sharoff. 2006. Creating general-purpose corpora using automated search engine queries. In Marco Baroni and Silvia Bernardini, editors, *Wacky! Working Papers on the Web as Corpus*. GEDIT, Bologna. Cited on p. 25.

Vésteinn Snæbjarnarson, Haukur Barri Símonarson, Pétur Orri Ragnarsson, Svanhvít Lilja Ingólfsdóttir, Haukur Jónsson, Vilhjalmur Thorsteinsson, and Hafsteinn Einarsson. 2022. A warm start and a clean crawled corpus - a recipe for good language models. In *Proceedings of the Thirteenth Language Resources and Evaluation Conference*, pages 4356–4366, Marseille, France. European Language Resources Association.

Unicode Consortium. 2021. *The Unicode® Standard: Version 14.0 – Core Specification*, version 14.0 edition. Unicode, Inc., Mountain View, CA.

Turkish Delights: a Dataset on Turkish Euphemisms

Hasan Can Biyik and **Patrick Lee** and **Anna Feldman**
Montclair State University
New Jersey, USA
{biyikh1,leep,feldmana}@montclair.edu

Abstract

Euphemisms are a form of figurative language relatively understudied in natural language processing. This research extends the current computational work on potentially euphemistic terms (PETs) to Turkish. We introduce the Turkish PET dataset, the first available of its kind in the field. By creating a list of euphemisms in Turkish, collecting example contexts, and annotating them, we provide both euphemistic and non-euphemistic examples of PETs in Turkish. We describe the dataset and methodologies, and also experiment with transformer-based models on Turkish euphemism detection by using our dataset for binary classification. We compare performances across models using F1, accuracy, and precision as evaluation metrics.

1 Introduction

Euphemisms are polite or indirect words or expressions used in substitution of unpleasant or more offensive ones. They can be used to show kindness while discussing sensitive or taboo topics (Bakhriddionova, 2021) such as saying *between jobs* instead of *unemployed*, or as a way to make unpleasant or unappealing things sound less harsh (Karam, 2011), such as saying *passed away,* instead of *died.* Similar to the word *died* in English, Turkish makes use of many substitutions for the word *öl-mek/öl-dü (to die/died)*, which is considered unpleasant. The substitutions for this word could be given as *vefat etmek (to pass away)*, *öbür dünyaya göçmek (to migrate to the other world)*, *hakkın rahmetine kavuşmak (to go to kingdom come)*. Euphemisms can be used to conceal the truth (Rababah, 2014); for instance, if one were to use the expression *enhanced interrogation techniques*, one would mean *torture* (Lee et al., 2022b). Furthermore, humans may not agree on what a euphemism is (Gavidia et al., 2022a). There are various challenges regarding euphemisms. For instance, in some cases, words or expressions might develop or lose euphemistic meanings in time (Pinker, 1994, 2003). Due to the aforementioned reasons, the words and phrases in this research will be referred to as *potentially euphemistic terms (PETs)* (Lee et al., 2022c). Euphemisms pose a challenge to Natural Language Processing (NLP) due to this figurative behavior as they might also have a non-euphemistic interpretation in certain contexts. For example, while the Turkish PET *mercimeği fırına vermek* means *to put the lentil in the oven* literally, it could mean *to have sex/to get someone pregnant* euphemistically. In the following sentence, this PET used literally: "Günümüzde hem <mercimeği fırına vermek> daha kolay, hem de fırında makarna yemek..." which can be translated as "Nowadays, it's easier to <put the lentils in the oven> and to eat mac and cheese..." However, it was used euphemistically in the following sentence: "Gel gör ki kasabanın yegane doktoru ile pişiren bu kadın, zaman zaman <mercimeği fırına veriyorlarmış>" which can be translated as "However, it turns out that this woman, who is having an affair with the town's only doctor, sometimes <puts the lentils in the oven>" meaning that the doctor and woman are involved in a secretive or intimate sexual intercourse.

Conducting a euphemism detection task in Turkish has several challenges to overcome. Firstly, as far as we are aware of, there are no available datasets for automatic euphemism detection task in Turkish. Academic research, published books, articles, and other resources on this topic are very limited, making the collection of PETs difficult. In this research, we aim to identify PETs in Turkish and create a dataset of Turkish PETs by making use of native speaking Turkish annotators who have a linguistics background. We aim to fine-tune language models (LMs) such as BERTurk (DBMDZ, 2019; Beyhan et al., 2022) and Electra (Clark et al., 2020) and large language models (LLMs), such as XLM-RoBERTa (AI, 2019; Conneau et al., 2020)

Proceedings of the First Workshop on Natural Language Processing for Turkic Languages (SIGTURK 2024), pages 71–80
August 15, 2024

and mBERT (AI, 2018; Devlin et al., 2019) for euphemism detection in Turkish. Therefore, the significant contributions of this paper are as follows:

- Introduction of the Turkish PETs dataset, which we plan to make publicly available later,
- Overview of the Turkish PETs and how they were collected and annotated,
- Comparison of the performances of XLM-RoBERTa, mBERT, BERTurk, and ELECTRA in detecting PETs in Turkish, using F1, accuracy, and precision as evaluation metrics,
- This research will compare the PETs in Turkish and other languages and analyze potentially interesting patterns.

Additionally, through extending euphemism detection task to a new language, we contribute to a better understanding of how euphemisms are utilized and interpreted across different linguistic and cultural contexts.

2 Turkish Language

Agglutinative languages, such as Turkish, form words by adding multiple affixes to a stem, with each affix representing a distinct morphological feature (Comrie, 1988). This morphological productivity creates a vast number of possible word forms, making it difficult to develop comprehensive dictionaries or rule-based systems for tasks like euphemism detection. For instance, the PET *hayata gözlerini yummak* (*to close one's eyes to life*) can be formed as yum-*du*, yum-*muş*, yum-*duğunda*" and many other variations. See Table 1 for more examples regarding morphological variations.

The free word order in Turkish, where the position of words in a sentence can vary without significantly changing the meaning (Göksel and Kerslake, 2004), poses another challenge for euphemism detection. This flexibility makes it difficult to rely on fixed patterns or word sequences to identify euphemisms. For example, the PET *uyutmak* (*to put to sleep*) can appear in various positions within a sentence, making it harder to detect reliably.

Similar to euphemisms in other languages, the meaning of words and expressions are context dependent in Turkish. While one word can be used euphemistically in one sentence, it might not have euphemistic meaning in another. For instance, the PET *engelli* might be used euphemistically to indicate that the person is *disabled*, but it might also have its non-euphemistic meaning of *blocked*.

Moreover, Turkish is considered to be a low-resource language because of the limited availability of annotated datasets. It was also stated by various researchers that collecting data from various sources and labeling them was a challenging process (Mutlu and Özgür, 2022). Since there was no available dataset that contained euphemisms in Turkish with examples, it was necessary for us to build a dataset and get it annotated by native Turkish annotators.

3 Automatic Euphemism Detection

Euphemism detection can be viewed as a classification task in which an input text is classified as containing a euphemism or not.

While this can be theoretically done at at the phrase-level or sentence-level euphemism detection, previous work has focused on classifying examples containing specific multi-word expressions, which may or may not be used euphemistically depending on the context (Lee et al., 2022a). A number of approaches have performed decently at the task using language models such as transformers, improving upon baselines using various techniques. For example, Keh et al. (2022) use an ensemble of models each utilizing a combination of data and contextual augmentations to improve performance by 5 Macro-F1 points. Kesen et al. (2022) achieve similar improvements by incorporating non-euphemistic meanings and image embeddings associated with PETs. Maimaitituoheti et al. (2022) propose a prompt-based approach for euphemism detection utilizing the language model RoBERTa, achieving an F1 score of 85.2%, demonstrating the effectiveness of prompt-based learning. Similar to our initial dataset, which contained more than 6,000 examples, the dataset they used was imbalanced and had more euphemistic examples than non-euphemistic. They noted the model's superior performance on euphemistic sentences compared to non-euphemistic ones due to this imbalance.

Given the nuanced nature of these expressions in the Turkish language and the lack of previous work on figurative language processing in Turkish, this study aims to investigate how well different language models identify and categorize PETs in Turkish. We fine-tuned two large multilingual

PET	Variations (Turkish)	Variations (English Equivalents)
aramızdan ayrıldı (left us)	aramızdan ayrıldı, aramızdan ayrılışının, aramızdan ayrılan, aramızdan ayrılanlar, aramızdan ayrılması, aramızdan ayrılalı	(has) left us, of his/her/their departure from us, the one who left us, those who left us, his/her/its departure from us, since he/she/they left us
beklemek (to expect)	bekliyor, bekliyoruz, bekleyen, bekledikleri, bekleniyor, bekleyeceğiz, bekliyorsunuz (...)	is expecting, we are expecting, the one who is expecting, what they are expecting for/whom they are expecting for/that they are expecting for, is being expected/is expected, we will expect, you are expecting (plural or formal)
hakka yürümek (to walk to God)	hakka yürüyen, hakka yürümesinden, hakka yürüdü, hakka yürümüştür	the one who walked to God, from his/her/their walking to God, walked to God, has walked to God

Table 1: Examples and morphological variations of Turkish PETs

models, XLM-RoBERTa and mBERT, along with language models specifically trained on extensive corpora of Turkish text data: bert-base-turkish-cased and electra-base-turkish-cased-discriminator. These models were chosen to examine the impact of model size, training data, and architecture on euphemism detection performance. We hypothesized that XLM-RoBERTa and mBERT would provide strong general language understanding capabilities, as large multilingual models are trained on vast amounts of diverse data. On the other hand, bert-base-turkish-cased and electra-base-turkish-cased-discriminator, being specifically trained on Turkish text, were hypothesized to capture more nuanced aspects of euphemistic language in Turkish due to their exposure to a wider range of Turkish expressions and linguistic patterns.

Our focus on the Turkish language addresses a gap in existing research, as most previous studies have primarily concentrated on English euphemisms (Felt and Riloff, 2020; Zhu and Bhat, 2021; Zhu et al., 2021; Gavidia et al., 2022a,b; Lee et al., 2022a, 2023). By extending the euphemism detection task to a new language, we contribute to a better understanding of how euphemisms are utilized and interpreted across different linguistic and cultural contexts. The recent Multilingual Euphemism Detection Shared Task by Lee and Feldman (2024) has encouraged researchers to explore multilingual and cross-lingual methods for identifying euphemisms. This research emphasizes the importance of understanding euphemisms in different languages.

4 Data Collection and Annotation

4.1 Data Collection

To find PETs in Turkish, we analyzed the PETs in other languages described in previous work (Lee et al., 2023, 2024), such as American English, Mandarin Chinese, Yorùbá, and a mix of Spanish dialects to see whether there were overlapping words or expressions used euphemistically (see Table 2). As a result, we were able to compile an initial list of Turkish PETs.

Through reviewing published articles and papers related to euphemisms in Turkish, such as those by Aksan (1994); Karabulut and Ospanova (2013); Çabuk (2015), we expanded our list of PETs. Another method we used to collect PETs was by posting polls on social media. Initially, we explained the concept of "PETs" and provided examples. We then utilized social media to share these polls, where Turkish native speakers could share their ideas for new PETs. As a result, our Turkish PETs list now comprises a total of 122 entries. We also included detailed information for each PET, such as euphemistic category (e.g. bodily functions), meaning, non-euphemistic meaning, literal translation, and the source it was from. The list is categorized into 10 groups with varying frequencies, which can be seen in Table 4 . These categories were created based on the characteristics of the PETs. For example, the PET "*görme engelli*" (*visually impaired*) is related to physical attributes, and therefore it was added to the "physical/mental attributes" category.

Once the PETs list was finalized, we utilized a

English	Chinese	Spanish	Turkish	Yoruba
adult beverage	-	✓	✓	✓
birds and the bees	-	-	-	-
economical	✓	✓	✓	✓
pass away	✓	✓	✓	✓
pro-life	-	✓	-	-
under the weather	-	-	-	-

Table 2: Examples of (non-)overlapping PETs across the five languages.

Turkish corpus known as the TS Corpus Project (Sezer, 2017). We selected TS Corpus v2 and TS Timeline Corpus. TS Corpus v2 drew from the BOUN Web Corpus and included 491,360,398 tokens and 4,950,407 word types. TS Timeline Corpus contained more than 700 million tokens and over 2.2 million news and articles. To search for texts containing PETs for binary classification purposes, we utilized regular expressions, accounting for the agglutinative nature of the Turkish language. This approach allowed us to capture various word forms effectively. For instance, for the PET *hamileliği sonlandırmak* (*to terminate pregnancy*), we designed a regular expression to detect all variations of hamile-*lik* (pregnancy), hamile-*liğini* (her pregnancy), hamile-*liğimi* (my pregnancy), sonlan-*dırdı* (terminated/has terminated), sonlan-*dıracakmış* (I heard that she will terminate), sonlan-*dıramadı* (she could not terminate), etc., r"(hamileli\w+ sonlan\w+)". As a result, we successfully captured variations of each PET were successfully captured. These captured PETs were extracted and highlighted within their sentences using brackets, as shown: "Duyduğuma göre arkadaşı <hamileliğini sonlandırmış>." (I heard that her/his friend will <terminate her pregnancy>.) Additionally, we included preceding and succeeding sentence(s), if available, to form the entire example context for that PET. These contexts usually consisted of four sentences at most. Not all PETs on the initial list were found in the corpus; of the 122, only 58 were found and have at least one example. These examples were then compiled for the annotation phase.

4.2 Annotation

Annotators were provided text examples (~1-4 sentences) of PETs in context, as can be seen in Table 3. To recruit Turkish annotators, we utilized social media platforms to find volunteers with a background in linguistics or an interest in the field. After several informational meetings, the annotators were briefed about the research purpose, the annotation process, and the concept of PETs. These meetings were recorded with the consent of the annotators. They were instructed to label the examples as "1" if the highlighted word or expression was used euphemistically, and as "0" if it was not. Following the completion of all annotations, an additional meeting was held to address any disagreements. During this discussion, some labels were revised. Notably, examples that received conflicting labels from the annotators—euphemistic by two and non-euphemistic by another two—had to be excluded from the dataset. This underscored the inherent challenges humans face in consistently interpreting whether a word or expression is used euphemistically.

For the annotation task, we divided the volunteers into five groups, with each group comprising three annotators. The first group annotated 975 examples, the second group annotated 1200 examples, the third group annotated 1300 examples, the fourth group annotated 1099 examples, and the fifth group annotated 1500 examples. As a result, there were 6,074 annotated examples at the end of the annotation task. Subsequently, each group's examples were annotated by one annotator from another group—for instance, an annotator from the first group annotated the second group's examples, and so on, ensuring each example was annotated by four different people. Throughout this process, examples with discrepancies were highlighted for further discussion during a recorded meeting with the available annotators. Disagreements were resolved by majority vote to finalize the labels. However, examples receiving split decisions (two annotators labeling euphemistic and two labeling non-euphemistic) were removed from the dataset. Sample examples and their final annotated labels can be found in Table 3.

While each example ultimately had four sepa-

PET	Label	Example
uyutmak	*euphemistic*	(...) Hollywood'un en çok tanınan köpekleri arasında yer alan Jack Russell cinsi Uggie <uyutularak> yaşamına son verildi. Uggie, katıldığı Oscar gecesiyle ününe ün katmış ve Cannes'da Palm Dog Ödülü'nün de bulunduğu birçok ödül kazanmıştı. (...) / One of Hollywood's most well-known dogs, the Jack Russell Terrier named Uggie, was <put to sleep>. Uggie gained even more fame by attending the Oscars and won many awards, including the Palm Dog Award at Cannes.
	non-euphemistic	İNSANA en çok benzeyen hayvan olarak bilinen şempanzeler, yavrularını titizlikle büyütüyor. Anne şempanze, yavrusunu kucağında <uyutuyor> ve gerektiğinde battaniyeyle üstünü örtüyor. (...) / Chimpanzees, known as the animals most similar to humans, meticulously raise their young. A mother chimpanzee <puts her baby to sleep> in her arms and covers it with a blanket when necessary.
muayyen günü	*euphemistic*	Kadınların <muayyen günleri> ya da hamilelik dönemlerinin de gözetilmesi amacıyla, nöbet ve görevlendirme sürelerine yeni esaslar getirilirken, muharebe eğitiminde el bombasını atma kurallarının bile kadınlar gözetilerek yeniden düzenlenmesi, Askerlik erkek işidir diyenleri dehşete düşürüyor." / In order to account for women's <specific days> or pregnancy periods, new principles have been introduced regarding the duration of duty and assignments. Even the rules for throwing grenades in combat training have been rearranged with women in mind, which horrifies those who say "military service is a man's job."
	non-euphemistic	Davetiyede, dispeç ile müsbit vesikaların mahkeme kaleminde incelenebileceği ve çağırılanın daha önce de dispeçe karşı mahkemede itirazda bulunabileceği <muayyen günde> gelmediği takdirde dispeçe muvafakat etmiş sayılacağı yazılır." / The invitation states that the dispatch and supporting documents can be reviewed in the court clerk's office, and that if the summoned party, who could have previously objected to the dispatch in court, does not appear on the <specified day>, they will be deemed to have consented to the dispatch.
ince hastalık	*euphemistic*	Eleni zamanında Eftelya'nın anneannesini yakalandığı <ince hastalık>tan Kerim hocanın iyileştirdiğini ve bunu da aileden gizli yaptığını anlatır. / Eleni explains that in the past, Kerim Hoca cured Eftelya's grandmother of <thin disease> and that he did this secretly, without the family's knowledge.
	non-euphemistic	Burdaki balların her derde deva olduğunu, <ince hastalık>lara iyi geldiğine inaüñak';bu nedenle de ilaç olarak kullanılmaktadır. / The honey here is believed to be a cure for every ailment and is therefore used as medicine, particularly for treating <thin diseases>.

Table 3: Euphemistic and Non-euphemistic Usages of PETs

rate annotations, the annotators were allowed to collaborate and influence each others' opinions, nullifying potential inter-rater agreement analyses. We instead conducted inter-rater agreement analysis on a subset of 396 examples, labeled by two annotators who primarily worked separately. Cohen's kappa for these two raters was 0.696, which is rated as moderate to substantial agreement (Cohen, 1960). Interestingly, Krippendorf's alpha was 0.693, which is higher but still largely comparable to the degrees of agreement reported for euphemism datasets in Lee et al. (2024).

4.3 Balanced Dataset

For our text classification experiments, we sampled a portion of the main dataset. This was because some PETs had a disproportionately high number of examples compared to others, or a very skewed label imbalance (e.g., 100 euphemistic instances and 1 non-euphemistic). These factors were not ideal for text classification, and we wanted to assess models' abilities to classify texts for a variety of different PETs with different labels. Therefore, we randomly sample a maximum of 40 euphemistic and 40 non-euphemistic examples for each PET. In addition, some annotated examples, such as *apartman görevlisi* (*apartment attendant*), *inme* (*landing*), and *toplu* (*bulk*), were never used euphemistically, so we chose not to select those. The final result was a subset of 908 instances (521 euphemistic and 387 non-euphemistic) used for the euphemism detection task.

4.4 Dataset Statistics

We conducted a detailed statistical analysis of both the main and balanced datasets to better understand their differences and characteristics. Firstly, we provide the distribution of sensitive topics in Table 4. This table categorizes PETs into various groups, such as bodily functions, death, employment/finances, illness, miscellaneous, physical/mental attributes, politics, sexual activity, substances, and social topics. Each category is accompanied by the count of entries and examples of PETs within that category. Table 5 further highlights key metrics such as average sentences per example, number of tokens, and lexical density. Notably, we also compute an "PET ambiguity" score, which measures the degree of ambiguity, or class balance, for examples of a particular PET. For each PET, this was computed as follows:

$$1 - \frac{|N_{euph} - N_{noneuph}|}{N_{euph} + N_{noneuph}} \quad (1)$$

where N_{euph} and $N_{noneuph}$ is the number of euphemistic and non-euphemistic examples for that PET, respectively. Higher values indicate a higher degree of ambiguity. For example, if there were 5 euphemistic and 5 non-euphemistic examples of a particular PET, then it is maximally ambiguous (score = 1); if there were 10 euphemistic examples and 0 non-euphemistic, then the PET is not ambiguous at all (score = 0). We compute the average ambiguity score across all PETs in the main and balanced datasets for comparison. As expected, the main dataset has a significantly lower ambiguity score (0.076) compared to the balanced dataset (0.46), suggesting more consistent usage of terms in either euphemistic or non-euphemistic contexts and confirming that balanced dataset is better suited for the euphemisms detection task.

5 Methodology

5.1 Experiments

Since one of our goals were to extend the euphemism detection task to Turkish, classification experiments were conducted. Therefore, transformer-based models pre-trained on Turkish text like XLM-RoBERTa and mBERT were chosen due to their capability of capturing and understanding the linguistic nuances.

The balanced dataset described in the previous section was then randomly split into training (80%), testing (10%), and validation (10%) sets, resulting in 726 examples for training and 91 examples each for testing and validation. The 80-10-10 split is a common practice in machine learning for dividing a dataset into training, validation, and testing sets.

The fine-tuning process involved training each model on our prepared dataset for a maximum of 30 epochs with a learning rate of 1e-5 and a batch size of 4. We employed early stopping with a patience of 5 to prevent overfitting. No layers were frozen during fine-tuning, allowing the models to adapt fully to the euphemism detection task. Hyperparameter optimization was not explicitly performed in this initial exploration; however, the chosen hyperparameters are common for fine-tuning BERT-based models. The primary metric for evaluating model performance during training and validation was the macro-averaged F1 score, a balanced measure of precision and recall that is suitable for binary classification tasks with potentially imbalanced classes. The fine-tuned models were then evaluated on the held-out test sets, and their performance was assessed using various metrics, including accuracy, precision, recall, and F1 score.

Category	Count	PET Examples
bodily functions	2244	*sulamak* (to water), *aybaşı* (month's beginning), *hacet görmek*(to meet the need)
death	2564	*kaybetmek* (to lose), *vefat etmek* (pass away), *aramızdan ayrıldı* (left us)
employment/finances	276	*yoksul* (to be lacking), *ekonomik* (economical), *ihtiyaç sahibi* (in need)
illness	8	*amansız hastalık* (relentless disease), *ince hastalık* (thin disease)
misc.	10	*iyi saatte olsunlar* (may they be in a good hour)
physical/mental attributes	627	*görme engelli* (visually impaired), *işitme engelli* (hearing impaired)
politics	26	*sığınmacı* (seeking asylum), *gelişmekte olan ülke* (developing country)
sexual activity	190	*seks işçisi* (sex worker), *mercimeği fırına vermek* (put the lentils in the oven)
substances	143	*madde* (subtance)
social	27	*sıkmak* (to squeeze)

Table 4: Sensitive Topics with PET examples

5.2 Results

We gathered the results of all the test sets of each model and calculated the average of 20 trials (different train-validation-test splits). The findings demonstrated that monolingual models (bert-base-turkish-cased and electra-base-turkish-cased-discriminator) outperformed the multilingual models (BERT-Base-Multilingual-Cased and XLM-RoBERTa). This suggests that for automatic euphemism detection in Turkish, models specifically pre-trained on Turkish text data have an advantage due to their familiarity with the nuances of the language.

Additionally, the ELECTRA architecture appears to be slightly more effective for this task than the BERT architecture, as evidenced by the higher scores of electra-base-turkish-cased-discriminator compared to bert-base-turkish-cased. This could be attributed to the discriminator's ability to better distinguish between real and fake input data during training, which might be beneficial in identifying the subtle differences between euphemistic and non-euphemistic expressions. The results obtained from the models can be seen in Table 4.

The findings of this research have several potential real-world applications. The developed models could be integrated into NLP tools for automatic euphemism detection in various types of text data, including social media posts, news articles, and other online content. This could be particularly valuable in fields such as social media monitoring to analyze the insight into public sentiment, opinions, and attitudes towards sensitive topics. For content moderation, flagging potentially harmful or offensive content that uses euphemisms to disguise its true intent could be beneficial for online platforms and communities seeking to maintain a respectful and safe environment.

Moreover, the cross-lingual capabilities of the models demonstrated in this study open up possibilities for developing euphemism detection systems for low-resource languages, where labeled data might be limited. This could contribute to a more inclusive and equitable representation of different languages and cultures in NLP research and applications.

6 Conclusion and Future Work

In this study, we created a Turkish PETs dataset from scratch and through utilizing the dataset, we investigated the effectiveness of various language models in identifying and categorizing euphemisms in Turkish. Our findings indicate that models trained on multilingual data, particularly XLM-RoBERTa, generally outperform monolingual models, suggesting the benefits of cross-lingual transfer learning in capturing euphemistic nuances. However, for the Turkish language specifically, models trained on Turkish text data, such as bert-base-turkish-cased and electra-base-turkish-cased-discriminator, demonstrated superior performance,

Metric	Main Dataset	Balanced Dataset
Total Examples	6115	908
Euphemistic Examples	1876	521
Non-Euphemistic Examples	4239	387
Avg. PET Ambiguity	**0.076**	**0.46**
Avg. Sentences per Example	3.60	3.28
Avg. Sentences (Euphemistic)	3.51	3.16
Avg. Sentences (Non-euphemistic)	3.63	3.43
Avg. Number of Tokens per Example	96.22	90.42
Avg. Number of Unique Tokens per Example	78.63	74.24
Avg. Lexical Density	0.82	0.84
Notable PETs (Only Non-euphemistic Examples)	18 PETs (e.g., *toplu/bulk, işini bitirmek/to finish his/her job, inme/landing*)	1 PET (*e.g. muhtaç/in need*)

Table 5: Comparison of Main and Balanced Datasets

	Accuracy	F1	Precision	Recall
mBERT	0.81	0.80	0.80	0.80
XLM-RoBERTa	0.82	0.82	0.82	0.81
BERTurk	0.84	0.84	0.84	0.84
Electra	0.86	0.86	0.86	0.86

Table 6: Performance of the models on the Turkish euphemisms.

emphasizing the importance of language-specific training for this task.

Future research could investigate the impact of model size, architecture, and training data on euphemism detection performance. Additionally, exploring the use of explainability techniques could provide valuable insights into the decision-making processes of these models to better comprehend the specific linguistic features they rely on for euphemism detection. Experimenting with different model architectures or training techniques might also further improve the performance of euphemism detection systems in Turkish. Additionally, expanding the dataset to include a wider range of euphemisms and exploring their application in downstream tasks like sentiment analysis and content moderation could be useful for future work. It is important to acknowledge that the results are based on a limited dataset and may not generalize to all types of euphemisms in Turkish. Future work could involve testing the models on a larger and more diverse dataset to confirm these findings.

Lastly, exploring the cross-lingual transferability of euphemism detection models trained on Turkish data to other languages, similar to the work done in Lee et al. (2023, 2024) would provide valuable insights. This could involve fine-tuning multilingual models on Turkish euphemisms and evaluating their performance on other languages. As highlighted in Gavidia et al. (2022a), the ambiguity of potentially euphemistic terms (PETs) is a major challenge; therefore, future work could focus on developing methods to disambiguate PETs and distinguish between their euphemistic and non-euphemistic usages more effectively.

Limitations

While this study highlights the potential of language models in euphemism detection in Turkish, the results are based on a limited dataset that may not encompass the full spectrum of euphemistic language usage in Turkish, potentially affecting the generalizability of our findings.

Ethics Statement

The authors foresee no ethical concerns with the work presented in this paper.

Acknowledgments

Thanks to the annotators, whose names are Kader Teke, Devran Sarısu, Sümeyye Sena Şahin, Fitnat Filiz Bal, Kübra Aksoy, Ecem Küçükler, Azra Almira Kılıç, Özge Bilik, Mihriban Kandemir, Nazan Demir, Şüheda Nur Ünal, Özlem Özer, Salih Hamza Küpeli it was possible for us to create this dataset quickly.

This material is based upon work supported by the National Science Foundation under Grant No. 2226006.

References

Facebook AI. 2019. Unsupervised cross-lingual representation learning at scale. `https://huggingface.co/xlm-roberta-base`.

Google AI. 2018. Multilingual bert: A universal language model. `https://huggingface.co/google/bert-base-multilingual-cased`.

Doğan Aksan. 1994. Göktürk yazitlarinda söz sanatlari güçlü anlatim yollari. *Türk Dili Araştırmaları Yıllığı-Belleten*, 38(1990):1–12.

Rie Kubota Ando and Tong Zhang. 2005. A framework for learning predictive structures from multiple tasks and unlabeled data. *Journal of Machine Learning Research*, 6:1817–1853.

Galen Andrew and Jianfeng Gao. 2007. Scalable training of L1-regularized log-linear models. In *Proceedings of the 24th International Conference on Machine Learning*, pages 33–40.

Dildora Oktamovna Bakhriddionova. 2021. The needs of using euphemisms. *Mental Enlightenment Scientific-Methodological Journal*, 2021(06):55–64.

Fatih Beyhan, Buse Çarık, Inanç Arın, Ayşecan Terzioğlu, Berrin Yanikoglu, and Reyyan Yeniterzi. 2022. A turkish hate speech dataset and detection system. In *Proceedings of the thirteenth language resources and evaluation conference*, pages 4177–4185.

Arzu ÇĠFTOĞLU Çabuk. 2015. Türkçedekġ örtmece sözlerġn oluğum yollari. *Manas Journal of Social Studies*, 4(5):136–160.

Kevin Clark, Minh-Thang Luong, Quoc V Le, and Christopher D Manning. 2020. Electra: Pre-training text encoders as discriminators rather than generators. In *International Conference on Learning Representations*.

Jacob Cohen. 1960. A coefficient of agreement for nominal scales. *Educational and Psychological Measurement*, 20(1):37–46.

Bernard Comrie. 1988. Linguistic typology. *Annual Review of Anthropology*, 17(1):145–159.

Alexis Conneau, Kartikay Khandelwal, Naman Goyal, Vishrav Chaudhary, Guillaume Wenzek, Francisco Guzmán, Edouard Grave, Myle Ott, Luke Zettlemoyer, and Veselin Stoyanov. 2020. Unsupervised cross-lingual representation learning at scale. In *Proceedings of the 58th Annual Meeting of the Association for Computational Linguistics*, pages 8440–8451.

DBMDZ. 2019. Berturk: Bert models for turkish. `https://huggingface.co/dbmdz/bert-base-turkish-cased`.

Jacob Devlin, Ming-Wei Chang, Kenton Lee, and Kristina Toutanova. 2019. Bert: Pre-training of deep bidirectional transformers for language understanding. In *Proceedings of the 2019 Conference of the North American Chapter of the Association for Computational Linguistics: Human Language Technologies, Volume 1 (Long and Short Papers)*, pages 4171–4186.

Christian Felt and Ellen Riloff. 2020. Recognizing euphemisms and dysphemisms using sentiment analysis. In *Proceedings of the Second Workshop on Figurative Language Processing*, pages 136–145.

Martha Gavidia, Patrick Lee, Anna Feldman, and JIng Peng. 2022a. CATs are fuzzy PETs: A corpus and analysis of potentially euphemistic terms. In *Proceedings of the Thirteenth Language Resources and Evaluation Conference*, pages 2658–2671, Marseille, France. European Language Resources Association.

Martha Gavidia, Patrick Lee, Anna Feldman, and Jing Peng. 2022b. CATs are Fuzzy PETs: A Corpus and Analysis of Potentially Euphemistic Terms. In *Proceedings of the 13th Language and Resources Conference*. ELRA.

Aslı Göksel and Celia Kerslake. 2004. *Turkish: A comprehensive grammar*. Routledge.

Ferhat Karabulut and Gulmira Ospanova. 2013. Örtmece sözlerin mantığı: Kazak türkçesi ile türkiye türkçesinde karşılaştırmalı model analizi. *Uluslararası Türkçe Edebiyat Kültür Eğitim (TEKE) Dergisi*, 2(2):122–146.

Savo Karam. 2011. Truths and euphemisms: How euphemisms are used in the political arena. 17.

Sedrick Scott Keh, Rohit Bharadwaj, Emmy Liu, Simone Tedeschi, Varun Gangal, and Roberto Navigli. 2022. EUREKA: EUphemism recognition enhanced through knn-based methods and augmentation. In *Proceedings of the 3rd Workshop on Figurative Language Processing (FLP)*, pages 111–117, Abu Dhabi, United Arab Emirates (Hybrid). Association for Computational Linguistics.

Ilker Kesen, Aykut Erdem, Erkut Erdem, and Iacer Calixto. 2022. Detecting euphemisms with literal descriptions and visual imagery. In *Proceedings of the 3rd Workshop on Figurative Language Processing (FLP)*, pages 61–67, Abu Dhabi, United Arab Emirates (Hybrid). Association for Computational Linguistics.

Patrick Lee, Alain Chirino Trujillo, Diana Cuevas Plancarte, Olumide Ojo, Xinyi Liu, Iyanuoluwa Shode, Yuan Zhao, Anna Feldman, and Jing Peng. 2024. MEDs for PETs: Multilingual euphemism disambiguation for potentially euphemistic terms. In *Findings of the Association for Computational Linguistics: EACL 2024*, pages 875–881, St. Julian's, Malta. Association for Computational Linguistics.

Patrick Lee and Anna Feldman. 2024. Multilingual euphemism detection shared task: Fourth workshop on figurative language processing. `https://msuweb.montclair.edu/~feldmana/`.

Patrick Lee, Anna Feldman, and Jing Peng. 2022a. A report on the euphemisms detection shared task. *arXiv preprint arXiv:2211.13327*.

Patrick Lee, Martha Gavidia, Anna Feldman, and Jing Peng. 2022b. Searching for PETs: Using distributional and sentiment-based methods to find potentially euphemistic terms. In *Proceedings of the Second Workshop on Understanding Implicit and Underspecified Language*, pages 22–32, Seattle, USA. Association for Computational Linguistics.

Patrick Lee, Martha Gavidia, Anna Feldman, and Jing Peng. 2022c. Searching for pets: Using distributional and sentiment-based methods to find potentially euphemistic terms. *Preprint*, arXiv:2205.10451.

Patrick Lee, Iyanuoluwa Shode, Alain Trujillo, Yuan Zhao, Olumide Ojo, Diana Plancarte, Anna Feldman, and Jing Peng. 2023. FEED PETs: Further experimentation and expansion on the disambiguation of potentially euphemistic terms. In *Proceedings of the 12th Joint Conference on Lexical and Computational Semantics (*SEM 2023)*, pages 437–448, Toronto, Canada. Association for Computational Linguistics.

Abulimiti Maimaitituoheti, Yang Yong, and Fan Xiaochao. 2022. A prompt based approach for euphemism detection. In *Proceedings of the 3rd Workshop on Figurative Language Processing (FLP)*, pages 8–12, Abu Dhabi, United Arab Emirates (Hybrid). Association for Computational Linguistics.

Mustafa Melih Mutlu and Arzucan Özgür. 2022. A dataset and BERT-based models for targeted sentiment analysis on Turkish texts. In *Proceedings of the 60th Annual Meeting of the Association for Computational Linguistics: Student Research Workshop*, pages 467–472, Dublin, Ireland. Association for Computational Linguistics.

Steven Pinker. 1994. The Game of the Name. *The New York Times*.

Steven Pinker. 2003. *The Blank Slate: The Modern Denial of Human Nature*. Penguin.

Hussein Rababah. 2014. The translatability and use of x-phemism expressions (x-phemization): Euphemisms, dysphemisms and orthophemisms) in the medical discourse. *Studies in Literature and Language*, 9:1–12.

Mohammad Sadegh Rasooli and Joel R. Tetreault. 2015. Yara parser: A fast and accurate dependency parser. *Computing Research Repository*, arXiv:1503.06733. Version 2.

Taner Sezer. 2017. Ts corpus project: An online turkish dictionary and ts diy corpus. *European Journal of Language and Literature*, 9:18.

Wanzheng Zhu and Suma Bhat. 2021. Euphemistic phrase detection by masked language model. *Preprint*, arXiv:2109.04666.

Wanzheng Zhu, Hongyu Gong, Rohan Bansal, Zachary Weinberg, Nicolas Christin, Giulia Fanti, and Suma Bhat. 2021. Self-supervised euphemism detection and identification for content moderation. *arXiv preprint arXiv:2103.16808*.

Do LLMs Speak Kazakh? A Pilot Evaluation of Seven Models

Akylbek Maxutov[1], Ayan Myrzakhmet[2], Pavel Braslavski[2]
[1]Institute of Smart Systems and Artificial Intelligence, Astana, Kazakhstan
[2]School of Engineering and Digital Sciences, Nazarbayev University, Astana, Kazakhstan
pavel.braslavskii@nu.edu.kz

Abstract

We conducted a systematic evaluation of seven large language models (LLMs) on tasks in Kazakh, a Turkic language spoken by approximately 13 million native speakers in Kazakhstan and abroad. We used six datasets corresponding to different tasks – questions answering, causal reasoning, middle school math problems, machine translation, and spelling correction. Three of the datasets were prepared for this study. As expected, the quality of the LLMs on the Kazakh tasks is lower than on the parallel English tasks. GPT-4 shows the best results, followed by Gemini and AYA. In general, LLMs perform better on classification tasks and struggle with generative tasks. Our results provide valuable insights into the applicability of currently available LLMs for Kazakh. We made the data collected for this study publicly available: https://github.com/akylbekmaxutov/LLM-eval-using-Kazakh.

1 Introduction

Large Language Models (LLMs) increase human productivity and eliminate routine tasks in many areas, making them a powerful economic driver (Eloundou et al., 2023; Butler et al., 2023). At the same time, LLMs can lead to an inequality between different language communities and a widening gap between developed and developing countries (Khowaja et al., 2024). Creating LLMs requires huge amounts of text and computation, as well as skilled engineers. Most LLMs are trained for high-resource languages with large populations of speakers, primarily English. Training language models for low-resource languages can be technically and economically problematic – there is little training data, and it is unclear whether potential users can amortize the cost of collecting data and training the model. Although models trained primarily on English data express capabilities in other languages, their quality in these secondary languages is lower than in English (Ahuja et al., 2023). Recently, thanks to the advent of open LLMs, their adaptations to less-resourced languages are emerging (Qin et al., 2024). Evaluating LLMs in different languages is crucial in this situation.

Source	en	tr	kk
CulturaX	2.8T	64.3B	2.8B
Wiki pages	6.8M	610K	236K
HF datasets	10,889	402	120
HF models	51,365	1,403	458

Table 1: Overview of available Kazakh (kk) language resources compared to English (en) and Turkish (tr): # tokens in the CulturaX (Nguyen et al., 2023) dataset, # Wikipedia pages, and datasets/models on Huggingface.

In this study, we make the first attempt to evaluate the quality of available LLMs in Kazakh. Kazakh belongs to the Turkic language family and is the official language of the Republic of Kazakhstan (Campbell and King, 2020). Estimated 10 million Kazakh native speakers live in Kazakhstan, and about 3 million more abroad, predominantly in north-western China and western Mongolia. The language employs an extended Cyrillic alphabet with 42 letters. Kazakh is an agglutinative language, meaning that words are formed by adding various suffixes to root words. The language's rich inflectional morphology is reflected in the complex interaction of suffixes for number, possession, and case. For instance, the plural form, possessive affixes, and various case endings are layered sequentially onto noun roots. Kazakh has eight types of possessive agreements, adding complexity to its morphological structure. Kazakh verbs exhibit similar tenses and moods as Turkish ones but include unique tenses such as the goal-oriented future tense. Kazakh consonant and vowel harmony rules significantly affect its morphological structure. Consonant harmony determines the form of suffixes based on the voicing of the final consonant of the root word, while vowel harmony aligns suf-

Proceedings of the First Workshop on Natural Language Processing for Turkic Languages (SIGTURK 2024), pages 81–91
August 15, 2024 ©2024 Association for Computational Linguistics

fix vowels with the vowel type (front or back) of the root. Kazakh is considered a mid-resourced language (Joshi et al., 2020). Table 1 provides a brief statistics of resources available for Kazakh along with the figures for English and Turkish for comparison.

We experimented with *seven* models in total – five closed (GPT 3.5 and 4, Gemini 1.5 Pro, YandexGPT 2 and 3) and two open (LLAMA 2 and AYA) ones.[1] We focused on automatic benchmark-based evaluation, while trying to make the set of tasks diverse. We used a collection of six datasets sourced in different ways: 1) existing multilingual benchmarks that include Kazakh data (machine translation and multiple-choice question answering), 2) the recently published monolingual question answering dataset KazQAD (both open- and closed-book scenarios), 3) machine-translated COPA dataset[2] (commonsense causal reasoning), 4) original math school problems in Kazakh that we scraped online and post-processed, and 5) a Kazakh spelling correction dataset that we created from scratch within this study.

Based on our experiments, we can conclude that the GPT-4 is the most capable of all the models in the experiment. Gemini is the runner-up in the classification tasks. AYA is quite competitive, especially if we take into account its relatively small size and a long list of supported languages. All models show a lower quality in the generative tasks. As expected, the quality on Kazakh tasks is significantly lower than on English tasks, as we can see on parallel multilingual datasets (multiple-choice question answering, causal reasoning). Specialized models may still provide better quality for downstream tasks, such as machine translation or classification tasks. We cannot confirm previous findings that English prompts systematically improve LLM quality on non-English tasks: our results are mixed across tasks and models.

Our findings provide valuable insights into the applicability of currently available LLMs for Kazakh. We also anticipate that the study will contribute to the methodology of evaluating LLMs and improving the quality of LLMs in mid- and low-resource languages. The methods introduced in our work can be used to experiment with other languages and LLMs. We made the data and evaluation code publicly available.[3]

2 Related Work

As has been shown by Blevins and Zettlemoyer (2022), multilingual abilities of language models emerge when they are exposed even to a tiny fraction of non-English data in a large pre-training corpus. Earlier studies demonstrated that multilingual models learn high-level abstractions common to all languages, which make cross-lingual transfer possible even when languages share no vocabulary (Wu and Dredze, 2019). Open LLMs such as LLAMA (Touvron et al., 2023) and Qwen (Bai et al., 2023) can be adapted to other languages by expanding their vocabularies, continual pre-training and subsequent aligning on the data in target language (Qin et al., 2024). Another approach is to train a model from scratch: for example, Jais model was trained on a mixture of English and Arabic data in ratio 2:1 (Sengupta et al., 2023). Despite the development of non-English and multilingual models, many languages remain underrepresented in the modern LLM landscape. This situation is partly due to objective reasons (lack of training data), but also to inequalities in economic and technological development.

LLM evaluation is a complex and multifaceted problem (Chang et al., 2024). LLMs are truly multitasking, and users can leverage them to solve non-standard and creative problems, for example, brainstorming ideas or generating jokes. For generative tasks, the variety of formulations can be very large, making it difficult to automatically compare the answer to a "gold standard." With the proliferation of LLMs and their active use, evaluation of models becomes relevant not only at the task level, but also from their safety and security perspectives. The main approach to automatic LLM evaluation is based on ensembles of annotated benchmarks covering a wide range of usage scenarios (Liang et al., 2022). Popular benchmarks include MMLU (Massive Multitask Language Understanding) (Hendrycks et al., 2021) that measures LLM's knowledge across 57 subjects and GSM8K (Grade School Math) (Cobbe et al., 2021), aimed at evaluating multi-step math reasoning. MMLU contains multiple-choice ques-

[1] mGPT (Shliazhko et al., 2024) is another LLM that officially supports Kazakh. However, only a pre-trained mGPT is available, while the models in the study are instruction tuned.

[2] In the spring of 2024, while our study was underway, the Kardeş-NLU for five Turkic languages, including Kazakh, was published (Senel et al., 2024). The dataset includes a post-edited version of COPA.

[3] https://github.com/akylbekmaxutov/LLM-eval-using-Kazakh

tions, while GSM8K accepts numerical answers. There are multilingual adaptions of these datasets: Lai et al. (2023b) employed ChatGPT to translate the original MMLU dataset in multiple languages; MGSM dataset contains 250 problems from the GSM8K manually translated into 10 typologically diverse languages (Shi et al., 2023).

Studies that evaluate LLMs on non-English tasks are fewer that those targeting English and vary in their scope (Chang et al., 2024; Laskar et al., 2023). Some focus on multilingual datasets (Lai et al., 2023a; Ahuja et al., 2023), while others concentrate on a specific language, e.g. Arabic (Abdelali et al., 2024) or Russian (Fenogenova et al., 2024). Our study belongs to the latter type. LLMs, as expected, are better in solving problems formulated in English than in other languages. Moreover, fine-tuned models such as XLM-R (Conneau et al., 2020) in general outperform LLMs on specific tasks. The quality on non-English tasks can be improved by preceding actual task formulation with English prompts, or by explicitly stating in the prompt that the task must first be translated into English (Huang et al., 2023; Zhang et al., 2023). The multilingual abilities of LLMs also depend on the task type. It can be concluded that LLMs are better at "understanding" a language other than English than at generating a non-English answer (Bang et al., 2023). Thus, models do better in multilingual classification, reasoning, and multiple-choice question answering and struggle with generative tasks. Based on experiments with LLAMA 2, Wendler et al. (2024) hypothesize that the model first solves the task using English as a pivotal language, then generates the answer in the target language. This process can be seen as an implicit translate-test approach. These observations are partially confirmed by our experiments.

Recently, several annotated Kazakh datasets (Yeshpanov et al., 2022, 2024) and multilingual datasets including Kazakh (Bandarkar et al., 2023; Senel et al., 2024) have been published. However, we are not aware of any studies that have systematically evaluated the quality of existing LLMs in Kazakh.

3 Data

The data used in our experiments is summarized in Table 2. Due to limited resources, we could not afford to create large/numerous datasets from scratch or manually translate existing English datasets. In compiling the set, we were guided by the following criteria: 1) reuse existing datasets whenever possible; 2) avoid the massive use of machine translation; 3) include tasks that are potentially of practical use to the end user (rather than specific NLP tasks like NER or POS tagging); 4) make the set as diverse as possible.

Belebele is a massively multilingual machine reading comprehension dataset that spans 122 languages, including Kazakh (Bandarkar et al., 2023). Belebele contains 900 multiple-choice questions, each associated with one of 488 distinct passages originating from the Flores-200 dataset (Costa-jussà et al., 2022). First, the English multiple choice questions and answers were manually created using English passages from the Flores dataset. Later, questions and answers were translated in other languages and aligned with corresponding passages from Flores-200. Each question has four answer options, one of which is correct. So, a random guessing would result in accuracy of 0.25. All 900 Belebele questions are intended exclusively for testing, there is no training supplement to the dataset. Authors report performance of GPT-3.5-turbo and LLAMA2-CHAT 70B in zero-shot fashion on Kazakh/English Belebele subsets: 35.0/87.7 and 32.4/78.8 accuracy points, respectively.

kkWikiSpell is a manually collected dataset of correct/incorrect sentence pairs designed to test the spelling ability of LLMs in Kazakh. The sentences in the dataset are taken from randomly selected Kazakh Wikipedia pages, with 10 sentences extracted from each page. Note that there is a possibility that the LLMs "saw" these sentences during their pre-training. Each sentence was deliberately altered to include mistakes. According to Dhakal et al. (2018), people tend to make three types of mistakes when typing: substitution (changing letters), omission (missing letters), and insertion (adding extra letters). In kkWikiSpell, we manually injected these three types of mistakes into the sampled sentences, for example:

> Original Sentence: Содан бері бұл есіммен Абай тарихқа енді.
> Sentence with mistakes: Содан бері бұл есімнең Абай тарихқа енд.

The distribution of mistakes in the dataset is as follows: 89 sentences contain one mistake, 61 sentences contain two mistakes, and the remaining 10 sentences contain three mistakes. Letter substitutions occur in 93 sentences, missing letters in 73

	Dataset	Task	Size	Metric	Language
Class.	Belebele (Bandarkar et al., 2023)	Multiple-choice QA	900	Accuracy	Human-translated
	kkCOPA*	Causal reasoning	500	Accuracy	Machine-translated
	NIS Math*	School Math	100	Accuracy	Orig. in Kazakh
	KazQAD§ (Yeshpanov et al., 2024)	Reading comprehension	1,000	Token-level F1	Orig. in Kazakh
Gen.	kkWikiSpell*	Spelling correction	160	Token-level Jaccard	Orig. in Kazakh
	KazQAD§ (Yeshpanov et al., 2024)	Generative QA	1,927	Token-level recall	Orig. in Kazakh
	Flores-101 (Goyal et al., 2022)	Machine translation	500	BLEU	Human-translated

*Datasets prepared within this study. §KazQAD data was used both in open- and closed-book scenarios.

Table 2: Benchmarks in the study. The upper part of the table describes discriminative/classification tasks, whereas the bottom part – generative tasks.

sentences, extra letters in 17 sentences, missing spaces in 4 sentences, extra spaces in 2 sentences, capitalization mistakes and missing characters occur in one sentence each. The total dataset consists of 160 incorrect/correct sentence pairs. The sentences vary in length from 5 to 26 words, with an average sentence length of 11 words.

NIS Math. Math problems are one of the standard tests for large language models. We are not aware of any multilingual benchmarks that include math problems in Kazakh, so we downloaded the entrance tests used for admission to the Nazarbayev Intellectual Schools (NIS). The difficulty level corresponds to the sixth school grade. The tests, in PDF format, were automatically parsed and then manually checked; only textual questions (i.e., without illustrations) were retained. The final set consists of 100 problems, each with four possible answers, one of which is correct. Accuracy is used as a metric to evaluate the task (random guessing results in an accuracy of 0.25). An example from the NIS Math dataset along with an English translation:

```
Question: Егер шаршының қабырғасын
60%-ға арттырса, ауданы қалай өзгереді.
a: 2.56 есе өсті
b: 2.56 есе кеміді
c: 0.36 есе өсті
d: 0.16 есе өсті
correct: a
```

```
Question: If the side of a square is increased
by 60%, the area of the square changes as
follows.
a: increased by 2.56 times
b: decreased by 2.56 times
c: increased by 0.36 times
d: increased by 0.16 times
correct: a
```

kkCOPA is a machine translation of the *test* subset of the English *Choice Of Plausible Alternatives* (COPA) dataset (Roemmele et al., 2011) using the Google Translate API.[4] COPA is designed to evaluate the ability of models to identify real-world cause-effect relationships. In this respect, it differs from question-answering datasets, which, depending on the scenario, evaluate the model's language understanding and/or factual knowledge. Each COPA item is a triple containing a premise and two alternatives corresponding to either to *effect* or *cause*. Thus, given a premise, a direction (i.e., forward or backward causal reasoning), and two alternatives, the task is to choose the correct option from two. COPA has 500 items in its balanced test set, so random guessing will result in an accuracy of 0.5. An example of a COPA item and its corresponding kkCOPA entry:

Premise: The band played their hit song.
Question: What happened as a *result*?
Alt1: The audience clapped along to the music.
Alt2: The audience politely listened in silence.

```
Premise: Топтар хит әндерін ойнады.
Question: әсері ретінде не болды?
Alt1: Аудитория музыкаға сәйкес келеді.
Alt2: Көрермендер үнсіз тыңдады.
```

Laskar et al. (2023) report that the zero-shot performance of GPT-3.5 on COPA is 94. XCOPA (Ponti et al., 2020) is a multilingual extension of the original dataset. It contains human translations of the COPA test set and 100 items from the development set into 11 languages (doesn't include Kazakh). GPT-3.5 and GPT-4 achieve an average accuracy across all languages on XCOPA of 79.1 and 89.7, respectively (Ahuja et al., 2023).

KazQAD is an open domain question answering (ODQA) dataset in Kazakh (Yeshpanov et al., 2024). The dataset can be used in various scenarios – for training and evaluation of information retrieval, reading comprehension, and open/generative question answering. The dataset contains questions, annotated passages from

[4]https://cloud.google.com/translate/

Kazakh Wikipedia and short answers extracted from the relevant passages. The training subset contains questions from the English NaturalQuestions dataset (Kwiatkowski et al., 2019) which have been machine translated into Kazakh. The test set contains 1,927 original questions from the Unified National Test (UNT) – a high school graduation exam in Kazakhstan in six subjects. The KazQAD test set is the largest benchmark in our study. We used the KazQAD data in two scenarios: open-book and closed-book question answering. In the first case, we provided the question and the relevant passage as context, along with the instruction that the LLM should return a span of the passage as the answer. Since the dataset was recently released, we hope that the KazQAD test set wasn't contaminated.

FLORES-101 is a dataset for machine translation evaluation covering 101 languages, including Kazakh (Goyal et al., 2022). To build the dataset, original English sentences were first extracted from three Mediawiki projects and then manually translated into 101 languages. The dataset contains 3,001 English sentences and their translations, divided into train (997), dev (1,012), and test (992) subsets. FLORES-101 enables the simultaneous evaluation of different translation pairs and directions. In this study, we evaluate LLM's ability to translate Kazakh sentences into English, Russian and Turkish. Note, however, that in the case of the Kazakh-Russian and Kazakh-Turkish pairs, both parts were created by translators and may contain translationese. The creators of FLORES-101 suspect that the way the data was created may, for example, lead to increased differences between cognate languages (e.g. Kazakh and Turkish, as they belong to the same language family). Zhu et al. (2023) report BLEU scores of zero-shot translation from Kazakh to English on FLORES-101 for LLAMA 2-CHAT, GPT-3.5 and GPT-4: 6.83, 21.74, and 30.65, respectively.

4 Models

In our work, we evaluated seven models. Since five of the seven models are closed, many of their aspects such as the number of parameters or the data on which they were trained are unknown. Table 3 lists the models in our experiment and presents official metrics on two common benchmarks – MMLU and GSM8K for GPTs, Gemini and LLAMA 2. In addition, we present the results of the evaluation of YandexGPTs and AYA on multilingual MMLU adaptations. The release date of the model may indirectly indicate the up-to-dateness of the information stored in its parameters (it should be noted that the pre-training of mT5, on which AYA is based, was conducted much earlier). We also report the vocabulary sizes of the models and the fertility rates of their tokenizers, i.e. the ratios of tokens and whitespace-tokenized words calculated on the kkCOPA data. Tokenization stronfgly influences the quality of subsequent task solving (Ahuja et al., 2023; Bandarkar et al., 2023) and may also introduce inequity between language communities, since LLM APIs charge on a per-token basis (Petrov et al., 2023).

GPT 3.5 and 4 are two generations of LLMs from OpenAI. Kazakh is included in the official list of languages that GPTs work with.[5] We access the models through their official APIs. We use `gpt-3.5-turbo-0125` and `gpt-4-0125-preview` versions in our study.

Gemini 1.5 Pro is the latest publicly available LLM from Google. Kazakh is not on the list of languages officially supported by Gemini.[6] This is probably the reason why Gemini returns empty results or error messages for a significant share of requests, see details in Section 5. We accessed `gemini-1.5-pro-preview-0409` model through Google Cloud's Vertex AI Studio.

LLAMA is a collection of open LLMs of different sizes. They have been pre-trained on 2T tokens, of which an estimated ~90% are English. Due to limited computational resources, we use an 8-bit quantized version of LLAMA 2-CHAT 7B, an aligned model for dialogue use cases. Although the model was mainly trained on English data, it has some multilingual capabilities, as shown by numerous experiments.

YandexGPT 2 and 3. Few technical details about Yandex' language models are disclosed, but the company's blog posts provide results of evaluating models on proprietary benchmarks and comparing YandexGPTs side-by-side with ChatGPT and LLAMA 2 on tasks in Russian. We could not find an official list of supported languages, but our

[5] `https://help.openai.com/en/articles/8357869#h_513834920e`

[6] `https://support.google.com/gemini/answer/13575153`

Model		xMMLU	GSM8K	Release date	|V|	T/W
GPT-3.5-turbo[1]	C	70.0†	57.1	11.2022	100k[4]	5.80
GPT-4-turbo (Achiam et al., 2023)	C	86.4†	92.0	03.2023		
LLAMA 2 (Touvron et al., 2023)	O	45.3†	56.8	02.2023	32k	4.78
Gemini 1.5 pro (Reid et al., 2024)	C	81.9†	91.7	02.2024	256k	3.63
AYA (Üstün et al., 2024)	O	37.3§	–	02.2024	250k	2.66
YandexGPT 2[2]	C	55.0*	–	09.2023	?	3.83
YandexGPT 3[3]	C	63.0*	–	03.2024		

[1] https://openai.com/blog/chatgpt [2] https://ya.ru/ai/gpt-2 [3] https://ya.ru/ai/gpt-3 (in Russian)
[4] https://github.com/openai/tiktoken † original English MMLU (Hendrycks et al., 2021)
§ multilingual MMLU (Lai et al., 2023b), averaged over 31 languages * proprietary Russian version of MMLU

Table 3: Open (O) and closed (C) LLMs in the study. Note that *xMMLU* scores correspond to different variants of the dataset and can only be used for comparison within subgroups of the models (e.g., YandexGPT 2 vs. 3). The last two columns report the vocabulary size and the token/word ratio calculated on kkCOPA.

experiments show that the models "understand" English and Kazakh to some extent. In March 2024, there were press reports that Yandex was planning to train YandexGPT in Kazakh language, but it is unclear whether these plans have already been implemented.[7]

AYA is a massively multilingual model based on the 13B mT5-xxl model (Xue et al., 2021) that supports 101 languages, including Kazakh. The main challenge of the Aya project was to prepare a large instruction dataset to cover all supported languages (Singh et al., 2024). We hosted the AYA model[8] on a cloud GPU.

5 Experimental Results

5.1 Experimental Design

All models and tasks were evaluated in a zero-shot scenario. We used two types of prompts – with English and Kazakh instructions (the main content – question, sentence to correct or translate, etc. – was always in Kazakh).[9] Since open-book question answering implies relatively long contexts when accessing the paid APIs, we randomly sampled 1,000 KazQAD test questions to stay within our limited budget.

For classification tasks, we implemented simple processing scripts for extracting actual answers from the LLM responses. For evaluation of open-book QA and machine translation we employed F1 and BLEU scores implemented in the Huggingface's `evaluate` library.[10] As a quality metric for spelling correction, we use the token-level Jaccard coefficient between the "gold standard" and the sentence returned by the model.

Automatic evaluation of closed-book QA is problematic because we need to assess the similarity of "golden" answers to the free-form response returned by the language model (Kamalloo et al., 2023). In particular, LLMs often return sentence-long answers to factoid questions, even though the prompt asks for concise answers. On the other hand, the LLM's response may be semantically close to the reference, but quite different in wording. We used the recall of lemmatized tokens as a metric to evaluate closed-book QA. For the lemmatization, we used the Stanza library (Qi et al., 2020). This approach makes it possible to ignore the length of the LLM response, as well as to match different morphological variants of a word, which is especially important in the case of the inflectionally rich Kazakh language. This metric does not take into account word order, synonyms and word meaning. However, manual inspection of the results confirms that this is a viable option for *comparing* different LLMs. In addition to the average recall over all questions, we report the absolute number of responses with a recall greater than 0.5. For similar values of averaged recall, this additional parameter indicates the number of more precise answers in the model's responses.

5.2 Results and Discussion

Table 4 summarizes results on six tasks, while Table 5 reports translation results.

Our results confirm the findings of previous studies – LLMs perform quite well on **classification tasks** in non-English languages. On the **Belebele** dataset, GPT-4 and Gemini show similarly high

[7] https://tass.ru/ekonomika/20390279 (in Russian)

[8] https://huggingface.co/CohereForAI/aya-101

[9] With the exception of the closed-book QA task, which we evaluated with English instructions only.

[10] https://huggingface.co/docs/evaluate/

Dataset	Instr.	GPT-3.5	GPT-4	YaGPT 2	YaGPT 3	LLAMA 2	Gemini	AYA
Belebele	en	0.37	**0.87**	0.65	0.64	0.12	0.86	0.70
	kk	0.33	0.85	0.64	0.59	0.01	0.86	0.63
kk-COPA	en	0.51	0.78	0.69	0.65	0.05	0.80	0.74
	kk	0.48	**0.82**	0.66	0.60	0.00	0.81	0.73
NIS Math	en	0.22	0.46	0.26	0.31	0.19	0.41	0.32
	kk	0.22	**0.48**	0.25	0.31	0.10	–	0.27
KazQAD OB	en	0.42	0.57	0.27	0.52	0.04	0.10	**0.61**
	kk	0.16	0.36	0.15	0.36	0.01	0.10	0.48
kkWikiSpell	en	0.07 (9)	**0.08 (51)**	0.06 (24)	0.08 (28)	0.02 (0)	–	0.08 (23)
	kk	0.07 (4)	0.08 (36)	0.07 (21)	0.06 (19)	0.00 (0)	–	0.08 (14)
KazQAD CB	en	0.08 (92)	**0.33 (695)**	0.01 (3)	0.01 (5)	0.07 (130)	0.05 (92)	0.09 (114)

Table 4: Main results. We report accuracy for Belebele, kkCOPA, and NIS Math and F1 for open-book QA; for spelling correction, we report average token-level Jaccard coefficient and the number of ideal responses out of 160; for closed-book question answering, we report average token-level recall, as well as the number of answers with recall > 0.5 out of the total 1,927 questions. Gemini returned no results for NIS Math tasks with Kazakh prompts and kkWikiSpell; in both versions of KazQAD questions the share of non-empty responses was also extremely low (10-13%). The best scores for each task are in **bold**, the second-best scores are underlined.

Instr.	Target	GT	GPT-3.5	GPT-4	YaGPT 2	YaGPT 3	LLAMA 2	Gemini	AYA
en	en	0.35	0.15	0.28	0.20	0.22	0.04	0.23	0.25
	ru	0.24	0.11	0.21	0.15	0.15	0.03	0.16	0.17
	tr	0.17	0.10	0.16	0.09	0.09	0.03	0.13	0.13
kk	en	0.35	0.13	0.29	0.21	0.23	0.00	0.22	0.14
	ru	0.24	0.09	0.20	0.16	0.16	0.00	0.16	0.08
	tr	0.17	0.05	0.16	0.10	0.10	0.00	0.13	0.04

Table 5: Translation results: BLEU scores on the FLORES dataset (GT: Google Translate).

results, followed by AYA with English prompts. There are 18 Belebele questions that none of the LLMs answered correctly with either English or Kazakh instructions. We didn't find any patterns in these "hard" questions. Furthermore, excluding LLAMA 2 with Kazakh instructions, there are 14 questions that all models answered correctly across 13 runs. Again, these questions and their passages show no noticeable similarities. Notably, two **kkCOPA** questions (#574 and #992) were answered incorrectly in all 14 configurations. In both cases, the Kazakh translations were incorrect. As a results, the models selected answers that, although incorrect in the original context, were logically consistent with the mistranslated versions. An interesting observation is that most models achieved higher accuracy in identifying *effects* than *causes*. In particular, AYA with English prompts showed the largest difference, achieving an accuracy of 66.4% for causes and 79.2% for effects. Out of 100 **NIS Math** questions, there were three where all models failed to provide correct answers. One of these (#44) was flawed because it erroneously showed the wrong answer as correct. On math problems, the results of YandexGPT 2 are approximately at the level of the random baseline (0.25), while GPT-3.5 and LLAMA 2 are below it.

On the **open-book question answering** task with English prompts, AYA is the winner, outperforming both GPT-4 and Gemini. GPT-4 and AYA outperform SOTA on this dataset – fine-tuned XML-V achieves $F1 = 0.54$ (Yeshpanov et al., 2024) (although we must treat these results with caution, since in our study, due to limited resources, the evaluation was performed on about half of the test set).

Tasks involving the generation of responses in Kazakh are more difficult for all models. The **spelling correction** task proved to be quite hard for all models, although the errors introduced can be considered simple. Again, GPT-4 is the leader in this task. The results of both Yandex models are comparable. YandexGPT 2 occasionally outputs some Kazakh words in Latin script or inserts ** in the output words as they were split into subword tokens. Gemini returned only empty responses. LLAMA 2, when instructed in Kazakh, does not solve the task at all, but sometimes provides a kind of analysis of the input, e.g. *The text is a poem and it has a specific structure and rhythm.* When instructed in English, LLAMA 2 performs slightly better, but still responded to only 55 out of 160 sentences, none of which were correct.

GPT-4's leadership is particularly evident in the **closed-book question answering**. The AYA model looks quite competitive compared to the closed models that are reportedly significantly larger. Note that the AYA's backbone model mT5 does not have the most advanced architecture and the model may be prone to the "curse of multilinguality" (Conneau et al., 2020). Interestingly, LLAMA 2 generates relatively many high-recall answers to KazQAD questions, ranking second in this respect after GPT-4. Manual inspection of the KazQAD closed-book answers revealed that GPT-3.5 tends to return incorrect *Kazakh* names as answers. For example, for the question *Who is the scientist who proposed the principle of naming the genus and species in Latin?* GPT-3.5 returned *Galim-Aibek Bolat*, while the correct answer is *Carl Linnaeus*. The other strange thing about GPT-3.5 is that about a fifth of the answers were just the questions themselves, but with some letters/words removed. The YandexGPT 2 returned most of the answers in Russian.

Machine translation results show that dedicated solutions are still a better alternative for this task and the considered language pairs. At the same time, GPT-4 approaches the quality of Google Translate on the Kazakh-Turkish pair (interestingly, translation between two languages belonging to the same family shows the lowest scores). The translation quality of the LLAMA 2 and AYA models drops significantly when using Kazakh prompts. Gemini appears to be competitive with GPT-4, returning non-empty translations for 64% and 62% of sentences following English and Kazakh prompts, respectively. AYA was even less responsive in the machine translation task with Kazakh prompts. After tweaking the prompt, we were only able to get Turkish translations for about 10% of the Kazakh sentences. GPT-3.5 also showed strange behavior in the Turkish translation task: in many cases, the model simply rephrased the Kazakh input.

It is interesting to note that, based on our results, we cannot draw a clear conclusion that English prompts improve results over Kazakh prompts. In rare cases, Kazakh prompts lead to slightly better scores (GPT-4 on **kkCOPA** and **NIS Math**). In other cases, the decrease is insignificant. However, the quality of the extractive question answering drops for all models. LLAMA 2's results decrease significantly when switching from English to Kazakh prompts on all tasks.

Gemini behaves very differently from, for example, GPT-4: in many cases the model returns empty responses or error messages. Gemini refused to return any answers to math problems with Kazakh prompts, as well as any spelling corrections. Gemini answered about half of the math questions with English prompts, i.e. its accuracy on the answered questions is about 80%. Gemini answered only a small fraction (10-13%) of KazQAD questions in all scenarios. **LLAMA 2** results are lower than we expected based on previous studies. For example, on Belebele with English prompts, our results differ significantly from those reported by Bandarkar et al. (2023) for LLAMA 2 70B: 12 vs. 34 accuracy points. There may be several reasons for this discrepancy, such as model size (8-bit quantized 7B vs. 70B) and a less optimal prompt. We will address this issue in our future work.

6 Conclusion

Our results provide valuable insights into the applicability of currently available LLMs for Kazakh. GPT-4 shows the best results, followed by Gemini and AYA. Gemini's results are promising, although the proportion of empty answers is quite high. AYA is very competitive compared to its supposedly larger closed counterparts. As expected, the quality of the LLMs on the Kazakh tasks is lower than on the parallel English tasks. In general, LLMs perform better on classification tasks and struggle with generative tasks. English instructions can improve results on some tasks/models.

Our evaluation showed that there is a steady progress in LLMs for Kazakh (GPT-3.5 vs. GPT-4). We expect the support of Kazakh by Gemini and YandexGPT to be strengthened, as well as the appearance of a Kazakh adaptation of an open LLM. We made the datasets prepared for the study and the collected LLM responses publicly available. These resources can form the basis for an LLM benchmark focused on the Kazakh language. In our future work, we plan to expand the list of LLMs and the set of benchmarks.

Acknowledgments

Pavel Braslavski acknowledges funding from the School of Engineering and Digital Sciences, Nazarbayev University. The experiments were partially supported by a Yandex Cloud grant.

References

Ahmed Abdelali, Hamdy Mubarak, Shammur Chowdhury, Maram Hasanain, Basel Mousi, Sabri Boughorbel, Samir Abdaljalil, Yassine El Kheir, Daniel Izham, Fahim Dalvi, Majd Hawasly, Nizi Nazar, Youssef Elshahawy, Ahmed Ali, Nadir Durrani, Natasa Milic-Frayling, and Firoj Alam. 2024. LAraBench: Benchmarking Arabic AI with large language models. In *Proceedings of the 18th Conference of the European Chapter of the Association for Computational Linguistics (Volume 1: Long Papers)*, pages 487–520, St. Julian's, Malta. Association for Computational Linguistics.

Josh Achiam, Steven Adler, Sandhini Agarwal, Lama Ahmad, Ilge Akkaya, Florencia Leoni Aleman, Diogo Almeida, Janko Altenschmidt, Sam Altman, Shyamal Anadkat, et al. 2023. Gpt-4 technical report. *arXiv preprint arXiv:2303.08774*.

Kabir Ahuja, Harshita Diddee, Rishav Hada, Millicent Ochieng, Krithika Ramesh, Prachi Jain, Akshay Nambi, Tanuja Ganu, Sameer Segal, Mohamed Ahmed, Kalika Bali, and Sunayana Sitaram. 2023. MEGA: Multilingual evaluation of generative AI. In *Proceedings of the 2023 Conference on Empirical Methods in Natural Language Processing*, pages 4232–4267.

Jinze Bai, Shuai Bai, Yunfei Chu, Zeyu Cui, Kai Dang, Xiaodong Deng, Yang Fan, Wenbin Ge, Yu Han, Fei Huang, et al. 2023. Qwen technical report. *arXiv preprint arXiv:2309.16609*.

Lucas Bandarkar, Davis Liang, Benjamin Muller, Mikel Artetxe, Satya Narayan Shukla, Donald Husa, Naman Goyal, Abhinandan Krishnan, Luke Zettlemoyer, and Madian Khabsa. 2023. The belebele benchmark: a parallel reading comprehension dataset in 122 language variants. *Preprint*, arXiv:2308.16884.

Yejin Bang, Samuel Cahyawijaya, Nayeon Lee, Wenliang Dai, Dan Su, Bryan Wilie, Holy Lovenia, Ziwei Ji, Tiezheng Yu, Willy Chung, Quyet V. Do, Yan Xu, and Pascale Fung. 2023. A multitask, multilingual, multimodal evaluation of ChatGPT on reasoning, hallucination, and interactivity. In *Proceedings of the 13th International Joint Conference on Natural Language Processing and the 3rd Conference of the Asia-Pacific Chapter of the Association for Computational Linguistics (Volume 1: Long Papers)*, pages 675–718, Nusa Dua, Bali. Association for Computational Linguistics.

Terra Blevins and Luke Zettlemoyer. 2022. Language contamination helps explains the cross-lingual capabilities of English pretrained models. In *Proceedings of the 2022 Conference on Empirical Methods in Natural Language Processing*, pages 3563–3574, Abu Dhabi, United Arab Emirates. Association for Computational Linguistics.

Jenna Butler, Sonia Jaffe, Nancy Baym, Mary Czerwinski, Shamsi Iqbal, Kate Nowak, Sean Rintel, Abigail Sellen, Mihaela Vorvoreanu, Najeeb G. Abdulhamid, Judith Amores, Reid Andersen, Kagonya Awori, Maxamed Axmed, danah boyd, James Brand, Georg Buscher, Dean Carignan, Martin Chan, Adam Coleman, Scott Counts, Madeleine Daepp, Adam Fourney, Daniel G. Goldstein, Andy Gordon, Aaron L Halfaker, Javier Hernandez, Jake Hofman, Jenny Lay-Flurrie, Vera Liao, SiÃ¢n Lindley, Sathish Manivannan, Charlton Mcilwain, Subigya Nepal, Jennifer Neville, Stephanie Nyairo, Jacki O'Neill, Victor Poznanski, Gonzalo Ramos, Nagu Rangan, Lacey Rosedale, David Rothschild, Tara Safavi, Advait Sarkar, Ava Scott, Chirag Shah, Neha Parikh Shah, Teny Shapiro, Ryland Shaw, Auste Simkute, Jina Suh, Siddharth Suri, Ioana Tanase, Lev Tankelevitch, Adam Troy, Mengting Wan, Ryen W. White, Longqi Yang, Brent Hecht, and Jaime Teevan. 2023. Microsoft new future of work report 2023. Technical Report MSR-TR-2023-34, Microsoft.

George L Campbell and Gareth King. 2020. *Compendium of the World's Languages*. Routledge.

Yupeng Chang, Xu Wang, Jindong Wang, Yuan Wu, Linyi Yang, Kaijie Zhu, Hao Chen, Xiaoyuan Yi, Cunxiang Wang, Yidong Wang, et al. 2024. A survey on evaluation of large language models. *ACM Transactions on Intelligent Systems and Technology*, 15(3):1–45.

Karl Cobbe, Vineet Kosaraju, Mohammad Bavarian, Mark Chen, Heewoo Jun, Lukasz Kaiser, Matthias Plappert, Jerry Tworek, Jacob Hilton, Reiichiro Nakano, et al. 2021. Training verifiers to solve math word problems. *arXiv preprint arXiv:2110.14168*.

Alexis Conneau, Kartikay Khandelwal, Naman Goyal, Vishrav Chaudhary, Guillaume Wenzek, Francisco Guzmán, Edouard Grave, Myle Ott, Luke Zettlemoyer, and Veselin Stoyanov. 2020. Unsupervised cross-lingual representation learning at scale. In *Proceedings of the 58th Annual Meeting of the Association for Computational Linguistics*, pages 8440–8451, Online. Association for Computational Linguistics.

Marta R Costa-jussà, James Cross, Onur Çelebi, Maha Elbayad, Kenneth Heafield, Kevin Heffernan, Elahe Kalbassi, Janice Lam, Daniel Licht, Jean Maillard, et al. 2022. No language left behind: Scaling human-centered machine translation. *arXiv preprint arXiv:2207.04672*.

Vivek Dhakal, Anna Maria Feit, Per Ola Kristensson, and Antti Oulasvirta. 2018. Observations on typing from 136 million keystrokes. In *Proceedings of the 2018 CHI conference on human factors in computing systems*, pages 1–12.

Tyna Eloundou, Sam Manning, Pamela Mishkin, and Daniel Rock. 2023. GPTs are GPTs: An early look at the labor market impact potential of large language models. *arXiv preprint arXiv:2303.10130*.

Alena Fenogenova, Artem Chervyakov, Nikita Martynov, Anastasia Kozlova, Maria Tikhonova, Albina

Akhmetgareeva, Anton Emelyanov, Denis Shevelev, Pavel Lebedev, Leonid Sinev, et al. 2024. Mera: A comprehensive llm evaluation in russian. *arXiv preprint arXiv:2401.04531*.

Naman Goyal, Cynthia Gao, Vishrav Chaudhary, Peng-Jen Chen, Guillaume Wenzek, Da Ju, Sanjana Krishnan, Marc'Aurelio Ranzato, Francisco Guzmán, and Angela Fan. 2022. The flores-101 evaluation benchmark for low-resource and multilingual machine translation. *Transactions of the Association for Computational Linguistics*, 10:522–538.

Dan Hendrycks, Collin Burns, Steven Basart, Andy Zou, Mantas Mazeika, Dawn Song, and Jacob Steinhardt. 2021. Measuring massive multitask language understanding. In *9th International Conference on Learning Representations, ICLR 2021, Virtual Event, Austria, May 3-7, 2021*.

Haoyang Huang, Tianyi Tang, Dongdong Zhang, Xin Zhao, Ting Song, Yan Xia, and Furu Wei. 2023. Not all languages are created equal in LLMs: Improving multilingual capability by cross-lingual-thought prompting. In *Findings of the Association for Computational Linguistics: EMNLP 2023*, pages 12365–12394, Singapore. Association for Computational Linguistics.

Pratik Joshi, Sebastin Santy, Amar Budhiraja, Kalika Bali, and Monojit Choudhury. 2020. The state and fate of linguistic diversity and inclusion in the NLP world. In *Proceedings of the 58th Annual Meeting of the Association for Computational Linguistics*, pages 6282–6293, Online. Association for Computational Linguistics.

Ehsan Kamalloo, Nouha Dziri, Charles Clarke, and Davood Rafiei. 2023. Evaluating open-domain question answering in the era of large language models. In *Proceedings of the 61st Annual Meeting of the Association for Computational Linguistics (Volume 1: Long Papers)*, pages 5591–5606, Toronto, Canada. Association for Computational Linguistics.

Sunder Ali Khowaja, Parus Khuwaja, Kapal Dev, Weizheng Wang, and Lewis Nkenyereye. 2024. Chatgpt needs spade (sustainability, privacy, digital divide, and ethics) evaluation: A review. *Cognitive Computation*, pages 1–23.

Tom Kwiatkowski, Jennimaria Palomaki, Olivia Redfield, Michael Collins, Ankur Parikh, Chris Alberti, Danielle Epstein, Illia Polosukhin, Jacob Devlin, Kenton Lee, Kristina Toutanova, Llion Jones, Matthew Kelcey, Ming-Wei Chang, Andrew M. Dai, Jakob Uszkoreit, Quoc Le, and Slav Petrov. 2019. Natural questions: A benchmark for question answering research. *Transactions of the Association for Computational Linguistics*, 7:452–466.

Viet Lai, Nghia Ngo, Amir Pouran Ben Veyseh, Hieu Man, Franck Dernoncourt, Trung Bui, and Thien Nguyen. 2023a. ChatGPT beyond English: Towards a comprehensive evaluation of large language models in multilingual learning. In *Findings of the Association for Computational Linguistics: EMNLP 2023*, pages 13171–13189, Singapore. Association for Computational Linguistics.

Viet Dac Lai, Chien Van Nguyen, Nghia Trung Ngo, Thuat Nguyen, Franck Dernoncourt, Ryan A Rossi, and Thien Huu Nguyen. 2023b. Okapi: Instruction-tuned large language models in multiple languages with reinforcement learning from human feedback. *arXiv preprint arXiv:2307.16039*.

Md Tahmid Rahman Laskar, M Saiful Bari, Mizanur Rahman, Md Amran Hossen Bhuiyan, Shafiq Joty, and Jimmy Huang. 2023. A systematic study and comprehensive evaluation of ChatGPT on benchmark datasets. In *Findings of the Association for Computational Linguistics: ACL 2023*, pages 431–469, Toronto, Canada. Association for Computational Linguistics.

Percy Liang, Rishi Bommasani, Tony Lee, Dimitris Tsipras, Dilara Soylu, Michihiro Yasunaga, Yian Zhang, Deepak Narayanan, Yuhuai Wu, Ananya Kumar, et al. 2022. Holistic evaluation of language models. *arXiv preprint arXiv:2211.09110*.

Thuat Nguyen, Chien Van Nguyen, Viet Dac Lai, Hieu Man, Nghia Trung Ngo, Franck Dernoncourt, Ryan A Rossi, and Thien Huu Nguyen. 2023. Culturax: A cleaned, enormous, and multilingual dataset for large language models in 167 languages. *arXiv preprint arXiv:2309.09400*.

Aleksandar Petrov, Emanuele La Malfa, Philip H. S. Torr, and Adel Bibi. 2023. Language model tokenizers introduce unfairness between languages. In *Advances in Neural Information Processing Systems 36: Annual Conference on Neural Information Processing Systems 2023, NeurIPS 2023, New Orleans, LA, USA, December 10 - 16, 2023*.

Edoardo Maria Ponti, Goran Glavaš, Olga Majewska, Qianchu Liu, Ivan Vulić, and Anna Korhonen. 2020. XCOPA: A multilingual dataset for causal commonsense reasoning. In *Proceedings of the 2020 Conference on Empirical Methods in Natural Language Processing (EMNLP)*, pages 2362–2376.

Peng Qi, Yuhao Zhang, Yuhui Zhang, Jason Bolton, and Christopher D. Manning. 2020. Stanza: A python natural language processing toolkit for many human languages. In *Proceedings of the 58th Annual Meeting of the Association for Computational Linguistics: System Demonstrations*, pages 101–108, Online. Association for Computational Linguistics.

Libo Qin, Qiguang Chen, Yuhang Zhou, Zhi Chen, Yinghui Li, Lizi Liao, Min Li, Wanxiang Che, and Philip S Yu. 2024. Multilingual large language model: A survey of resources, taxonomy and frontiers. *arXiv preprint arXiv:2404.04925*.

Machel Reid, Nikolay Savinov, Denis Teplyashin, Dmitry Lepikhin, Timothy Lillicrap, Jean-baptiste

Alayrac, Radu Soricut, Angeliki Lazaridou, Orhan Firat, Julian Schrittwieser, et al. 2024. Gemini 1.5: Unlocking multimodal understanding across millions of tokens of context. *arXiv preprint arXiv:2403.05530*.

Melissa Roemmele, Cosmin Adrian Bejan, and Andrew S Gordon. 2011. Choice of plausible alternatives: An evaluation of commonsense causal reasoning. In *2011 AAAI Spring Symposium Series*.

Lütfi Kerem Senel, Benedikt Ebing, Konul Baghirova, Hinrich Schuetze, and Goran Glavaš. 2024. Kardeş-NLU: Transfer to low-resource languages with big brother's help – a benchmark and evaluation for Turkic languages. In *Proceedings of the 18th Conference of the European Chapter of the Association for Computational Linguistics (Volume 1: Long Papers)*, pages 1672–1688, St. Julian's, Malta. Association for Computational Linguistics.

Neha Sengupta, Sunil Kumar Sahu, Bokang Jia, Satheesh Katipomu, Haonan Li, Fajri Koto, Osama Mohammed Afzal, Samta Kamboj, Onkar Pandit, Rahul Pal, et al. 2023. Jais and jais-chat: Arabic-centric foundation and instruction-tuned open generative large language models. *arXiv preprint arXiv:2308.16149*.

Freda Shi, Mirac Suzgun, Markus Freitag, Xuezhi Wang, Suraj Srivats, Soroush Vosoughi, Hyung Won Chung, Yi Tay, Sebastian Ruder, Denny Zhou, Dipanjan Das, and Jason Wei. 2023. Language models are multilingual chain-of-thought reasoners. In *The Eleventh International Conference on Learning Representations, ICLR 2023, Kigali, Rwanda, May 1-5, 2023*. OpenReview.net.

Oleh Shliazhko, Alena Fenogenova, Maria Tikhonova, Anastasia Kozlova, Vladislav Mikhailov, and Tatiana Shavrina. 2024. mgpt: Few-shot learners go multilingual. *Transactions of the Association for Computational Linguistics*, 12:58–79.

Shivalika Singh, Freddie Vargus, Daniel Dsouza, Börje F Karlsson, Abinaya Mahendiran, Wei-Yin Ko, Herumb Shandilya, Jay Patel, Deividas Mataciunas, Laura OMahony, et al. 2024. Aya dataset: An open-access collection for multilingual instruction tuning. *arXiv preprint arXiv:2402.06619*.

Hugo Touvron, Louis Martin, Kevin Stone, Peter Albert, Amjad Almahairi, Yasmine Babaei, Nikolay Bashlykov, Soumya Batra, Prajjwal Bhargava, Shruti Bhosale, et al. 2023. Llama 2: Open foundation and fine-tuned chat models. *arXiv preprint arXiv:2307.09288*.

Ahmet Üstün, Viraat Aryabumi, Zheng-Xin Yong, Wei-Yin Ko, Daniel D'souza, Gbemileke Onilude, Neel Bhandari, Shivalika Singh, Hui-Lee Ooi, Amr Kayid, et al. 2024. Aya model: An instruction finetuned open-access multilingual language model. *arXiv preprint arXiv:2402.07827*.

Chris Wendler, Veniamin Veselovsky, Giovanni Monea, and Robert West. 2024. Do llamas work in english? on the latent language of multilingual transformers. *arXiv preprint arXiv:2402.10588*.

Shijie Wu and Mark Dredze. 2019. Beto, bentz, becas: The surprising cross-lingual effectiveness of BERT. In *Proceedings of the 2019 Conference on Empirical Methods in Natural Language Processing and the 9th International Joint Conference on Natural Language Processing (EMNLP-IJCNLP)*, pages 833–844, Hong Kong, China. Association for Computational Linguistics.

Linting Xue, Noah Constant, Adam Roberts, Mihir Kale, Rami Al-Rfou, Aditya Siddhant, Aditya Barua, and Colin Raffel. 2021. mT5: A massively multilingual pre-trained text-to-text transformer. In *Proceedings of the 2021 Conference of the North American Chapter of the Association for Computational Linguistics: Human Language Technologies*, pages 483–498, Online. Association for Computational Linguistics.

Rustem Yeshpanov, Pavel Efimov, Leonid Boytsov, Ardak Shalkarbayuli, and Pavel Braslavski. 2024. KazQAD: Kazakh open-domain question answering dataset. In *Proceedings of the 2024 Joint International Conference on Computational Linguistics, Language Resources and Evaluation (LREC-COLING 2024)*, pages 9645–9656, Torino, Italia. ELRA and ICCL.

Rustem Yeshpanov, Yerbolat Khassanov, and Huseyin Atakan Varol. 2022. KazNERD: Kazakh named entity recognition dataset. In *Proceedings of the Thirteenth Language Resources and Evaluation Conference*, pages 417–426, Marseille, France. European Language Resources Association.

Xiang Zhang, Senyu Li, Bradley Hauer, Ning Shi, and Grzegorz Kondrak. 2023. Don't trust ChatGPT when your question is not in English: A study of multilingual abilities and types of LLMs. In *Proceedings of the 2023 Conference on Empirical Methods in Natural Language Processing*, pages 7915–7927, Singapore. Association for Computational Linguistics.

Wenhao Zhu, Hongyi Liu, Qingxiu Dong, Jingjing Xu, Shujian Huang, Lingpeng Kong, Jiajun Chen, and Lei Li. 2023. Multilingual machine translation with large language models: Empirical results and analysis. *arXiv preprint arXiv:2304.04675*.

Intelligent Tutor to Support Teaching and Learning of Tatar

Alsu Zakirova,[◇] **Jue Hou,**[†⋆] **Anisia Katinskaia,**[†⋆] **Anh-Duc Vu,**[†⋆] **Roman Yangarber**[⋆]
[◇]Moscow State University, Russia
[†]Department of Computer Science, University of Helsinki, Finland
[⋆]Department of Digital Humanities, University of Helsinki, Finland
zakirova.alsu112@student.msu.ru first.last@helsinki.fi

Abstract

This paper presents our work on tools to support the Tatar language, using Revita, a web-based Intelligent Tutoring System for language teaching and learning. The system allows the users—teachers and learners—to upload arbitrary authentic texts, and automatically creates exercises based on these texts that engage the learners in active production of language. It provides graduated feedback when they make mistakes, and performs continuous assessment, based on which the system selects exercises for the learners at the appropriate level. The assessment also helps the students maintain their learning pace, and helps the teachers to monitor their progress. The paper describes the functionality currently implemented for Tatar, which enables learners—who possess basic proficiency beyond the beginner level—to improve their competency, using texts of their choice as learning content. Support for Tatar is being developed to increase public interest in learning the language of this important regional minority, as well as to to provide tools for improving fluency to "heritage speakers"—those who have substantial passive competency, but lack active fluency and need support for regular practice.

1 Introduction

Tatar is a minority language spoken in the Russian Federation and by the Tatar diaspora worldwide. Although Tatar is an important Turkic language with over seven million speakers, it remains a low-resource language from the technological perspective, with little language technology to support its wider use online. This reduced online presence, in turn, limits and diminishes the overall vitality of the language.

Interest in second-language (L2) learning is continually increasing, with a growing number of resources available for learners at various proficiency levels. However, most of these resources either provide only an elementary introduction to the basics of the language, or try to increase proficiency by memorizing advanced vocabulary or complex grammatical structures, such as verb tenses. Despite this variety, it is difficult to find tools that make the learning process interactive and *personalized*—engaging the learners' interests and adapting to their level. The Revita approach to language learning and teaching[1] is founded on allowing the users themselves—students or teachers—to select any authentic material as learning content. The system then automatically generates exercises based on the chosen content, monitors the learner's performance on these exercises to assess the learner's proficiency in multiple dimensions, and adjusts the difficulty of the exercises according to the learner's current level. Currently, there is no similar online service for teaching Tatar to non-beginner students, using text material chosen by the students themselves. Implementing this plan will enable anyone to learn Tatar, using the latest methods from artificial intelligence and language technology.

Creating opportunities for learning Tatar and promoting its use within speaker communities is of great importance to supporting the language. Tatars form the largest linguistic minority in Russia, with diasporas in many other countries. It is crucial to stimulate interest in learning this language to preserve its heritage and expand its use geographically.

The need to create and maintain learning platforms such as Revita, as well as the importance of supporting the study of the Tatar language, underlies the relevance of this work. Intelligent support for language learning is a rapidly evolving and complex area of research. The problem becomes especially challenging in the case of *low-resource* languages: on one hand, the need is more urgent,

[1]revita.cs.helsinki.fi

Proceedings of the First Workshop on Natural Language Processing for Turkic Languages (SIGTURK 2024), pages 92–101
August 15, 2024

since many of the low-resource languages are endangered, and their speaker communities urgently require support. On the other hand, building intelligent tools for such languages is much more difficult due to the paucity of foundational tools and resources.

Some work is being done in this direction, e.g., by Apertium (Mirzakhalov et al., 2021; Forcada et al., 2011; Khanna et al., 2021). However, the availability of natural language processing (NLP) resources for Turkic languages, particularly the endangered ones, still lags far behind that of, e.g., the major European languages.

This paper introduces and describes the work on Tatar in the Revita system. Section 2 outlines the broad principles and capabilities of Revita, describes the work on the system, and explains the notion of "construct" within the framework. Section 3 details all the constructs implemented in the Revita platform and provides examples of exercises that can be created based on these constructs. Section 4 summarizes the results achieved during the adaptation of Revita to the Tatar language, and outlines the next steps for future work.

2 Features of the Revita system

2.1 System Capabilities

Tools for natural language processing (NLP) and automatic text analysis are understood to be central in the creation of platforms for language teaching and learning (Slavuj et al., 2015). Such platforms do not aim to *replace* the teacher, but rather aim to serve as an effective intelligent *assistant* to the teacher (Al Emran and Shaalan, 2014). Thanks to such systems, students can continue learning the language beyond school hours, and practice on their own time while tracking their progress independently. Developments focused on teaching rare languages are particularly valuable because it is more difficult to find teachers who speak these languages at the proper level.

At present, many platforms and applications exist for learners to get acquainted with a *new* language, and learn the basic structures using limited, pre-fabricated material. However, as students gradually acquire language skills, they often face a shortage of authentic and interesting material to practice more complex constructions at the intermediate to advanced level.

Further, learning a language is an ongoing process that requires a significant investment of time on the part of the learner. To achieve mastery, it is crucial to have a sufficient supply of practice material and exercises. Therefore, the automatic, intelligent generation of exercises, based on an unrestricted amount of text, can meet the needs of students aiming to reach advanced competency. Revita is designed to fulfill these requirements (Katinskaia et al., 2017, 2018).

Initially, the purpose of Revita, developed at the University of Helsinki, was to revitalize and support endangered Finno-Ugric languages (Katinskaia and Yangarber, 2018). More recently, this approach has been applied to language teaching and learning more generally, including for the "majority" languages. Currently, the Finnish and Russian languages are the most developed in terms of the richness of the kinds of exercises the system is able to generate, and the number of various grammatical concepts that it covers. It is used by teachers and students of Finnish and Russian at several universities. Other languages are under development, including major European languages (e.g., Italian, German, Swedish) and minority languages (e.g., Udmurt, Northern Sami). Revita has also been partially adapted for the endangered Turkic language Sakha (Ivanova et al., 2019).

An important aspect of Revita is that the approach is not intended for beginners, which distinguishes it from many other existing learning approaches and platforms. The approach assumes that the learner already knows some basic vocabulary (500–1000 words) and is familiar with elementary grammar. Revita tries to provide a "starter" library of texts for each language, but the main principle is to teach the language using materials that interest the learner. Students can independently choose the texts, based on which the exercises are generated, making use of the structure and vocabulary of the chosen material.

The system aims to act as a teacher's assistant: supporting continuous and effective learning, maintaining the students' motivation, and keeping their attention on the study objectives. To promote motivation and provide a variety of exercise modes, Revita employs various gamification features, as introduced in (Hou et al., 2022).

Before starting to work with texts, the student can take an adaptive test, usually consisting of 50–60 questions. This test estimates the level of language proficiency using several types of tasks: identifying a word by its meaning, choosing the correct structure, testing knowledge of phraseol-

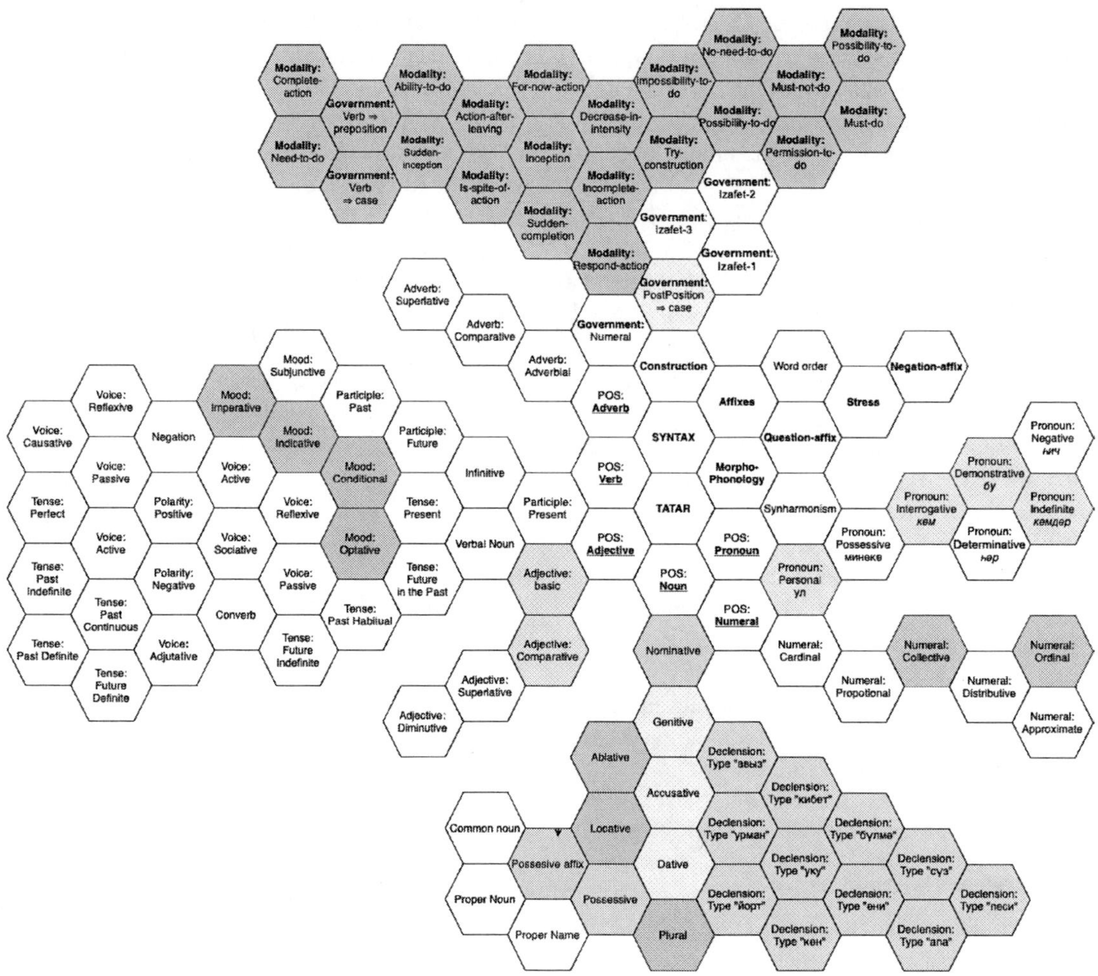

Figure 1: Heatmap of constructs for Tatar in Revita.

ogy and expressions, orthography, grammatical forms of words, etc.

To begin practicing within Revita, the student selects a text. Texts can be uploaded directly by the learner or by the teacher. Once the text has been analyzed and exercises have been created, the Preview mode allows the students to familiarize themselves with the grammatical structures (and vocabulary) present in the text. Since the platform adapts to the student's level over time, the learner can immediately start completing exercises proposed by the system. If the number of erroneous answers is high, the system will generate tasks based on easier grammatical topics.

Revita currently creates three types of exercises. "*Cloze*" (fill-in-the-gap) exercises require the student to produce the correct grammatical form based on the context of the word; the hint given to the student is the lemma (base form of the word). In multiple-choice (MC) tasks, the learner is asked to select the correct option from a drop-down list of answers. The challenge in generating MC questions is automatically finding appropriate "distractors"—options which are not suitable for the context, and yet not obviously incorrect (which would make the exercise too easy and uninteresting). Listening exercises are aimed at training auditory perception of spoken language. In auditory comprehension exercises, the student needs to enter the word pronounced by a speech generator. The system provides a set of settings to adjust the difficulty level of exercises. The student can select the type of exercises as desired.

Personalized feedback is a central aspect of the practice mode in Revita. The system analyzes learner errors and presents hints that help the student find the correct answer independently—rather than giving away the correct answer in case

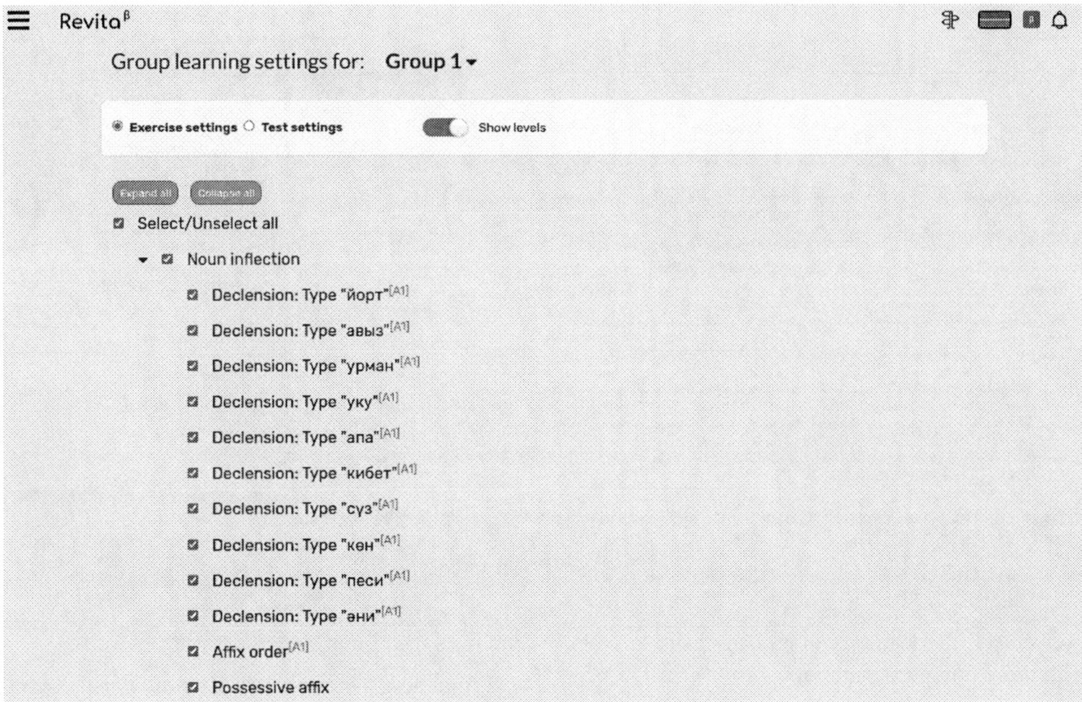

Figure 2: Selection of (top 12) constructs for learning during exercise sessions.

of a mistake. This way, the student not only discovers whether the answer is correct, but also understands which grammatical features need to be changed to complete the task correctly. After several incorrect attempts, the system will show the correct answer, with a detailed explanation of the correct form of the word or phrase.

2.2 Construct-centred Learning

The Revita approach treats *constructs* as the central unit of L2 teaching and learning, as introduced in prior research (Boas, 2022; Katinskaia et al., 2023). Language constructs may describe individual word forms, phrases, or clauses, and encompass topics on various linguistic levels—grammatical, lexical, orthographic, morphological, etc.—for each language (Katinskaia and Yangarber, 2018).

When developing a new language in Revita, we use the notion of a "chunk"—in linguistics, a chunk is a collocation or construction, which is regulated by certain rules. Chunks have a main word that controls and dependent ones, see, e.g., Figure 4. In this example, the analysis of the sentence Кояшка таба әйлән! (*"Turn towards the sun"*) is presented—the analyzer identifies the post-positional construction in the sentence, and highlights the components of the chunk: the post-position—таба ("towards"), which governs the noun—кояш=ка (*"sun"*)—which must be in the required (dative) case.

All constructs implemented for a given language can be graphically seen on the *heatmap*, which can be examined in the learner's profile. This allows both the student and the teacher to track progress, Figure 1. The size of the cell indicate how many times this construct has been practiced (relative to other constructs), and its color shows how well the construct is mastered over the selected period of time (which can be selected by the user). Using the heatmap, the teacher can visually assess the level of mastery of the lesson's topic (construct) by an individual student or by the group as a whole. As the number of constructs increases, the map also expands.

Constructs are linked to specific language proficiency levels. If a student believes her level is, e.g., B1, she can choose to study all constructs related to this level and below. In the system settings, it is possible to select constructs, which determines which exercises will be generated. In case a learner evaluates her level of language proficiency as insufficient for training a particular construct, she can disable exercises for this construct.

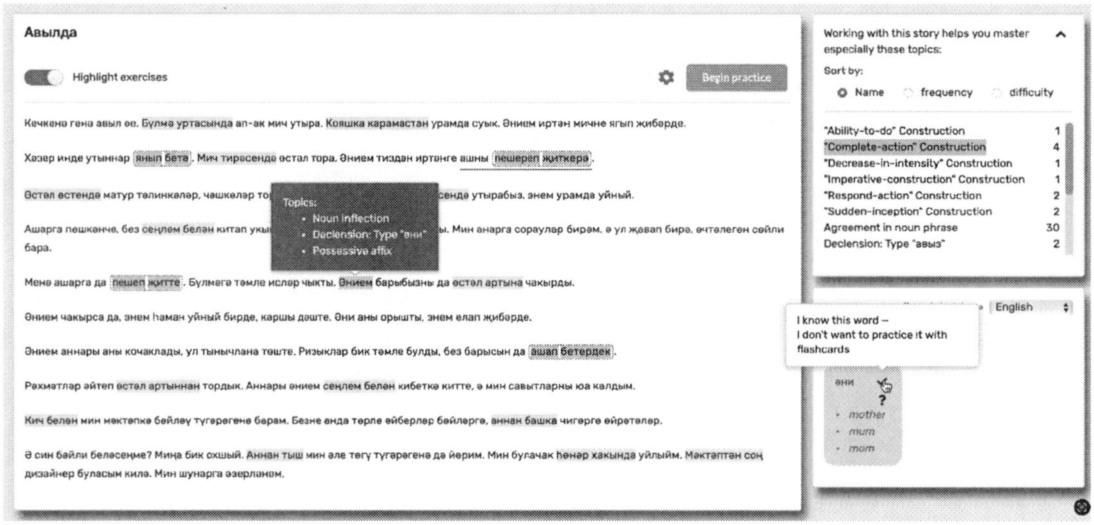

Figure 3: Preview Mode.

Conversely, the learner can request tasks to work with more complex material.

Exercises on finding the correct grammatical form of a word in its context (and on auditory perception) are tied to language constructs, allowing for the adjustment of task complexity. This is convenient for teachers—when working with a group of students, they can choose constructs relevant to the lesson and focus on training only those.

The system displays a tree structure of constructs, with each item attached to a CEFR level[2] corresponding to the construct, see Figure 2, and *topics* in upper-right box in Figure 3. The latter tells the learner which grammatical concepts will be presented during practice with this text.

To view all constructs contained in the chosen text, the system offers the Preview Mode, Figure 3. Hovering over each word brings up the list of constructs attached to it by Revita. The student can preview a selected text *before* practice, view the highlighted constructions and the of constructs identified for each word. Additionally, when the student clicks on a word, Revita displays its translation into a preferred language.

2.3 Technical Implementation of Constructs

To adapt the system to a new language (here: Tatar) we need to specify and implement the constructions of the language—e.g., rules for syntactic agreement, government, and many more. The system performs *chunking* based on these rules, and uses the chunks when creating exercises.

Syntactic government is a particularly important area in L2 teaching and learning. A government bank is a collection of declarative rules—each rule describes an essential pattern of interaction between, e.g., a head verb and its syntactic dependents which it governs—nouns, pre- or post-positional phrases, etc. These banks describing the government of adpositions, nouns, adjectives and verbs—as well as banks of more complex constructions—are, of course, language-specific, they must be created for each language separately. Currently, government banks in Revita are constructed manually, though our recent work attempts to extend government banks automatically by probing pre-trained large language models (Hou et al., 2024; Klyshinsky et al., 2023).

According to the defined rules, the system finds constructions in the text, as shown in Figure 3. The identified constrictions are then used to generate exercises. For example, the lemma of the governed noun can be used as the hint in the exercise (so the student must inflect it in the correct case), or the governed adposition (post-position in Tatar) can be replaced by a list of options from which the student must choose the correct one.

The distractors for multiple-choice exercises are also created using language-specific rules. This is a hard problem, since the tutor must avoid both those options that are a. *obviously incorrect* in the given context (which would make the exercise too easy), and b. those that could be *also correct* in the

[2]Common European Framework Reference

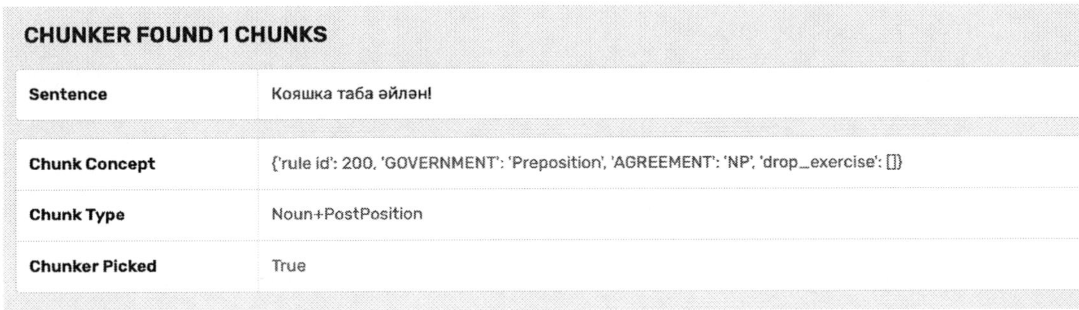

CHUNKER FOUND 1 CHUNKS

Sentence	Кояшка таба әйлән!
Chunk Concept	{'rule id': 200, 'GOVERNMENT': 'Preposition', 'AGREEMENT': 'NP', 'drop_exercise': []}
Chunk Type	Noun+PostPosition
Chunker Picked	True

Figure 4: Example of post-positional construction (in developer's user interface for testing constructions.

context (making the exercise too difficult or impossible to solve). Deciding which distractors are suitable in a given context is an important problem that we are actively researching (Katinskaia et al., 2019; Katinskaia and Yangarber, 2021, 2023).

At present, the Apertium morphological analyzer is used for Tatar. The analyzer can recognize the grammatical form of a word, and generate required forms based on a lemma, which will be used for constructing future exercises (in particular, distractors in MC questions). The analyzer is still under development, but it partially meets the needs for analyzing forms, recognizing structures and creating exercises.

As the quality of morphological analysis improves in the future, we can expect to be able to make enhancements to the quality of the exercises. As mentioned in the introduction, the lack of foundational resources for Turkic languages, and Tatar in particular, is a major bottleneck, ultimately limiting the quality of downstream applications.

3 Tatar Constructs Implemented in Revita

3.1 Basic Constructs

The list of constructs that are currently implemented can be viewed both in the heatmap and in the system's settings. The selectable constructs are shown in these views. Not all of them are fully recognized by the system at present. Basic constructs include, e.g., declension of nouns, degrees of comparison of adjectives, tenses of verbs, etc. Tatar constructs are listed based on the inventory in the *Guide to the Tatar language and Tatar grammar* (Guzev, 2015; Mansurova, 2018; Nigmatullina, 2011; Nurmukhametova, 2008; Sharafutdinova, 2018).

Basic constructs are formulated at the beginning of development stage, since they form the foundation for further development. On the heatmap, basic constructs are displayed as branching out from the main parts of speech. At the top of the heatmap, more complex constructs/constructions are highlighted in light red (in the Figure).

3.2 Constructions

The more complex constructions are developed based on their descriptions in the works listed above, Constructions implemented so far include:

- post-positional constructions;
- verbal constructions;
- and modality constructs.

At present, the system recognizes 67 post-positional constructions, 344 verbal constructions, and 18 modality constructs. A detailed analysis for these constructions can be explored in the "Grammar Tester" interface, as shown in the example for a post-positional construction, Figure 4.

This interface is intended exclusively *for developers*. It provides detailed insights into the functionality and performance of the system's analyzers, and helps the developers tune the recognition algorithms. The system highlights post-positional constructions (Galiyeva, 2020) in blue, showing a detailed analysis of these constructions.

The structure and analysis of verbs can also be examined using this tool, see the example in Figure 5. This demonstrates the analysis of the sentence containing a verb construction: Тәртипкә гадәтләнергә кирәк! (*"One must get used to the order!"*). The main word of the construction—the verb гадәтләнергә (*"to get used to"*)—and the noun dependent on it тәртип=кә (*"[to the] order"*), where case=Dative. Note, in the Preview Mode, for verb constructions that require post-positional control (Gatiatullin, 2012), both the entire verb-government construction and the

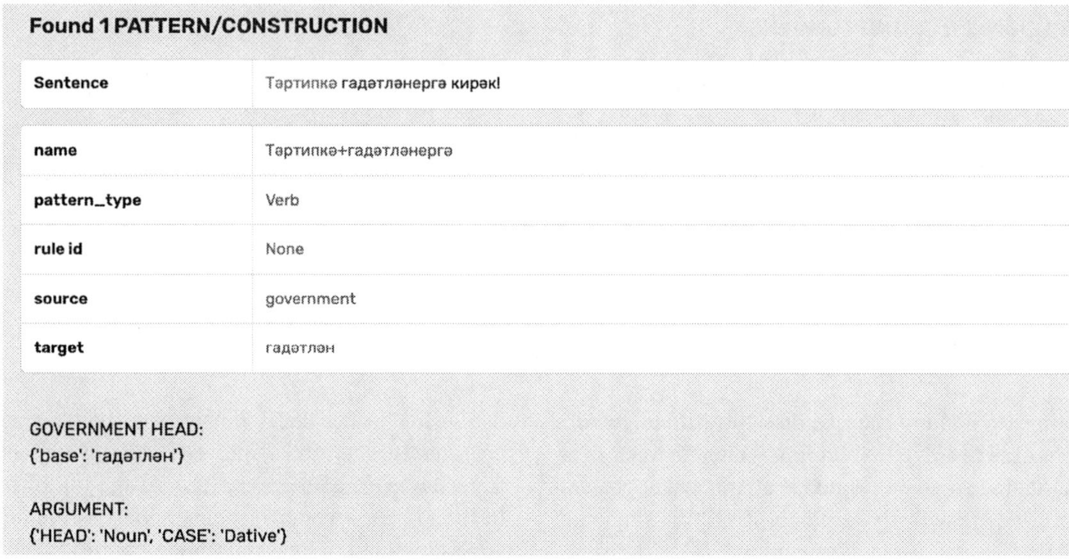

Found 1 PATTERN/CONSTRUCTION

Sentence	Тәртипкә гадәтләнергә кирәк!

name	Тәртипкә+гадәтләнергә
pattern_type	Verb
rule id	None
source	government
target	гадәтлән

GOVERNMENT HEAD:
{'base': 'гадәтлән'}

ARGUMENT:
{'HEAD': 'Noun', 'CASE': 'Dative'}

Figure 5: Verbal Construction.

post-positional construction inside it will be highlighted.

Modality constructions (Gatiatullin, 2012; Tatevosov, 2018) are of particular interest, as their correct use can indicate that language proficiency has progressed to a higher level. Each of these constructions has a logical, concise name, which helps the student remember its meaning, see Figure 6. This example shows the structure and characteristics of a modal construction in the sentence Мин кибеткә барам, ә син укый тор. (*"I will go to the store, and you stay here and study"*). The modal meaning is conveyed through the serial verb construction: the 3SG.PRS verb укый (*"study"*) followed by the imperative verb тор (*"stay"*).

3.2.1 Examples of Exercises

In this section, we present examples of exercises that can be generated using these constructs. Various types of exercises implemented in the system will be described, along with the various kinds of feedback that the student can receive.

When working with the selected text, the student may be asked to inflect a noun or pronoun into the correct form:

- Original text: Мәктәптән соң кунакка барам. (*"After school I will go for a visit"*).
- Task: [мәктәп] соң ("after [school]")—the *lemma* of the noun (мәктәп) is presented as the hint for this cloze exercise—which must be inflected correctly by the learner.
- Correct answer: мәктәптән (*"school"*), Case=ablative.
- If the learner answers incorrectly, the system will offer *graduated feedback*—a sequence of increasingly more specific hints on each attempt:
  1. Pay attention to the part of speech.
  2. Choose the correct case.
  3. Inflect the noun мәктәп into the correct case, as required by the following post-position.
  4. Inflect the noun мәктәп into the ablative case.

In multiple-choice exercises, the student may be offered several options as distractors: various post-positions or post-positional words, as well as different forms of a noun or a pronoun:

- Original text: Ул минем артыма яшеренде (*"He hid behind me"*).
- Task: [яныма/артыма/хакында] яшеренде—multiple-choice menu of options.
- Correct answer: артыма (*"behind"*).
- Graduated feedback:
  1. Which post-position can follow the pronoun in the genitive case?
  2. Recall the meaning of the post-position.
  3. Translate *hid behind me (behind my back)*.

In an exercise with *modality constructions*, the learner may be asked to select the correct auxil-

CHUNKER FOUND 1 CHUNKS	
Sentence	Мин кибеткә барам, ә син укый тор
Chunk Concept	{'MODALITY': 'imperative-construction', 'rule id': 113, 'ANALYTIC': True, 'NUMBER': 'Singular', 'PERSON': '2', 'TENSE': 'Imperative', 'CHUNK_RULE': 'respond-action', 'drop_exercise': []}
Chunk Type	Verb+Verb
Chunker Picked	True

Figure 6: Example of Modality Construct—in the Grammar Tester interface.

iary verb, or the form of the "semantic" (i.e., the meaning-bearing) verb.

- Original text: Мин кибеткә барам, ә син укый тор. (*"I'll go to the store, and you stay here and read"*).
- Task 1: син укый [тор/башла/ал]—multiple-choice menu of options.
- Task 2: син укый [...]—a gap.
- Correct answer: [тор].
- Graduated feedback:
    1. Recall how the imperative construction is formed.
    2. Try to translate the phrase *"stay and read."*
    3. Use an auxiliary verb appropriate for this context.

Since the choice of an auxiliary verb may not always be unambiguous, the name of the construction (or its translation) can be used as a hint.

4 Conclusions

This paper presents the current state of our work on adapting, Revita, a system for L2 teaching and learning, to Tatar—a low-resource Turkic language, spoken by over 7M people. It describes in some detail the constructs implemented to date. To the best of our knowledge, this is the first work dedicated to the development of L2 teaching and learning tools specifically for Tatar at the intermediate to advanced levels, based on state-of-the-art technologies available at present.

Work is on-going on identifying constructs most useful for teaching, and classifying them by proficiency levels, in accordance with the scale of assessment of language competencies. The next major development phase is to extend the inventory of constructions to include more complex syntactic constructs, with a particular interest in synthetic subordinate clauses (Zakharova, 2016).

We are also working on expanding the selection of texts on various topics to create a more complete open library, to give learners who do not have a source of their own texts a wider choice from the public library. Having more texts will increase the amount of content for training AI models—for example, using transfer learning from Turkish—a related, higher-resource language—which may help address problems of low-resource languages. An essential system component, found to be extremely useful in the development of other languages, is a syntactic dependency parser. Such a parser (of reasonable quality) is not available for Tatar at present. When one becomes available, the quality of the analysis—and the variety and quality of the automatically generated exercises—will progress to the next level.

Further work will focus on developing the platform to support Tatar. The ultimate goal is to bring the Tatar Revita to a level of functionality that can be deployed for teaching and learning Tatar, e.g., in schools with teachers, as is done for other languages for which richer resources are available—currently Finnish and Russian. We also hope that this work will contribute to stimulating global interest in the study and development of Tatar—and other low-resource languages in need of support—using the latest NLP technologies and theories of L2 acquisition.

References

Mustafa Al Emran and Khaled Shaalan. 2014. A survey of intelligent language tutoring systems. In *Advances in Computing, Communications and Informatics*, pages 393–399. IEEE.

Hans C Boas. 2022. From construction grammar(s) to pedagogical construction grammar. *Directions for pedagogical construction grammar. Learning and teaching (with) constructions*, pages 3–43.

Mikel L Forcada, Mireia Ginestí-Rosell, Jacob Nordfalk, Jim O'Regan, Sergio Ortiz-Rojas, Juan Antonio Pérez-Ortiz, Felipe Sánchez-Martínez, Gema Ramírez-Sánchez, and Francis M Tyers. 2011. Apertium: a free, open-source platform for rule-based machine translation. *Journal of machine translation*, 25(2).

Gatiatullin Galiyeva. 2020. Semantics of constructions with the postposition 'belan' in the Tatar language: analysis of corpus data. *Philological Sciences. Questions of theory and practice.*

Suleimanov Gatiatullin. 2012. Model of verbose constructions of the Tatar language: analytical forms. *Kazanskaya Nauka.*

Guzev. 2015. *Theoretical Grammar of the Turkish Language.*

Jue Hou, Anisia Katinskaia, Lari Kotilainen, Sathianpong Trangcasanchai, Anh-Duc Vu, and Roman Yangarber. 2024. What do transformers know about government? In *Proceedings of the Joint Conference on Computational Linguistics and Language Resources and Evaluation*, Torino, Italy.

Jue Hou, Ilmari Kylliäinen, Anisia Katinskaia, Giacomo Furlan, and Roman Yangarber. 2022. Applying gamification incentives in the Revita language-learning system. In *Proceedings of the 9th Workshop on Games and Natural Language Processing within the 13th Language Resources and Evaluation Conference*, pages 7–16, Marseille, France. European Language Resources Association.

Sardana Ivanova, Anisia Katinskaia, and Roman Yangarber. 2019. Tools for supporting language learning for Sakha. In *22nd Nordic Conference on Computational Linguistics (NoDaLiDa).*

Anisia Katinskaia, Jue Hou, Anh-duc Vu, and Roman Yangarber. 2023. Linguistic constructs represent the domain model in intelligent language tutoring. In *Proceedings of the 17th Conference of the European Chapter of the Association for Computational Linguistics: System Demonstrations*, pages 136–144, Dubrovnik, Croatia. Association for Computational Linguistics.

Anisia Katinskaia, Sardana Ivanova, and Roman Yangarber. 2019. Multiple admissibility in language learning:: Judging grammaticality using unlabeled data. In *Workshop onBalto-Slavic Natural Language Processing*, pages 12–22. The Association for Computational Linguistics.

Anisia Katinskaia, Javad Nouri, and Roman Yangarber. 2017. Revita: a system for language learning and supporting endangered languages. In *6th Workshop on NLP for CALL and 2nd Workshop on NLP for Research on Language Acquisition, at NoDaLiDa*, Gothenburg, Sweden.

Anisia Katinskaia, Javad Nouri, and Roman Yangarber. 2018. Revita: a language-learning platform at the intersection of ITS and CALL. In *Proceedings of the Eleventh International Conference on Language Resources and Evaluation (LREC 2018)*, Miyazaki, Japan. European Language Resources Association (ELRA).

Anisia Katinskaia and Roman Yangarber. 2018. Digital cultural heritage and revitalization of endangered Finno-Ugric languages. In *Proceedings of the 3rd Conference on Digital Humanities in the Nordic Countries*, Helsinki, Finland.

Anisia Katinskaia and Roman Yangarber. 2021. Assessing grammatical correctness in language learning. In *Proceedings of the 16th Workshop on Innovative Use of NLP for Building Educational Applications*, pages 135–146.

Anisia Katinskaia and Roman Yangarber. 2023. Grammatical error correction for sentence-level assessment in language learning. In *Workshop on Innovative Use of NLP for Building Educational Applications*, pages 488–502. The Association for Computational Linguistics.

Tanmai Khanna, Jonathan N Washington, Francis M Tyers, Sevilay Bayatlı, Daniel G Swanson, Tommi A Pirinen, Irene Tang, and Hèctor Alòs i Font. 2021. Recent advances in Apertium, a free/open-source rule-based machine translation platform for low-resource languages. *Journal of Machine Translation*, pages 1–28.

Eduard Klyshinsky, Anna Bogdanova, and Mikhail Kopotev. 2023. Towards a corpus-based dictionary of verbal government for the Russian language. *Journal of Linguistics/Jazykovedný casopis*, 74(1):173–181.

Mansurova. 2018. Agreement of numerals in Arabic and Tatar languages. *Modern Muslim World.*

Jamshidbek Mirzakhalov, Anoop Babu, Duygu Ataman, Sherzod Kariev, Francis Tyers, Otabek Abduraufov, Mammad Hajili, Sardana Ivanova, Abror Khaytbaev, Antonio Laverghetta Jr, et al. 2021. A large-scale study of machine translation in the Turkic languages. *arXiv preprint arXiv:2109.04593.*

Nigmatullina. 2011. *Learning the Tatar language (rules and exercises).*

Nurmukhametova. 2008. *Collection of rules on the Tatar language for Russian-speaking students.*

Sharafutdinova. 2018. Isafet constructions in the Tatar language. *Modern Muslim World.*

Vanja Slavuj, Božidar Kovačić, and Igor Jugo. 2015. Intelligent tutoring systems for language learning. In *Proceedings of the 38th International Convention on Information and Communication Technology, Electronics and Microelectronics (MIPRO).* IEEE.

Tatevosov. 2018. On the subparadigm of analytical forms of the Tatar verb. *Ural-Altai Research.*

Zakharova. 2016. Concessive clauses in the Yakut, Tatar and Turkish languages: a comparative analysis of synthetic and synthetic-analytic constructions. *New Science: Current State and Ways of Development*.

Author Index

Association for Computational Linguistics
209 N. Eighth Street
Stroudsburg, Pennsylvania 18360

ISBN 979-8-3313-0176-7

CURRAN ASSOCIATES INC.
proceedings.com